Java™ Testing Patterns

Java™ Testing Patterns

Jon Thomas
Matthew Young
Kyle Brown
Andrew Glover

WILEY

Wiley Publishing, Inc.

Executive Editor: Robert M. Elliott
Production Editor: Felicia Robinson
Book Producer: Ryan Publishing Group, Inc.
Copy Editors: Liz Welch and Linda Recktenwald
Compositor: Amy Hassos

Vice President and Executive Group Publisher:
  Richard Swadley
Vice President and Publisher: Joseph B. Wikert
Executive Editorial Director: Mary Bednarek
Editorial Manager: Kathryn A. Malm

Library of Congress Cataloging-in-Publication Data:

ISBN 0-471-44846-X

Printed in the United States of America

10 9 8 7 6 5 4 3 2 1

CONTENTS AT A GLANCE

CONTENTS

I would like to thank my wife and children for their continued support throughout this endeavor and dedicate this work herein to my father, teacher, and mentor Jay Thomas, who went to be with the Lord in 2002.

—Jon Thomas

Jon Thomas began his software development career at Intuit. In 1996 he began developing Java software for a wide range of Internet startups, corporate IT departments, and custom software development shops. From 1997 through 1999 he served on the Board of Directors for The Information Technology Association of Southern Arizona (ITASA). In 1998 while at SimplySay (formerly Parigon, formerly Authetix, now gone-- wasn't the dotCom boom grand?) he had a two-day session on Extreme Programming with Martin Fowler where he was introduced to testing before coding, continuous integration, and common code ownership. At this point the seeds of XP began to grow in his heart. When he moved to eBlox in 2000, he brought the concept of unit testing with him and became an XP evangelist. In 2001 he contributed to the first edition of the bestselling book *Java Tools for Extreme Programming*.

As a Senior Software Engineer for Healthtrio, Jon continued to practice integration between Ant and JUnit as he designed code to meet the interfaces defined by his unit tests, which in turn were defined by product specifications.

Today at ScriptSave he helps define processes and methodologies for a software development team using DotNet, and gets plenty of quality time in with NUnit. He also teaches master classes in UML and Extreme Programming methodologies.

When he's not programming, Jon spends as much time as possible with his family, his church, and in his community.

Matthew Young received a B.S. in Computer Science and Engineering from Bucknell and an M.S. in Systems Engineering from Johns Hopkins. Matthew has been leading software efforts since 1992. He spent most of his career as a defense contractor, working on such projects as Differential GPS and Force Structure Modeling and Simulation. As a software development manager, he focused teams on solid engineering principles and realistic software projects. Tired of the hustle and bustle of suburban Washington, D.C., Mr. Young relocated to the southwest desert and Tucson, AZ where he serves as the Sr. Java Architect for Healthtrio. He is currently focused on several efforts including complex and adaptive systems and software process improvement.

Kyle Brown is a Senior Technical Staff Member with IBM Software Services for WebSphere. He has written or contributed to six books on WebSphere, J2EE, and Design Patterns; has written over fifty published papers and articles on software-engineering topics; and speaks frequently at industry conferences.

Andrew Glover is the founder and CTO of Vanward Technologies, a company specializing in building automated testing frameworks on various platforms spanning the gamut from Java to C++ to .NET. When he's not in front of a computer, he attempts to strum a six-string for his two children; moreover, he's always trying to complete his ever growing "Honey-Do" list. He holds a BS in Computer Science from George Mason University.

Introduction

In 2000 and 2001 I was fortunate enough to work with an amazing team of software developers that included Rick Hightower, Nick Lesiecki, and Erik Hatcher. We were all at a company called eBlox and had one of those rare opportunities to build a useful product the way we wanted to. I'd had a little experience with extreme programming at a previous company and was enthusiastic about pursuing it on a wider scale. Andy Barton, eBlox's owner, afforded us a unique opportunity to truly experiment with implementation, and we went all out: paired programming, common code ownership, continuous refactoring, and continuous customer involvement. But the concept that has always struck me as the truest–and the one that has stayed with me the longest–is unit testing, and specifically test first development.

Our involvement with XP, and Rick's connections in the publishing industry, led us to write the book *Java Tools For Extreme Programming*. This book helped us further hone our software development methodologies. We also had to learn so much about the tools covered in the book that our appreciation for their usefulness grew phenomenally. Case in point: Who knows Ant better than Erik Hatcher? We realized that by using the tools and practicing the methodolgies they enabled, we were becoming better developers.

A year later saw me writing HealthCare software at HealthTrio and attending JavaOne in San Francisco. Hanging out with Rick one night, we decided to attend the Wiley Publishing author reception.

While hanging out with our publishers and editors, we all made plans to go to dinner and brainstorm.

At JavaOne that year there was absolutely no topic as hot as design patterns. Earlier in the day I had attended a session with Floyd Marinescu where he'd said something that really stuck with me. To paraphrase him:

> *A good indicator of the maturity of any platform is the implementation of best practices with and surrounding it. The maturity of the Java platform is one reason that design patterns in Java are gaining such a profound foothold.*

It occurred to me then and there that an important area in Java patterns that had not received enough attention was testing patterns. Testing patterns are vital tools for the developer: they help ensure the proper functionality of each software component; and, when implemented hand-in-hand with a design, can help ensure the effectiveness of development planning and execution, as well as code maintainability.

At dinner that night, thinking I might help Rick get another book, and that I might get to write a chapter or two and an appendix, I mentioned this to Tim Ryan and my editor at Wiley. They agreed, and the next thing I knew I was writing a proposal and signing a contract. Whew, that went fast!

The rest went not so fast. In the time since, I have switched jobs, had a son, and seen my father off to be with God. It has been a long road, but the patterns have kept coming. A good deal of credit goes to Bob Binder who did the original authoritative work on the subject of testing patterns in OOP. Additionally great thanks are offered to Mark Grand who was an invaluable technical resource. About a year and a half in, with my father in a coma and my wife pregnant, it became clear that I would need some help getting this book finished.

The only reason I am fortunate enough to know Matthew Young is that on the morning of September 11, 2001 he was supposed to have been in a server room of the Pentagon (a room that was completely destroyed by an airliner). I guess this dodged bullet was enough to make Tucson, Arizona seem pretty attractive to Mr. Young and his wife because it brought him into my life and this book. As far as I am concerned, Matt, there is one good thing that God has made out of the horrors of that day. I thank you for joining me on this book.

About this Book

Patterns provide a common vocabulary and formalized structure for discussing software development concepts. Software developers and engineers can use patterns to identify and resolve universal, recurring challenges in the software development process. The patterns discussed in this book focus on the challenges of software testing.

Testing is a process that provides a reasonable level of confidence in the system that you have created by demonstrating an understanding of the limits of that system. Testing is not simply debugging, nor is it a rubber stamp seal-of-approval that there are no bugs in the system. In the simplest sense, testing is checking to see that all of the pieces of the system fit together and that the system produced in the end is what you set out to build. It is an evaluation that you have built the right thing and that you have built the thing right.

Patterns alone are not enough to realize the goals of testing. For this reason, we have taken a slightly different approach to the topic in this book. Rather than discussing testing patterns singly and in isolation, we present them as the core of a complete software testing environment in which development methodologies such as Extreme Programming, tools such as Ant and JUnit, and the Java language combine to form a dynamic and powerful software testing system. Accordingly, this book is divided into three parts:

Chapters 1-5 discuss the core concepts of testing and Extreme Programming. It explains various types of testing–including unit testing, integration testing, end-to-end testing–and identifies the benefits and capabilities of each.

Chapters 6-16 describe a broad range of testing design patterns, describes how they are best used, and presents Java code for implementing each one.

Chapters 17-21 take the concepts and patterns from the first two parts of the book and builds a fully functional test suite for the Sun J2EE Petstore application. The process begins with defining use cases for the application, then proceeds to identifying components for testing, determining the types of tests that should be applied, building the actual tests, and then analyzing the results.

The Appendixes provide concise references to key tools and concepts such as Ant, JUnit, DbUnit, UML, and the advantages of using aspect-oriented programming techniques in your Java testing environment.

Along the way, this book offers practical solutions to a host of software development challenges such as:

- How can I know that my program/interface is doing what I intend it to when it is buried deep in interactions between a client and server?

- How can I know that my program is working when it has been placed in a new environment?

- After piecing an entire application together, how can I find an internal bug that seems to leave no traces?

- How have other programmers tested this situation before?

- How can I test data-dependent use cases against a dynamic database?

- When a tester/analyst/customer/manager tells me my code is broken, how can I determine if there is really a problem and what the problem is?

As a reader of this book you should come away with an easily referenced repertoire of solutions to the type of unit and functional testing problems that you will face in all aspects of software development, whether you are a one-man band or a programmer analyst for a Fortune 500 corporation.

Pattern Structure

I've given a great deal of thought to how patterns will be documented in this book. I considered the Alexandrian template and many others, but ultimately I settled on the Gang of Four template which was introduced in their book *Design Patterns: Elements of Reusable Object-Oriented Software*. Not only does the GoF design pattern template elegantly handle the unique problems inherent in, and addressed by, software design and development, but it has reached a high level of recognition within the software community. For those of you who may be meeting the GoF template for the first time, here is a brief key:

Description of the Design Pattern Template

1. Name
2. Intent
3. Also Known As
4. Motivation
5. Applicability
6. Structure
7. Participants
8. Collaborations
9. Consequences
10. Implementation
11. Sample Code
12. Known Uses
13. Related Patterns

Who This Book Is For

This book is designed for software engineers and engineering managers, in addition to software testers. To get the most from this book you should have a foundational knowledge of the core concepts of object-oriented programming. To understand the code examples, you will need to be an experienced Java developer.

Throughout the book we use the Unified Markup Language (UML) to document the design of our applications and test suites. Although we attempt to clearly explain the meaning of each UML chart, a working knowledge of the UML will enrich your understanding of this book. To that end, we've included a brief introduction to the UML in Appendix C.

Beyond these things, the only requirement is a basic knowledge of the software development lifecycle and the demands that it makes developers to understand how the code they write will behave in unexpected situations.

Downloading the Code

All the code in this book is available from the book's Web site: www.wiley.com/
compbooks/javatesting. Here you'll find the Java implementations of each pattern, code for the sample applications in the book, and the code for all the tests.

Many of the diagrams in this book are detailed and conceptually complex; some would be far better served as four-color posters than as 7.5 x 9.25" black-and-white book pages. To do the illustrations justice (and to save some eye fatigue), we have posted them on the book's Web site. We have also made a bonus chapter available for download; the chapter details more ideas and experiences we've had while working with patterns, open source tools, and methodologies to build an effective testing environment.

CHAPTER 1

Critical Testing Concepts

The test of a first-rate intelligence is the ability to hold two opposed ideas in mind at the same time and still retain the ability to function.

—*F. Scott Fitzgerald*

What Is Testing?

If you put together a puzzle, while it might not be apparent to you, you perform a process of testing and integration. You find a flat surface or table where you can assemble the puzzle and make sure it is clear. You take the contents of the box, bag, or other container that the puzzle came in and dump the contents out onto the table. Slowly, you begin turning the pieces over, displaying the picture side of each piece. You may start grouping the pieces by shape (corners, sides, and central), or by colors, or by combinations of these approaches. Some people begin assembling the edges; others tackle significant features of the puzzle (maybe the eyes of the animal depicted, or the horizontal separation between grass and sky, or other easily recognizable color change areas within the puzzle). If you're like me, you'll refer to the picture quite often either to pick additional areas to work on or to determine how the smaller picture representation may appear on a given piece.

When you build a puzzle, you have certain expectations. You expect that all the pieces are there, that each piece will fit together, and that, in the end, what you finally produce will look reasonably like the picture on the container. You can assemble all the pieces and be "done" but still not have a completed puzzle that looks like the intended picture. You might also try to jam the pieces together in a way that they are not intended to go. In fact, sometimes this may not be readily noticeable, until you attempt to fit other pieces into the erroneously joined pieces. Constantly, you need to check to see if the pieces are fitting together correctly and that the picture produced is what is expected.

This is the same for testing. Within any software project, from a simple "Hello World" application to the code that controls a satellite, testing is basically the same: It is a process that provides a reasonable level of confidence in the system that you have created by demonstrating an understanding of the limits of that system. In the simplest sense, testing is checking to see that all of the pieces of the system fit together and that the system produced in the end is what you set out to build. It is an evaluation that you have built the thing right and that you have built the right thing.

Formally, these two very *different* acts of testing are referred to as *verification* and *validation*. We want to show that we've built the widget to function correctly (verification) and that the widget we produced is what we set out to build in the first place (validation). Failure in either case is just as unacceptable within the software process. If the software product that we built doesn't function correctly, the system has a potential for failure, whereas if we built a different system than what we had intended, it may not be accepted by the customer or may result in failures due to a certain level of expectation on the customer's part.

But it is not such an easy thing to maintain the concepts of both verification and validation in a single plan. To show that we've built the software properly, we have to make a basic assumption that the specification we built the system to is correct, and we are simply checking to see that our software meets that specification. However, to show that we've built the right thing we have to throw out that notion and assume that the system works. It seems that testing is a huge paradox.

To add to this dichotomy, there are two opposed methods of testing: "white box" and "black box". White box testing involves conducting a test with the knowledge of the tested unit's internal functions. Black box tests, however, are designed to exercise the interface to a unit without regard for its internals. A white box test can often expose more errors in the system due to its ability to look into the actual implementation, whereas a black-box test can assist in identifying the most critical of system errors. Although the methods seem to be at odds with each other, they must be used together to adequately test a system and uncover system faults.

Testing at its heart is an analytical process, with the tester resembling a crime-scene investigator, charged with finding the faults within the system. It is apparent (or at least it should be) that the software is not totally perfect—just as at most scenes where a crime was committed. The tester has to dig behind the scenes to find those things that might not be so obvious. Doing so requires using many different tools and looking at the system from various angles. A tester must see that a system can be functionally correct and yet still have faults. It is this investigative process that gives the developer, tester, manager, and customer a higher degree of confidence in the system and ultimately allows us to release software that will perform to meet customer needs.

What Testing Is Not

Now that we have a simple understanding of what testing is, let's see what testing is *not*. I once worked in a software development shop where, after I happily submitted my first project to the testing organization, I received an email stating that my performance on this project was not adequate; testing was shocked that I would submit a program that had bugs. Naturally, I was stupefied, so I went to my new colleagues and asked about the "software process," in particular the "testing process."

"Oh, yeah," said one of the developers who had overheard my outburst of puzzlement at the chastising email. (Of course, nothing is a secret in the world of the cubicle dweller.) "Never submit anything to testing that has a bug in it—they don't know anything about coding and it will only get you 'written up' by management. In fact, I just got hauled into the project manager's office the other day because I had too many errors in my code."

"This is ridiculous!" I yelled. "Nothing can go to test that has a bug in it? Then what does testing do? How messed up is this place?" The more I thought about this question, the more I realized that in several of the organizations where I worked, there were some very messed-up notions of what testing entails. So just what are these ideas and where do they come from?

Testing Is Not Demonstrating the Lack of Bugs

Too many times, testing is used (quite incorrectly) via demonstrations to show that the "system has no bugs." In the aforementioned software shop, the testing organization was simply looked upon as the "customer demonstration" function. They were advocates for the customer, used to "beat up" the engineers and get what the customer wanted. From the start, testing was approached from the standpoint of demonstrating to the customer that the system works. The problem is that this one-sided view produced exactly what was planned: a demonstration that the system contains no bugs. That is not to say that the systems under test actually don't contain errors but just that the tests were skewed in a way to demonstrate only success.

Many organizations make this basic mistake. They attempt to show the absence of bugs to the customer, feeling that the customer would never buy a piece of software with errors in it. The truth is that we can't show the absence of bugs (at least not for every case). In a classic theoretical experiment, Allen Turing proved, mathematically, that it is impossible to always determine whether for any given input (program) that the system will halt (error) or not. So why then do organizations fall into this common trap?

It's a sense of customer perception versus mathematical reality. To tell you that the software that runs the 777, manages the flow of traffic on city streets, or controls the critical systems that keep patients alive during an operation contains fatal flaws would scare most people, but this may in fact be the case—we just can't prove that it doesn't have errors. Ask any engineer, mathematician, or scientist who has worked on any of these projects and they'll tell you, however, that the software is "statistically safe." Often organizations dismiss this mathematical notion of correctness and safety as too "techie" and academic. (Ask a mathematician to move closer to the wall by halving the distance with each move, and he'll tell you he never reaches the wall but gets "close enough for all practical purposes.") Customers, in most cases, are not concerned with the mathematical details and academic puzzles that are often brought about in formalized logic proofs. They just want to know that their software works (even if the fine print says "to a statistical proven degree").

This is not such a bad thing, however. The problem becomes apparent when companies (such as the software shop mentioned previously) base their entire testing organization around the single premise of showing the software works. This is but one aspect of testing and should not be taken as the entire purpose. Showing that something fails (when it's supposed to) or degrades gracefully under pressure (I don't want the ABS on my car to just stop if it encounters conditions out of tolerance) is just as important as demonstrating what is working within the system.

Testing Is Not Debugging

At the opposite extreme, we have those organizations and individuals who feel that testing should be removing bugs. This is not the case; while testing and debugging often go hand in hand, they are two distinct processes with two very different goals. Debugging is, just as the name implies, the removal of bugs or errors from the code. During the debugging activities of a software process, the emphasis is on finding ways to solve software problems. We already know that the system is faulty; we are trying to find a way to correct the system. Testing, on the other hand, is the discovery of these bugs. It is not focused on *removing* bugs but on *finding* bugs. We assume that the software is correct and document areas where our assumption is violated.

Combining testing and debugging is akin to weeding your garden by searching for an individual weed and pulling it out as soon as you find it. While this approach will work if there are only a few weeds and your garden is relatively small, it's not feasible for large fields or thickets of weeds—a closer analogy to the software project. There are just better, faster, and cheaper methods for removing weeds (i.e., software bugs). Activities such as pair programming and peer review have shown that they are far more effective at detecting and eliminating bugs than the traditional and formal methods of testing.

But this just seems contradictory to logic: If I spend all this time identifying a bug, shouldn't I also invest the time to remove it? The answer is yes and no. In a managed software process, there are trade-offs to every action that we take; in other words, the cost to fix that bug is not only the time spent in fixing the detected error but also the opportunity cost of the time lost searching for other bugs and the potential for other errors injected into the system during the fix. This is not to say that we shouldn't fix the errors that are found, just that there is an entire process that must be taken into account when fixing errors. If you are testing, test; if you are debugging, debug—but don't combine the two functions and expect quality software.

Testing Is Not Someone Else's Job

Within software projects, traditionally there is a separate testing organization, often lumped into a Quality Assurance (QA) division. Developers finish their development process and toss their code over the proverbial wall to the QA team. Testing is viewed by the developer as "someone else's job." The testing team performs its tests on the system and tosses it back over the wall to the programmers with a list of errors.

This traditional approach is costly and prone to failure.

The QA team must often reproduce modules and environments that have either already been created or that are more easily created by the development organization. Developers know the code, having often spent months writing it. They are intimately familiar with the software (to the extreme of not seeing its faults, which is the chief reason for separating the two teams). But do we simply throw out all of this knowledge just for the sake of maintaining a clean environment? It is in fact this separation of duties that often weakens the software quality.

Developers, seeing an entire division dedicated to quality and testing, often don't bother to test their code. The QA and testing division, under the guise of remaining pure, knows very little about the code or what is actually being written, so they can only scratch the surface of testing. As a division justifying its existence, QA must find errors—so it concentrates on the easy ones to detect. The result is that only the very obvious errors are caught and the rest are released—to be found by the customer and eventually blamed on the engineer. "Why are you writing code with bugs in it! We tested what we could, but we can't be expected to test every line of code!" is often the cry of the QA folks.

In one organization in which I worked, I had a known bug in my software—I admit it, I knew that there was a bug but I released it to the testing organization anyway. Why? Because it was going to take me too long to fix the error (well beyond the schedule) and it was a function that would only cause an error in a very distinct way. Chances were that no one would find this error and I was a betting man. The code went through the testing process, and just as I had assumed, the error was never caught. Eventually, the code was released to the customer, who detected the error almost immediately. Almost as quick was the finger-pointing within our organization. QA claimed to have tested everything, engineering claimed to have written to spec, and (after all) QA had tested it. When I was finally tasked to fix the error, it had escalated to a "critical" bug that could jeopardize customer relations and cause a possible cancellation of a contract.

So, how should this have been handled? OK, I'll accept some blame on this; I took a shortcut and made an engineering decision without documenting and without telling anyone. I didn't do my job and complete the code; I didn't completely test my portion of the code. But QA didn't do its job either. As the safety valve of the software development process, the QA people failed to catch a bug that the customer did. Maybe instead of pointing fingers at one another, we should have worked together to test the software. Engineer to engineer, I would have gladly pointed out to testing engineers that this code was missing, giving me time in maintenance to fix the issue. I could have also steered them in the direction to catch some (if not a majority) of the other issues that were written against that component. The peer programming model should extend to the testing of components as well. Testing (when properly defined) is everyone's concern.

In the same vein, you can see why the break is established. QA and testing are separated from the direct reporting chain of the development process to assure that they are an "honest broker" in the software development process, capable of pointing out faults and failures in the software product and process without fear of reprisal from the development project management authority. This is a good idea and is not in debate; what is in question, however, is the common practice of totally separate and isolated divisions. There is nothing that says the two teams cannot talk or share information. We aren't competitors working against one another but rather teammates with a common goal of improving the quality of the software. Although the development engineers shouldn't be the *only* ones to conduct tests, they should assist in conducting tests. Especially in white-box testing, the engineer can often point out potential flaws or identify instances of "I did it this way because…"

Testing Is Not A Single Phase

Too often on a project testing is conducted as a development phase completely separate from development. It is viewed as the final hurdle to clear prior to release of the software. Software organizations wait until the system has been completed before conducting any testing. Just as we have come to recognize that requirements are not all thoroughly defined at the start of a project, not all testing can be defined at the tail end of a project. Testing starts with the acceptance of the contract and continues throughout the life of the project.

More often than not, testing is the last element on the schedule and as such suffers the most cuts of time, personnel, and money. When (not if) the project falls behind, the testing is usually the first thing cut. This concept often goes hand and hand with the separation of development and testing divisions. The misconception is that we can recoup resources (time, personnel, and money) when we fall behind by pushing all testing into the development phase. This is akin to the idea that to lose weight, you should eat everything you would typically eat at all meals at breakfast versus spreading the food out over the day. The belief is that if you eat everything that early, you'll have more time to digest your food. Developers already have a job: developing code. If you force them to do all the testing, they either won't do any testing or will try to do some—at a cost to development.

Testing at the end phases of a project also makes the job of the testing division more difficult. In the early stages of a project, small, manageable units are constructed. As the system is built up, the simplicity (and knowledge of the workings of the manageable pieces) is lost. Testing as an end phase requires testers to tear down through the layers of abstraction and complexity to get at the routines that actually do the work. When you're faced with a shrinking budget and a complex stack of code and hardware, and project managers are breathing down your neck to deliver this software to the customer, is it any wonder that testers can look only at the highest level of functionality?

Testing's Place in the Development Process

One of the most important questions that I have run into in defining software development plans is when testing should occur. If we test a system too early, we run the risk of building up a test structure and conducting tests on subsystems that are in flux. On the other hand, if we test a system too late in its life cycle, we may have too large of a system to adequately cover.

Ideally, testing should occur throughout the development process but at varying levels. Testing is usually approached as a "bottom-up" task. That is, during the early phases of a project we are concerned more with the low-level workings of the system, and as the project proceeds (as shown in Figure 1.1), testing begins to shift focus toward interfaces and eventually on to the higher-level business and user-based functions of the system. This is not to say that testing (or software development for that matter) is a waterfall-like process, but rather that the project and testing should proceed through various discrete phases of the project life cycle and grow and change over time.

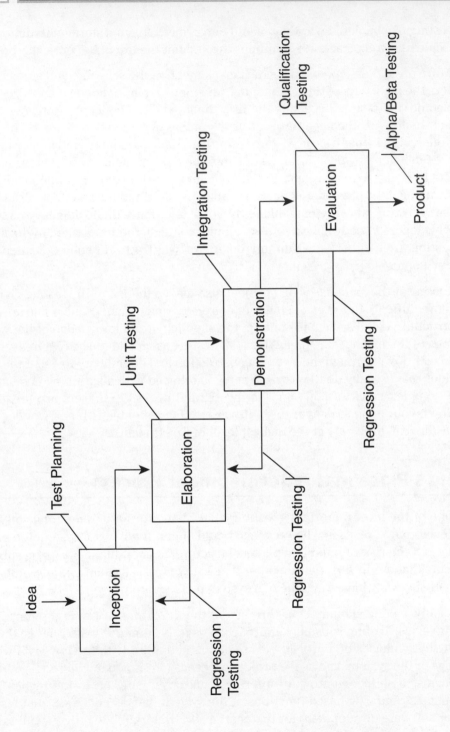

Figure 1.1 Testing from idea to product.

No matter what software development methodology (waterfall, evolutionary, iterative, time-boxed, etc.) you choose (or have chosen for you), the project will evolve through these phases.

Unit Level Testing

Software testing at the lowest level is referred to as *unit testing*. At this level, individual classes and methods are tested. More emphasis is placed on verification and black-box testing at this level.

Here, the concern is that algorithms work as directed and that individual classes have captured the requirement(s) assigned to them. Typically, you are working with an individual class and developing a method or two to exercise the functionality of each method. This type of testing is often conducted in an informal way (System.out.println statements scattered throughout the code, creating a main() method and compiling/running during development, etc.). While these methods are effective for an individual programmer, they often fall into the traps of "bad testing":

- **Demonstrating lack of bugs:** Developer tests are all too often geared toward showing that the system works instead of identifying the faults. After writing the routine, they write a simple "test" that shows the system works for a given case (or maybe even for a few simple cases). Testing is done to show that the method "works." This might give the developer some confidence in the system, but it does nothing to instill overall system confidence and quality. To avoid this type of scenario, it is suggested that developers "write the test first." By creating a testing harness and focusing on possible modes of failure, the developer can then write a routine that will pass the test. This method of "bugging" (the opposite of debugging) allows the developer (or pairs of developers and testers) to prioritize and analyze the failure modes of the method sooner rather than later.

- **Debugging during testing:** At the method level, you may be too far into the details to effectively debug a system. Just because a method does not operate as you think it should doesn't mean that it has failed. Operation in a certain way may be defined as part of the system as a whole or in part with other integrated parts. Too much emphasis on debugging the system might begin to affect higher-level system functions (speed, performance, allocated runtimes, etc.). Often, a well-placed (and carefully worded) "FIXME" or "TODO" comment can suffice to indicate that further attention may be required. This will also give you a chance to assess all the problems as a whole and assign priority to the major issues. There's no sense making a low-use, low-priority routine bulletproof while the major system functionality goes unaddressed.

- **Passing the buck testing:** This is an all-too-common problem at the unit level of testing. After all, in a lot of organizations, the testing division either is too swamped or just doesn't have the programming skills to look into the code for problems. So why bother? From my experiences with improving software processes and assisting large organizations in maturing their software practices, one key point sticks in my mind: "If you don't have time to do it right, how will you make time to do it over?" If you are not testing your units because your testers are swamped or (you feel) that they won't find it, what makes you think that your testers will have time to do the testing? They hold the same opinions about the people they hand the software to next (your paying customers). By avoiding testing, you are starting a cycle that you (and your company) won't recover from. This software is only coming back to you to rewrite, so why not do it right from the start and avoid the emails, late nights, and frantic phone calls (unless you really enjoy these things)?

- **Single-phase view:** I've seen too many developers insert unit-testing code into the system, then pass it on to integrators who insert more tests and code, and then on to qualification testers who will strip out all the testing code before they package for shipping. If you really are concerned with "code-bloat," I can see why this practice is appealing, but a carefully planned test at all levels can reuse knowledge, code, and results to devise higher levels of testing. Coding as an integrated approach (involving qualification testers, QA personnel, and developers) can allow for a reusable testing framework (first across the application and later across all products). Patterns (as you'll see later) can greatly assist in this endeavor, making testing constructs easier to establish, easier to execute, and easier to interpret.

Pair programming is an excellent mechanism to employ at this level. Two developers (or a developer and a member of the test organization) can sit down and side by side construct the tests that are needed. The algorithm developer will have intimate knowledge of the module under construction, and the tester will focus on what could potentially go wrong with the system. If the "bugging" approach of testing before coding is taken, one member of the pair can write a test (or a series of tests) while the other writes code to pass the test—a separation of concerns without a separation of knowledge.

Integration Testing

As the system progresses, classes and methods are linked together into logical and physical system components. Testing at this level involves checking to see that interactions and interfaces are meeting their responsibilities.

Here, you are shifting focus from the work of individual methods to how classes interact. Instead of worrying about algorithms working as a whole, developers focus on the robustness, error handling, and overall communications of two or more components. But why perform this level of testing? It seems that if the individual pieces operate correctly, the system should operate as a whole. Ah, how soon we forget software failures such as the Mars Climate Orbiter, which landed rather ungracefully (and quite fatally) on the Martian surface. The reason: interfaces. Some systems were sending data in metric form (meters per second, grams, etc.) while others were expecting English units (feet per second, pounds, etc.). The individual unit systems worked just as designed, calculating acceleration, stress, and such to their proper degree of certainty. Unit tests on these systems would have not shown any anomalies. However, when the units were assembled into larger components, integration tests (when properly constructed) should have detected these anomalies.

Of course, this form of testing is vulnerable to the same "bad testing" issues that plague all testing phases. With a shift from building low-level components into locking those components together, there is also a tendency to forget the lessons of the unit-test phase and build not only software components but also software errors. Even though the integration phase is often more formalized and controlled, it is still burdened by these faulty testing strategies:

- **Yes, we have no errors:** If the tests are written to "prove the system has no errors," then you will get only tests that don't show errors. In the case of the Mars Climate Orbiter, perhaps tests were written that checked a few random values passed to and from the various components. As long as those values were in the "middle range" (values that were acceptable both as English and metric units), the integration tests would have passed. It is only when the developers tested the extremes of each side that they would generate failures. A knowledgeable tester with a little planning can start to recognize areas where systems fail (passing null values to objects, passing 0 or negative numbers to integer functions) and create common tests and scenarios around those areas.

- **Slap it together and see if it works:** It much more fun to build up the code that tests little pieces of it; at least, that's the philosophy I've seen from most developers. Integration testing is nothing more than linking Module A to Module B and running through the unit tests for both. But this just leads to the "proving we have no errors" approach that we know will fail. We've seen it work; we want to see *how* it works. Integration is often the first time that the "-ilities" are introduced. These are the requirements (which often end in *ility*) that are less quantitative in nature and more qualitative. Things like usability, reliability, and scalability are important aspects that need to be tested and built up.

- **We'll test that later when it's easier:** Especially at the lower levels of integration, it may seem impossible to test certain combinations of components. Especially in larger J2EE applications, it's a lot easier to test a system when it's completed than it is to test individual interfaces. On one system we had the standard data access object (DAO) layer built on a service framework on which individual services were built, which led to Web-based JSP tags for each functional area. For a lot of the code, we were able to use code-generation tools (XDoclet and the like), which took much of the burden of creating these systems away from the developer. And with that we all got lazy. Instead of testing the service-DAO interface, we just ran our complex Ant tasks and generated the tags and tested from that end. This was all well and good until we started to detect little errors in the framework layer—not specific unit test errors, but those errors that only materialized because we started to use the program in a specific way. Now we were faced with having to change the DAOs and framework while the services were still in flux. As a result, developers began to lose confidence in our system. The lesson? You can't skip over the middle integration testing, no matter how automated your build system becomes. Improvements in coding efficiency shouldn't translate to shortcuts in testing. Even if you didn't write it, you have to interface to it and you still should test it.

It is during this phase that you, as the tester, must start to think about building confidence in the system versus showing that things work. But wait; isn't the job of a tester to break things? How can you build confidence in a system by breaking things? During integration testing, you should be less concerned about breaking the system and more focused on testing its boundaries. Issues of robustness, failure mode, and graceful degradation must be considered. You will most certainly find instances where the interfaces fail, the system grinds to a halt, or the interactions do not behave as expected. You need to test the boundaries of the system to know what the system can and cannot do.

What makes integration and integration testing so hard is that the process begins the shift from determining if the module does its work correctly toward determining if it does the right work. By gluing components together, you can begin to see not only if the module is operating properly but also if it is doing what it is supposed to do. It is entirely possible to have components (such as those in the Mars Climate Orbiter) that do their individual tasks quite well but fail to meet the overall system requirements. When I once asked one of my developers to tell me the difference between X and Y, he described it like a factory. If the factory produces widgets, we can pull individual widgets off the line and test to see that they work, but this doesn't do any good if the factory wasn't supposed to be producing widgets in the first place. The same holds true for software. At the unit-testing level, we were more concerned with the details of how the job was done, but at integration we focus on what job is to be done.

Engineers in Great Britain constructed what was to be one of the modern marvels of engineering, architecture, and artistry. Just west of the town of Hull, they constructed (at the time) the world's largest single-span suspension bridge. The Humber Bridge was truly a model engineering program, exceeding schedules and milestones. However, it had one serious flaw: There was no need for a bridge in Hull. The residents of Hull refer to the monstrosity as the "bridge to nowhere" as it has never carried the traffic levels that it was originally designed to carry. Even its revenues from tolls have not met the levels required to save the project from the debt incurred to construct it. There is no question that the bridge was well constructed—it just wasn't needed. Building something correctly isn't enough to declare success; we also need to say that we've built the right thing for the environment and users.

Qualification Testing

The culmination of all these tests is *qualification testing*. At this level, focus has shifted entirely toward the validation of the system. Tests are conducted that address the developed requirements and business use cases for the system. In qualification testing, both formalized and informal methods are used to show that the system works.

On the formal side, there are (often contractually dictated) tests for customer acceptance. Often at these tests, the customer is working from a standard script and just wants to see the system function. Although this form of testing only scratches the surface of all testing, it is the confidence in what the system can and cannot do that will allow you to stand before the customer and push that button firing the rocket engines. It is rumored that for early qualification tests of the nuclear submarine program, U.S. Navy Admiral Hyman George Rickover used to require that the senior staff of the contract's companies go on the maiden underwater voyage. What better way to require that a company's testing organization is up to snuff than to have management bet their lives on it!

Informally, on one project that I worked on a manager played a similar game. During lunchtime, my program manager had the habit of "banging on" the application. Without much knowledge of what the application was designed to do (or without any regard for the layers and layers of user-friendly controls that my team slaved to put into place), he would sit down with his ham and cheese sandwich and proceed to press buttons, do queries, and "work the system." Occasionally, he'd ask a member of my staff to join him for this lunchtime effort. Programmers thought he'd lost it—flipping through screens, tearing through data. They complained that he didn't know anything about testing and was leading to the downfall of our software process. He knew exactly what he was doing. Capitalizing on the fear that every programmer has of sitting with the boss, he was playing a form of "you bet your life" or at least you bet your job (not that he'd actually fire anyone for errors) with the programmers. The end result? I'd never seen programmers test so diligently. No one wanted to be cornered with the program manager over lunch when their system went dead. My program manager just sat back and smiled and ate his ham sandwiches in peace—knowing that the testing was being done.

Regression Testing

Although not an entire level within itself, *regression testing* involves the rerunning and reevaluation of tests (or subsets of tests) when there is a change to the system. Something that was introduced might have broken a module or function that was previously working. While the system is changing, there is always a chance of introducing more bugs into the system.

One of the chief reasons for regression testing is that most errors in maintenance programming are introduced within small changes to the system. It is these changes that often go untested. Popular thinking says that since the systems are so small they can't possibly contain errors. But that can be deceiving. In 1990, the entire eastern seaboard was without telephone service for several hours. Upon examination, it was determined that there was a minor software error within one of the telephone switches. This code was introduced as part of a simple three-line software fix. As a result, it was estimated that nearly $1 billion was lost due to the outage. This costly mistake could have been avoided by running a series of regression tests on the affected code areas. No matter how small the change, the interfaces and entanglements of large-scale software projects have a way of piling up, regardless of how well managed or well documented they are.

However, regression testing is a lot more than just rerunning the same tests—it requires analyzing the affected code base to determine what could go wrong. You may have to incorporate new tests because of that changing situation that you just introduced. On one project, I had to change my primitives (*int, long, float*, etc.) into their cousin Object values (*Integer, Long, Float*, etc.). This was relatively easy even without an IDE with fancy code-management tools. Just a search and replace, and things were back to compiling. I did a refactoring on all my tests to replace those simple constants with constructors to my new objects and ran the tests—and passed! I checked it all into the repository and marked the issue as ready for use (it was part of a larger API). I was shocked to get emails from everyone complaining about failures in the API. What happened? Well, I forgot about testing things like passing null values into the methods and those "special" values like *NaN* (Not a Number) that can lead to errors. Clearly, I needed more checks in my test suite.

What Are We Looking for in Testing?

We've pretty much established what testing *isn't* and what *not* to do when you test. So what *should* you look for when you test? This isn't an easy question to answer. Knowing what to test for and how to push a system to its limits is as much a black art as turning lead to gold. I can't just tell you to always test for a certain set of values or for a particular functionality. It just doesn't work that way. But you can become familiar with the types of things to look for. As you test your systems more and more, you'll be able to build up the knowledge and experience required to just look at a system and know whether it will work.

Correctness: The System Does Its Function Properly

This is the most obvious thing to test for—after all, we know what the function of the system/module/method is, so we can make sure the outputs are correct relative to the inputs. We test the fundamental laws of the system, making sure that the proverbial 2 + 2 equals 4. If the system should process 30,000 messages in one minute, we feed in 30,000 messages and verify that they are all processed within a minute. This is the most basic of all the tests.

Completeness: The System Does Everything It's Supposed to Do

A task that's a little more complex—as we've pointed out—is making sure the system does what it is intended to do. In the case of our 30,000-message-processing system, we need to make sure that it indeed processes all 30,000 messages. In addition, we should verify that it works for values less than 30,000 —in other words, can it process only one message fed to it per minute as well? While that may seem obvious, it might be the case that the developer has hard-coded a value. In one such system that I worked on, the system did indeed work fine for 30,000 messages, but when we started sending smaller and smaller messages volumes to the system, it began to fail. The reason is that there was an internal constraint on a buffer that would only forward the contents of the message queue to the processor once the queue was full. So my 29,999 messages sat in the queue for a full minute without processing until the next message from the next set of inputs was received, triggering the buffer to release its contents to the processor. Had we only tested the 30,000 messages, we would have been unaware of the bug.

Failures: The System Knows when It Fails

This is one thing that is often overlooked in testing: Systems will need to recognize a failure and act accordingly. One of the worst things for a system to do is to incorrectly report success when indeed there was a failure. This undermines everyone's trust and confidence in the system. We once had a complex build process based on Ant that failed this test. Anyone who has used Ant before knows that it generally will stop with a message of BUILD FAILED if one of the executed tasks fails. But we were experiencing a problem. Developers would generate the system, receive the BUILD SUCCESS message, and deploy the application only to find that the system wasn't working. On closer examination, we found that the deployed JAR files didn't contain all of the necessary code to run the system. Further assessment of the system showed that one of the intermediate processes was failing but not reporting its failure. Sure enough, the system was running out of memory, but that was not considered a fatal error, so the system continued on, unable to do anything else until it finally reached the end and reported SUCCESS. However, it's not just external processes that should do this. Consider modules that multiply, divide, subtract, or add numbers. Because of the finite representation limit of computers (we can only store so much in the space allocated to an integer, byte, or long), we might run into issues where the maximum (or minimum) values are exceeded. And what programmer hasn't seen the error of division by zero? As our systems get increasingly complex and we build more functionality into each module, we tend to lose track of these simple errors.

"Grace Under Pressure": The System Can Fail and Not Flop

Along with the idea of knowing when it fails, a system should fail gracefully. This isn't something this is specified in most requirements documents but rather is taken for granted. Although this might not be the best practice, it is for the most part a reality; the exception is "man-rated" systems (systems that involve human contact whose failure may result in the loss of life). In these critical systems it is evident that subcomponents just shouldn't stop working (oxygen ventilators shouldn't halt if they get unexpected monitor values, the brakes on my car shouldn't stop functioning if the temperature falls below the specification values, etc.). With these systems, it is expected that they will still perform (although in a diminished capacity) when the specification is exceeded; in most cases this is clearly specified in the system planning documentation. But what about noncritical systems? We've come to expect a certain "grace under pressure" from these systems as well. When my word processor fails (as it does so often), I expect that my work will be saved in some capacity, either through backup files or intermediate differences. While my system might not be able to store the full details of my masterpiece of a novel, it should at least preserve as much of the work as possible. As a tester, you must look at not only what causes a failure to the system but also how the system reacts to a failure.

Confidence: The System Is Ready

This is the key element to testing. As we explained before, you can never show the absence of all the bugs; at best what you can do is instill the confidence in your system that, given the specification and operational parameters, it will function as intended and better yet will not function as not intended. Testing all comes down to trust and believing that the system will work.

I worked on a system once that performed analysis of data for the users. It was a direct replacement for their old systems, which involved using pen and paper and pouring over the numbers all night. To help with user acceptance, we hired as consultants several of the retired former "pen and paper" analysts as customer liaisons. We spent several months growing a very professional-looking interface and query generator that would allow the users to point and click their way through the volumes of data associated with our system. We demonstrated the user interface to the customer; the analysts loved it and suggested many changes that would make their jobs easier. We knew we had a winning application. At release time, I stood in front of the roomful of analysts and performed, using our tool, a data correlation and analysis effort that would have typically taken weeks, all in the span of 5 minutes. Our analysts were amazed. They immediately took to the new system, but months later, during a push to get out some critical analysis, I was shocked to see my analyst team creating SQL queries and doing analysis not with our tool but with pen and paper again. When I asked them why they weren't using the tool, they responded with "We just don't know if we can trust those numbers." I realized that we had made a critical mistake. We had focused too much on the user interface acceptance and not on the building of confidence in the system. After the critical analysis was over, I spent some time "retesting" the system, walking the analysts through the smallest pieces of the code and building up their confidence in the system. I needed to sell them on the fact that our system was built to their specification and could do just what they wanted. In the end, we didn't change one line of code (we did come up with a new list of enhancements for the system), but at the next analysis exercise, people not only used our tool but also our system became the central element in the exercise. Now when this yearly undertaking comes around, they can't think of doing it any other way.

Putting It All Together

So, after all of this, you must certainly get the impression that testing is an impossible job—one that requires you to believe the system is broken yet also instills confidence that it works. As a developer, you are the first line of testing in any organization. From my practice, I've seen that, more often than not, the amount of testing that you perform will be the most thorough and most effective in identifying the limits of the system. After all, you wrote it, so who better to start building confidence in the system?

2

Unit Testing

I find that the harder I work, the more luck I seem to have.

—*Thomas Jefferson*

This chapter is an introduction to unit testing, extreme programming, and the tools that a Java developer needs to perform unit testing. In addition, we cover JUnit and offer further resources for unit testing.

What Is Unit Testing?

A *unit test* is a test designed to evaluate a single element of code. The code's behavior is examined independently of other elements in order to determine whether the code element meets expectations. A suite of unit tests can be used to evaluate an entire solution (one unit at a time); then, if the solution itself ceases to be effective, it can be broken down into its component actions (or units) to see where the failure occurs.

When you're integrating code in an application or identifying bugs that have migrated into production code unexpectedly, unit tests can save developers and project managers many hours of work (and bottles of Excedrin). Additionally, when a new bug arises in code, sometimes six or more months after deployment, having unit tests available can diminish the time required to remember what the offending code actually does (or should be doing). In this way, unit tests are also an effective part of any documentation effort.

Let's illustrate a unit test in real-world terms by solving the following problem:

Problem: You are sitting on your couch, and you see one of your children's shoes on the floor in the middle of the living room. The shoe needs to be placed at the bottom of the stairs.

Solution: Get the shoe to the staircase.

Implementation: You as a designer decide that the most economic implementation of this solution is to get up off the couch, walk over to the middle of the floor, pick up the shoe, place it on the bottom stair, and then return to your original position on the couch.

The units of the solution are:

- Get up off the couch.
- Forward step left.
- Forward step right.
- Bend over and pick up the shoe.
- Straighten.
- Turn to face the stairs.
- Forward step to the stairs.
- Bend down and place the shoe on the stairs.
- Turn to face the couch.
- Forward step to the couch.
- Sit down and gripe about how much you do around here.

There are two types of units in object-oriented programming (OOP) that apply to unit testing. Unit testing will always be defined as being within the scope of one of these two elements: *class* and *method*. A class is constructed of properties and methods; a method is a behavior taken by a class. Since a class is defined as the sum of its members and methods (in a static state), it is logical to assume that a class-level unit test will accomplish the needs of unit testing; however, in the case of static utility classes or specific objects (instances of these classes with their own statefulness), tests at class level may not be appropriate to your needs.

It is important to note that if your objective is to create a testing framework for your project, then it is highly desirable to evaluate these two scopes before deciding which one to use throughout your project. If you try to integrate both class and method scope testing for the same project, it will become increasingly difficult to manage your test suites in your code-promotion process. It is also much more likely that you will end up with redundant tests and/or have whole sections of code without unit tests at all. Your testing framework should always be designed in such a way that you can examine it (like a file system) to ensure that the core elements of your application are covered by unit tests.

Class Scope Testing

Class-level testing can be categorized in terms of testing for implementation or testing for inheritance.

The goal of class-level testing is to define the interfaces for classes and then establish and maintain their effectiveness throughout the development, implementation, and support phases. As indicated by its name, class-level testing involves creating a test case for each class. This test case class will evaluate the members of the class to ensure that they behave as designed.

Why unit test at class level? Here are some reasons:

- Provides great documentation for the intended behavior of a class
- Easily integrates into a deployment/build process
- Communicates progress to customers/managers
- Can be used in team code ownership situations to regression test changes to classes
- Provides a more high-level system overview than method scope testing and is easier to maintain

To illustrate class-level testing, we will create two hypothetical classes. The class Dog consists of the properties dateOf Birth, eyeColor, isSeeingEyeDog, isHandicapped, heightUpperBound, heightLowerBound, weightUpperBound, and weightLowerBound. The Leonberger class inherits all these attributes from Dog (overwriting the height and weight information) but also includes attributes for hairstyle, haircolor, and a collection of faults (see Figure 2.1). For the sake of this illustration, we will assume they exist within a larger framework and are used as business objects to add some new functionality.

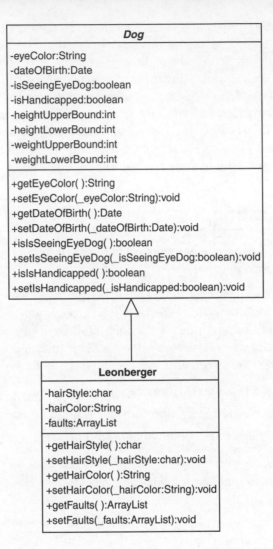

Figure 2.1 The Dog and Leonberger classes.

Inheritance-Level Class Scope Testing

Testing a class in terms of its full inheritance is referred to as *flattened class testing*. Suppose that the Dog class has been in production for two years, so you as a developer do not feel the need to test its functionality. In this case, you will define a unit test to test only the newly implemented members and methods of the Leonberger class.

If, however, you are concerned with regression testing of the Dog class under its new implementation as a Leonberger, you will want to "flatten" the class for the purposes of testing and then evaluate all of the members of the newly created Leonberger class, including those inherited from the Dog class (see Figure 2.2).

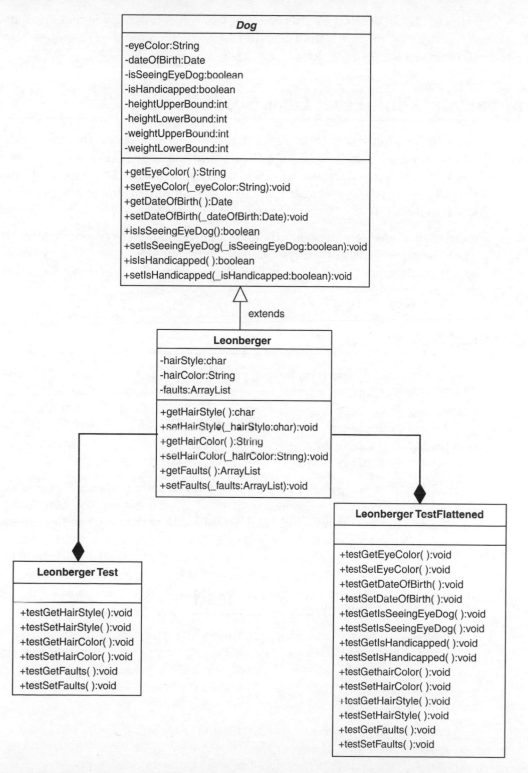

Figure 2.2 The difference between flattened class and implementation-level testing.

By testing Leonberger as a flattened class, you can determine whether anything you did by creating it as a child class of Dog has had unintended or undesirable effects on its superclass (Dog).

Implementation-Level Class Scope Testing

Testing a class in terms of its implementation means testing only those methods implemented specifically by it (or one of its objects), and no methods or members whose implementation is inherited from superclasses. These methods are either defined in the class under test (CUT) or defined in a superclass and overridden in the CUT.

In the case where your class is extending a core component of your system (a component for which extensive unit tests may already exist), it may make sense to write a unit test that tests only the newly implemented members and methods of this class.

Method Scope Testing

As an alternative to class-level testing, you may decide to test your applications at *method scope*. This means that instead of designing a test for all methods in a class, you design a test case to run only a single method. You then design a suite to run multiple test cases together. This is a paradigm shift from class-level testing. If you have a framework that has a few core classes that do a great deal of work in static context, this scope may make more sense for you.

Method-level testing can be extremely useful in evaluating robustness (in other words, how unexpected situations are handled). These tests can be used to validate passed arguments or values, and determine how they are handled within a method. For example, say the Dog class's setDateOfBirth() method needs to make sure dates can be parsed before assigning them to the dateOfBirth field. By creating a method-level test for setDateOfBirth(), you can evaluate how this situation is handled in many different date formats. Figure 2.3 shows the Dog class and DogSetDateOfBirth test case; Listing 2.1 contains the test code.

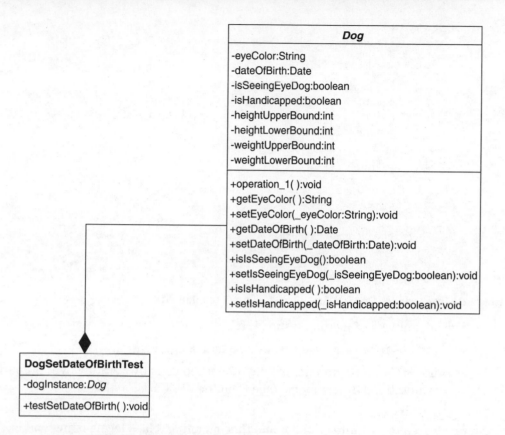

Figure 2.3 Dog class and DogSetDateOfBirth test case.

```
public class DogSetDateOfBirthTest {

    private Dog dogInstance;
    private static DogSetDateOfBirthTest testCase;


    public static void main(String[] args){
        testCase = new DogSetDateOfBirthTest();
        testCase.testSetDateOfBirth();
    }

    public void testSetDateOfBirth() throws AssertionError{
        /* note that Dog is an abstract class
         * and cannot be instantiated in and of
         * itself.  So we will instantiate a concrete
         * class that does not override the default
```

Listing 2.1 Test code for DogSetDateOfBirth test case. (continues)

```
      * functionality to test it.
      */
     dogInstance = new Leonberger();
     String eyeColor = "brown";
     dogInstance.setEyeColor(eyeColor);
     boolean assertion = (dogInstance.getEyeColor().equals(eyeColor));
     if(assertion){

         System.out.println("Test Passed.");
     }else{
         System.out.println("Test Failed.");
     }

   } // end testSetDateOfBirth

 } // end DogSetDateOfBirthTest
```

Listing 2.1 Test code for DogSetDateOfBirth test case. (continued)

The advantages of method testing are:

- Provides for testing use cases through test aggregation
- Allows for more granular testing of method calls by iterating over potential permutations of arguments (see Chapter 13, "Category-Partition Pattern")
- Proves to be more granular and thorough than class-level testing and is great for robustness testing and exception handling

Why Unit Test?

If a solution is not tested at the unit level, many bugs can slip through during the testing phase because they do not fit within the realm of the use cases. By implementing a unit test, you can change the parameters passed to the CUT or MUT to see how it behaves under different parameters.

One of the goals of OOP is to write solid, reusable code. It stands to reason, then, that unit testing encourages the decoupling of classes from their solution and the implementation of a more toolbox-based approach to the design of solutions. By thinking of a class as a unit of accomplishment, you can more easily identify where its contract can be used again in similar (or even dissimilar) solutions.

Developers will be much more comfortable refactoring existing code when they have a test to run against it that proves the code meets defined requirements. You can also use test suites as a baseline to prove the effectiveness of refactoring (e.g., before refactoring, it took 3.3 seconds to accomplish this task, but after the refactoring the unit test is accomplished in 55 milliseconds.

If a class falls within the middle of a three-tier or Model-View-Controller (MVC) architecture, it is testable separate from its view layer. When you have a unit test for your middle-tier business object, and a tester tells you that your code is broken, you can immediately test and determine if the error is in your code, in the data model, or in the view code (GUI).

XP: Test First Driven Development

Early in the 1990s, Kent Beck and Ward Cunningham developed a new team-driven approach to software development called Extreme Programming (XP). Their approach was designed to make the process of building software more successful in terms of product quality and quality of life for developers.

In the area of product quality, XP incorporates enhanced communication between development teams and managers, a better process of teamwork within development teams, constant communication between developers and customers, and a testing regimen that keeps stakeholders aware of progress.

Quality-of-life improvements are achieved by keeping customers in the loop throughout the design and development phase of a project, which helps manage expectations and provides constant feedback that the project is going in the intended direction. One of the fundamental premises of XP is that by team members taking the time to communicate throughout the process, time spent rehashing and refactoring is kept to a minimum. Another principle of XP that is attractive to development teams is a commitment that planning projects be developed inside a 40-hour workweek.

The success of this new paradigm shift in software development is attributed to improved levels of communication, simplicity of design, constant feedback from all stakeholders, and the courage and commitment to find a better way to work. Therefore, the four core values of XP are defined as communication, simplicity, feedback, and courage.

XP has attracted a strong following among many software developers and continues to gain followers and evangelists. It is far beyond the scope of this book to discuss all the principles and practices of XP. Instead I will list them here as well as some good XP resources, and then move on to the principle that falls within the scope of this book: Test First Driven Development.

Note that the following XP principles are tightly coupled; they are designed to work together.

Coding standard: It's a given that any sports team works better when everyone approaches the game with the same mindset. In order to do that, the team agrees on a strategy and practices together. This principle should be applied to teams of software developers as well. As a team, developers can make decisions about how to approach solutions, what design patterns to apply, and which common utility libraries can be used and refactored by the team. Teams should even take the time to define a standard way to name variables and methods and agree where to put the curly braces.

Collective code ownership: Wilt Chamberlain once scored over 100 points in a single basketball game, yet his team lost. If you work on a development team, your code will be more cohesive and easier to refactor if common code ownership is practiced. The principle is simple. The team owns the code base. No developer owns any particular module or package. At any point, any developer should be able to pick up a piece of the code and add functionality or refactor to fit the needs of the project.

Continuous integration: Integrating and building an application is critical and can cause great stress if the process is ignored until the end of the development phase. An XP team should check in source code to integrate and build on a regular (even daily) basis. This helps the team to quickly identify and fix changes in code that affect other parts of the application. It also helps developers keep a slightly more elevated perspective on the whole project. Finally, when it is time to deploy the entire application, everyone on the development team will be much more confident in the results.

Forty-hour workweek: Thorough planning enables the team to accomplish development in a standard 40-hour week. This keeps the developers more rested and effective; it also leaves room to work in extra time for the real emergencies that may crop up.

Metaphor: Developers working on a team need to speak the same language. Everyone must have a solid understanding of buzzwords and acronyms used by the team. Metaphors should also be used for business requirements and use cases.

On-site customers: Having a representative for the customer on site makes a huge difference in defining requirements and measuring achievement through design and development. Since the onset of XP, instant messaging has become prevalent enough to make this requirement a little easier to accomplish. If the customer cannot be on site, he or she should at least be always available to the development leader. The customer also needs to be empowered to make decisions and evaluate solutions.

Pair programming: Pair programming involves two programmers working together at one computer. At times, one programmer may be taking notes, brainstorming, or planning a unit test, but it is important that they work together so that they both determine the direction the code takes. This is a principle that must be planned for. Remember, if you are a small firm you may have to justify billing for two people when only one set of code is being produced. The principle here is sound. Two qualified people will usually develop a better solution than one alone and will be twice as prepared to refactor or support it.

Planning process: Customers define requirements and weigh the relative value of features. Programmers define time estimates. Let me say that one again: *Programmers define time estimates!* Programming managers use the time estimates to provide cost estimates for the customer.

Refactoring: If something looks like it needs to be refactored, do it. Make the changes necessary to improve the code, document those changes, and communicate with the team. Unit tests will help you get there and know that the contractual requirements of the interfaces continue to be met.

Small releases: Deploy the system early to find potential patterns of problems that arise in deployment. Deploy the application often to demonstrate new functionality and progress.

Simple design: Occam's razor is the principle that one should not multiply entities unnecessarily, or make further assumptions than are needed, and that in general one should pursue the simplest hypothesis. Likewise, an XP program should be the simplest solution to the proposed problem. Anything that needs to be added will be facilitated by common code ownership and refactoring.

Test First Driven Development: At design time developers determine the contractual requirements for their interfaces. These interfaces will pass the expected requirements to a given method and expect a valid return value (or effect). These tests will continue to fail until the interface is correct. This process helps immediately by clearly communicating what each unit of an application should accomplish. They also aid tremendously in documenting the application's design and communicating progress to customers.

Applying Test First Driven Development

As you know, applications are built from hundreds or thousands of discrete units of execution. Suppose your task is to develop a catalog Web site for an e-commerce business. You have a single requirement: the site's homepage must display one random product per page load, and it must label that product as an "Internet Special." In designing this function, you may determine that you require a single interface that will be passed an integer that represents the number of products in the catalog (call it maxProducts) and from it derive a random number between 1 and maxProducts. Your application will then use that number to look up one of the products in the database. Let's look at a use case for this unit of work:

Requirements: We need an interface that will take a primitive integer in Java (x) and return a random number (also a primitive integer) between 1 and x. This number should always be greater than 1 and less than the largest primary key in the catalog table (for simplicity's sake we will assume this field is an auto-incrementing counter and there are no deleted records).

Solution: Add a static method to our CatalogMathUtils class to achieve this requirement.

First we should crack open our CatalogMathUtil class and implement a method to test. For now we will have it return (-1) since primitives cannot be null and the method must return some value.

The code will look something like this:

```
public static int getRandomPositiveInteger(int upperBound){
        return -1;
}
```

Now we write our test case to evaluate the effectiveness of this method. Again, for simplicity's sake, assume that we are writing an implementation-specific class-level unit test, and that ours is the first method in our CatalogMathUtil class. See also Appendix A.

NOTE

The following code is written in the JUnit framework; we will cover JUnit in greater detail later in this chapter.

```
import junit.framework.TestCase;

public class CatalogMathUtilsTest extends TestCase {
    private int upperBound;

    /**
     * Constructor for CatalogMathUtilsTest.
     * @param arg0
     */
    public CatalogMathUtilsTest(String arg0) {
        super(arg0);
    }

    /**
     * @see TestCase#setUp()
     */
```

```
    protected void setUp() throws Exception {
        super.setUp();
        upperBound = 10;
    }


    /**
     * @see TestCase#tearDown()
     */
    protected void tearDown() throws Exception {
        super.tearDown();
    }


    public void testGetRandomPositiveInteger(){
        int randomNumber =
CatalogMathUtils.getRandomPositiveInteger(upperBound);
        assertTrue("The value returned was less than 1",
(randomNumber>0));
        assertTrue("The value returned was greater than the
upperbound",(randomNumber<=upperBound));
                //implement test of randomness of the returned integer
here
    }
}
```

Now if we run this test it will (and should) fail because we have not yet written the actual code for this. Here are the results:

```
junit.framework.AssertionFailedError: The value returned was less than 1
```

While this is a failure, it is also exactly what we expect and want to see at this point.

Next we have to actually write the code to solve the problem. In this case it is pretty straightforward:

```
import java.lang.Math;

public class CatalogMathUtils {

    public static int getRandomPositiveInteger(int upperBound){
        int randomNumber = (int)Math.rint((Math.random())*upperBound);
        System.out.println(String.valueOf(randomNumber));
        return randomNumber;
    }

}
```

Now when we run our unit test it passes.

The advantages to writing code this way are numerous. First, it helps us define exactly the results we expect to see before we even begin to code. Second, if the solution is more complicated than this one, we are less likely to lose sight of our goal. By continually testing our code, we can quickly see how our present work is getting us closer to the final goal of passing the unit test. At any point our development manager or another developer can evaluate our progress and implementation for refactoring or adding functionality. For example, if another developer needs to generate a random number without an upper bound, she may implement a method with the same name as ours that takes no arguments. That method may then turn and call ours with an argument of Integer.MAX_VALUE:

```
public static int getRandomPositiveInteger(){
        return getRandomPositiveInteger(Integer.MAX_VALUE);
}
```

After adding this method, which calls ours, the developer will want to run our unit test again to regression test her own. If her code were to negatively affect ours, it could create a bug nested deep in an application that might occur only sporadically after deployment. With a solid unit test for the CatalogMathUtils class that includes both methods, such a bug would be found and fixed at development time, saving a great deal of time and resources down the road.

What Is JUnit?

JUnit is a unit-testing framework that was originally developed by Kent Beck and Erich Gamma for testing at class-level scope. Many of the testing patterns described in detail in this book have been implemented in JUnit. It is lauded by the extreme programming community because of its reliance on unit testing, and it is written entirely in Java. JUnit is completely open-source software, and has been expanded and improved by a community of developers who contribute to the code base. It is based on the xUnit architecture for unit-testing frameworks. Information on JUnit can always be found on the Web at http://junit.org/. (See also Appendix A.)

JUnit features include the following:

- Assertions for testing expected results (see Chapter 6, "Assertion Pattern" for a detailed description of this concept)
- Test fixtures for sharing common test data
- Suites of tests for easily organizing and running tests
- Graphical and textual test runners

Working with JUnit involves building TestCases (which contain TestFixtures) and aggregating them into TestSuites.

What Is a TestCase?

A TestCase (in its simplest form) is designed to evaluate the execution of a single class. If we have a class Name that has three public methods and two member variables, as shown in Figure 2.4:

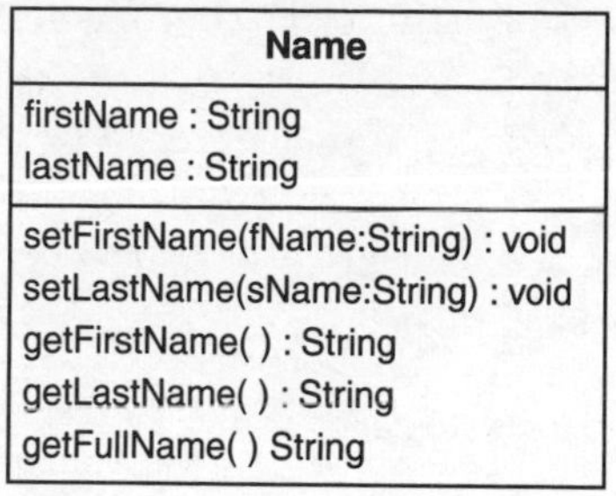

Name
firstName : String
lastName : String
setFirstName(fName:String) : void
setLastName(sName:String) : void
getFirstName( ) : String
getLastName( ) : String
getFullName( ) String

Figure 2.4 A simple test case.

then its TestCase will be a new class inheriting from junit.framework.TestCase (which itself inherits from junit.framework.Test). This new class will be called NameTest (the class name is important because JUnit uses reflection to aggregate TestCases into TestSuites) and it will have three subroutines, called testSetFirstname, testSetLastName, and testGetFullName.

NOTE

This is an extremely abbreviated and simplified version of TestCase. For more detailed information on JUnit's API, see the API Documents section at junit.org.

Any class extending junit.TestCase will inherit the following methods:

```
/**
 * Primitive int representing the number of test cases executed by run.
 */
int     countTestCases()


/**
 * Creates a default TestResult object
 */
protected TestResult    createResult()


/**
 * Returns the name of the TestCase
 */
String     getName()


/**
 * Runs this test
 */
TestResult     run()
/**
 * Runs the test given an existing TestResult
 */
void     run(TestResult result)
/**
 * Runs the bare test sequence
 */
```

```
void    runBare()

/**
 * Run the test and assert its state
 */
protected void runTest()

/**
 * Set the name of the TestCase
 */
void    setName(String name)

/**
 * Initialize the TestCase for each method to run
 */
protected void    setUp()

/**
 * Tears down the fixture for each Test Method
 */
protected void    tearDown()
```

What Is a TestFixture?

Just as classes depend on composite member variable objects, any TestCases that evaluate them will depend on their existence and state. For example, for the Name class we discussed in the previous section, we can see that it contains two composite variables (java.lang.String FirstName and java.lang.String Last-Name). If the TestCase we design is to evaluate Name's methods properly, then it will need to instantiate Strings and populate the Name class's fields with them. These values are TestFixtures of the NameTest class. Any objects that are needed to implement a test for the CUT are considered TestFixtures. Figure 2.5 shows a simple TestFixture.

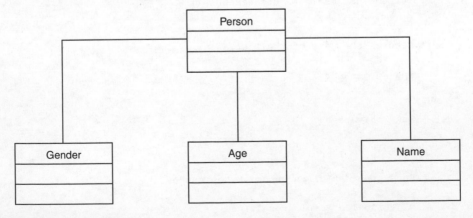

Figure 2.5 A simple TestFixture.

What Is a TestSuite?

Now let's say that the Name class lives in the "people" package along with three other classes, namely Gender, Age, and Person. It is good that we have a Test-Case for Name, but what we really need is to make sure that TestName is run concurrently with the TestCases for Age, Gender, and Person. That way, at test completion we can know that each test is meeting its individual contractual requirements and the package itself is coherent.

In order to achieve these goals, let's create a TestSuite that will run each Test-Case in the package and report on all of the results at the same time. The benefit here is in recognizing that while the people package may fail on some tests, we can see how the TestCase for each component fares on its own and how it fares in interacting with the Person class. In JUnit this is done by creating a new class that extends junit.framework.TestSuite (which itself inherits from junit.framework.Test). A TestSuite is a composite of TestCases with the following methods:

```
/**
 * Adds the given test to the suite.
 */
 voidaddTest(Test test)


/**
 * Add a new TestMethod to the Suite
 */
private void   addTestMethod(java.lang.reflect.Method m, java.util.
Vector names, Class theClass)
/**
 * Adds all the test methods from, the class to the Suite using
reflection.
 */
 voidaddTestSuite(Class testClass)


/**
 * Returns an int representing the number of testcases to be run by this
suite
 */
 int    countTestCases()

static Test    createTest(Class theClass,.String name)
/**
 * Converts the stack trace of the given Throwable to a string
 */
private static java.lang.String
exceptionToString(java.lang.Throwable t)


/**
 * Returns the name of the suite
 */
```

```
java.lang.String     getName()


/**
* Gets a constructor that takes a single string as its argument or a no
arg constructor
*/
static java.lang.reflect.Constructor    getTestConstructor(Class
theClass)


private  Boolean    isPublicTestMethod(java.lang.reflect.Method m)
private  Boolean    isTestMethod(java.lang.reflect.Method m)
/**
* Runs the test and collects their results in a given testresult.
*/
 voidrun(TestResult result)
          Runs the tests and collects their result in the given Test
Result.
 voidrunTest(Test test, TestResult result)
/**
* Sets the name of the TestSuite
*/
 voidsetName(java.lang.String name)


/**
* Returns the Test stored at the given index.
*/
 TesttestAt(int index)


/**
* Returns an int representing the number of tests in the suite
*/
 int     testCount()


/**
* Returns the tests in the TestSuite as an enumeration.
*/
 java.util.Enumeration    tests()


/**
* Returns a test that will fail and log a warning message
*/
private static Test    warning(String message)
```

Building a TestCase (Using the Eclipse IDE)

Here is a brief example that shows you how to build a TestCase. We use Eclipse in our example, but the basic steps are the same no matter what integrated development environment (IDE) you use.

1. First download and unpack JUnit (from http://www.junit.org).

2. Next, make sure whatever integrated environment you are working in includes JUnit.jar. For example, in the Eclipse IDE (http://www.eclipse.org), you open your project properties, select Java Build Path, and then select the Libraries tab. Now click Add External Jar and point to your *< junit install Directory >*/lib/junit.jar.

3. Create a new class extending junit.framework.TestCase.

4. Use the setUp method for any TestFixtures.

5. Create void test methods for each method you want to test in the actual class (Name.java).

6. Use the tearDown method to release any resources or fixtures that will not be GC'd (e.g., database connections).

```java
import junit.framework.TestCase;

public class NameTest extends TestCase {

    private String fixtureFirstName;
    private String fixtureLastName;
    private Name classUnderTest;

    public NameTest(String arg0) {
        super(arg0);
    }

    protected void setUp() throws Exception {
        classUnderTest = new Name();
        fixtureFirstName = "Ruder";
        fixtureLastName = "Daley";
    }

    protected void tearDown() throws Exception {
        super.tearDown();
    }

    public void testSetFirstName() {
        classUnderTest.setFirstName(fixtureFirstName);
    }

    public void testSetLastName() {
        classUnderTest.setLastName(fixtureLastName);
    }


    public void testGetFirstName() {
        classUnderTest.setFirstName(fixtureFirstName);
        assertEquals(fixtureFirstName,classUnderTest.getFirstName());
    }

    public void testGetLastName() {
```

```
        classUnderTest.setLastName(fixtureLastName);
        assertEquals(fixtureLastName,classUnderTest.getLastName());
    }


    public void testGetFullName() {
        classUnderTest.setFirstName(fixtureFirstName);
        classUnderTest.setLastName(fixtureLastName);
        assertEquals(fixtureFirstName + " " + fixtureLastName,class
UnderTest.getFullName());
    }
}
```

Unit Testing Resources

Following are additional unit testing resources that you may find valuable in your work.

- AsUnitForAppleScript—AppleScript (http://www.testdriven.com/modules/mylinks/singlelink.php?lid=101)

- AsUnit (ASUnit) for ActionScriptphysicalBuild *[in progress]* (http://c2.com/cgi/like?AsUnit)

- AspUnit—Test ActiveServerPages (from Visual Basic) (http://aspunit.sourceforge.net/)

- CLOS-unit—A CLOS implementation for CLOS/Lisp unit testing. See http://a.die.supsi.ch/~pedrazz/clos-unit

- C++—WhySoManyCplusplusTestFrameworks, ConsiderationsForAndComparisonOfCplusplusTestFrameworks (http://c2.com/cgi/like?WhyWiki)

    - CppUnit—C++ C#

    - CppUtxOverview—An excellent alternative to CppUnit, though you need to implement parts yourself (http://c2.com/cgi/wiki?CppUtxOverview)

    - CxxTest (http://cxxtest.sourceforge.net/)

    - RwCppUnit—C++ with RogueWave and no StandardTemplateLibrary (http://c2.com/cgi/like?RwCppUnit)

- C

    - CeeUnit—"cUnit" for C (http://c2.com/cgi/wiki?CeeUnit)

    - CheckFramework—Another unit test framework for C (http://c2.com/cgi/wiki?CheckFramework)

- CUT—C Unit Tester system. See http://www.xpsd.com/CUT. Portable across all platforms that support Python; does not rely on any libraries. Not an SUnit-clone
- CuTest—C. Works on Windows with MSVC and BCC32 (does not depend on glibc)
- C#
  - CppUnit—Does C# as well as C++
  - CsUnit—C# (http://www.csunit.org/index.php)
- CommonLispXpTest (http://c2.com/cgi/like?CommonLispWiki)
- ComUnit—for Microsoft Visual Basic and COM (http://comunit.source-forge.net/)
- DejaGnu—The GNU testing framework, based on Expect (which in turn is built on Tcl) (http://www.gnu.org/software/dejagnu/)
- DelphiUnit—A couple of different Delphi testing frameworks (http://c2.com/cgi/like?DelphiUnit)
- DocTest—for Python: test cases serve as documentation examples and vice versa (http://c2.com/cgi/wiki?DocTest)
- DotNetUnit—for the .NET platform
- DotUnit—for the .NET platform
- DtmlUnit—for the ZopeApplicationServer (see also ZopeTestCase)
- EmacsLisp (RegressEl), LispUnit, CommonLispUnit—(Not "StarUnit" libraries, but useful nonetheless)
- EiffelUnit—Unit test framework for Eiffel (formally known as ETest or EiffelTest)
- ExUnity— "X-Unity" testing for .NET platform (named Wikized)
- ForteToolUnit—Forte 4GL (TOOL)
- HarnessIt—.NET languages (Beta is free; production will have "a modest fee")
- HttpUnit—for Web server testing
- HtmlUnit—for Web server testing
- JavaUnit—"JUnit" library for Java (a Wiki-unfriendly name). There's also CactusUnit, a server-side unit testing framework that extends JUnit
- JavascriptUnit (JsUnit)—Javascript testing framework
- KayUnit—for K (KayLanguage) and KSQL
- LingoUnit—(LUnit) for LingoScriptingLanguage
- NunitFramework—NUnit for the .NET platform

- Objective C
    - ObjcUnit—Objective C
    - OcUnit—Objective C
- PerlUnit—for Perl (in development)
- PhpUnit—for PHP3
- PlSqlUnit—(a.k.a. utPLSQL) for PL/SQL (Oracle 7.3.4 and higher)
- PowerBuilderUnit (PBUnit)—for PowerBuilder
- PythonUnit—for PythonLanguage (various offerings)
- QeTest—for Java, hosted in Xalan-J
- RebolUnit—for RebolLanguage
- RubyTestUnit—for RubyLanguage
- RwCppUnit—C++ with RogueWave and no StandardTemplateLibrary
- SchemeUnit—as minimalistic as Scheme itself
- SmalltalkUnit—the original; for the SmalltalkLanguage
- TetWorks—(a.k.a. TET) Open Group multi-lingual test framework
- TsqlUnit—for Transact-SQL (Microsoft SQL Server)
- VbUnit—Visual Basic (for VB6)
- VbaUnit—for VisualBasicForApplications (which gets around VbUnit's incompatibility with VBA)
- WoUnitTest—for WebObjects
- XbUnit—for Xbase++
- XmlUnit—for assertions about XML using Junit and Java JAXP
- XsltUnit—for XSLT Stylesheets
- ZopeTestCase—for the ZopeApplicationServer
- ZopeUnit (ZUnit)—for the ZopeApplicationServer

Integration Testing

Integration is the combination of discrete elements. When the resulting combination proves greater than the sum of the individual elements, you have achieved synergy. Integration testing is an evaluation of the synergy inherent in software development. For software engineers, integration testing, then, is the evaluation of a combination of units to ensure that they produce a desired result when used either together or concurrently. This can be accomplished in one of three ways:

- Package testing
- Strict collaboration testing
- Functional testing

Each of these approaches is designed to accomplish specific goals, and each can play an important role in defining the test suite for an application. This chapter first discusses the specifics of each of these approaches, and then provides an example of a test-suite model that is structured to accomplish each approach.

Package Testing

Java classes are aggregated together into packages. When we're dealing with source code, a package is analogous to a subdirectory or a folder. When the source is compiled into archives, packages become a roadmap to the location of a specific bit of code within the application. In referring to packages, a file called StringUtils.java in a package might look like the one shown in Figure 3.1.

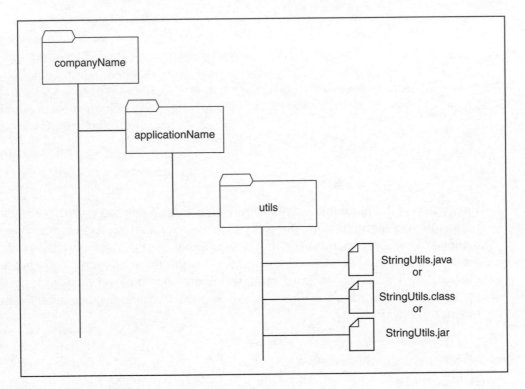

Figure 3.1 A source file in a package (File Explorer view).

Alternatively, companyName.applicationName.utils.StringUtils can be used as a direct reference to a package in code.

Generally a developer will organize classes together into logical groupings, and the package structures in the application will reflect this. For example, when designing an application to manage a music store a developer might create the following package:

- companyName (company root)
- companyName.MusicStore (the application root)

- companyName.MusicStore.products, with classes like
    - companyName.MusicStore.products.CD.java
    - companyName.MusicStore.products.Tape.java
- companyName.MusicStore.styles, with classes like
    - companyName.MusicStore.styles.Country.java
    - companyName.MusicStore.styles.ContemporaryChristian.java
- companyName.MusicStore.artists, with classes like
    - companyName.MusicStore.artists.ThirdDay.java

Upon closer inspection we might see that the products package contains many classes with varying levels of relationships, but all of them are related to Music-Store products. Figure 3.2 shows the structure for the products package, as well as the TestCases and TestSuite.

Each class in this package may have dependencies outside its package (for example, an instance of CD will have a related style in the styles package), but generally the classes in each package are grouped together because of a perceived commonality in the mind of the designer.

Package level testing is an implementation of unit testing that mirrors the existing package structure of the application under test, so that unit tests can be aggregated into the same underlying structure as the code base itself. In an automated testing environment, this can facilitate team awareness of where unit tests belong in the code base. Additionally, it can help a great deal during the maintenance portion of the software development life cycle to have unit tests organized in the same logical structures as the application itself.

When the developer creates a test suite, his MusicStore application will be a compilation of these packages. Each package will have many classes (or units), and the sum of all the packages (along with library dependencies) will be the application.

Once the developer has designed unit tests for each class, he could create a TestSuite whose purpose would be to methodically evaluate each class's success or failure. These test suites can then be integrated into a master TestSuite that can be run every time the application is built, or periodically whenever a class in source control is updated.

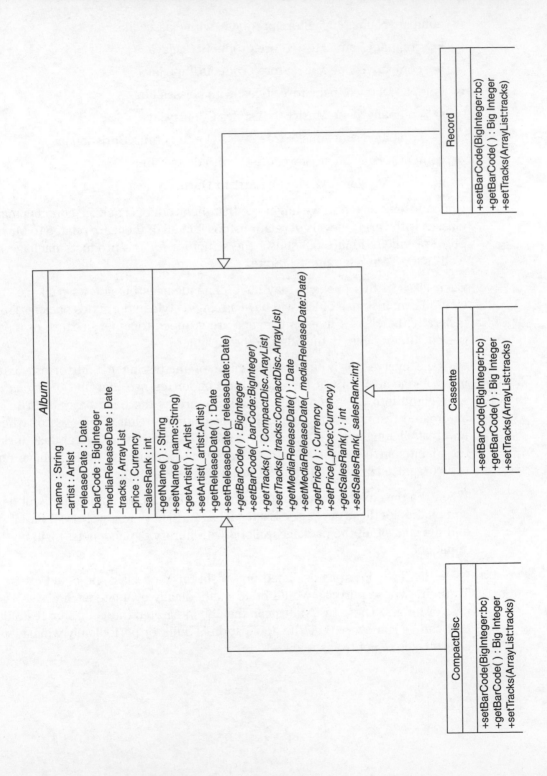

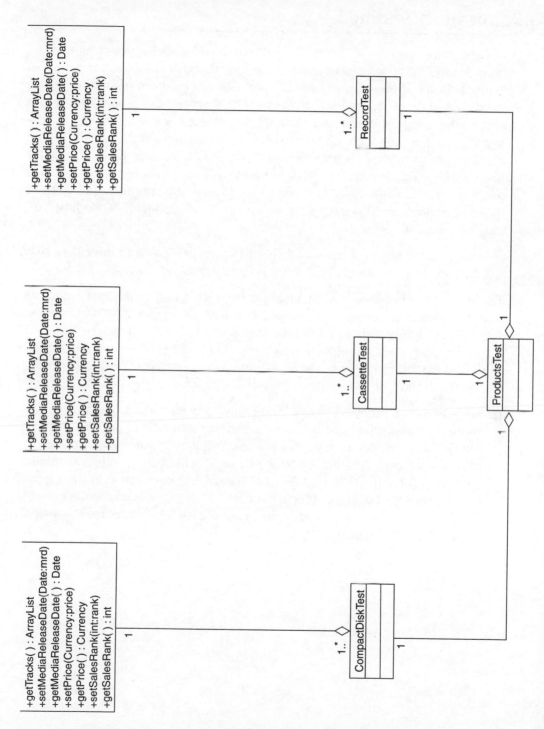

Figure 3.2 The structure for the products package, including TestCases and TestSuite.

Collaboration Testing

Collaboration testing—also called *functional testing*—is the act of integrating units for the purpose of evaluating a behavior that the units work together to achieve. For instance, in the example we used for package testing there is a great deal of functionality for the classes (CD, cassette, and record) that is not encapsulated into the package: How would someone add an instance of cassette to a shopping cart, or how would someone perform a search for all instances of an album for a particular artist or in a musical particular style? Both of these examples are behaviors that involve the classes in the products package, but they also involve classes that, presumably, are not in it. Both of these behaviors are also integral to any music store application. So how will they be tested?

In collaboration testing you logically choose a set of classes or interfaces that will be used to evaluate a behavior across packages.

The difference between strict collaboration testing and functional testing is that collaboration testing is developer driven. A developer may need to test some functionality that is required by the application but not strictly required by the product specification, whereas functional testing is use case driven. Figure 3.3 shows the structure of the MusicStore business Object packages in relation to the dataAccess package and database.

As an example of strict collaboration testing, consider again our MusicStore example. In the previous section, we examined the products package. Notice that in this package there are no classes that facilitate any database access for the business objects. Presumably these classes would be filled in by a database of some kind (be it RDBMS, LDAP, or flat files). The classes that do this (if not collocated with the business objects themselves) might be (and for the sake of our example, will be) in a package called dataAccess. The model for this might look something like Figure 3.4.

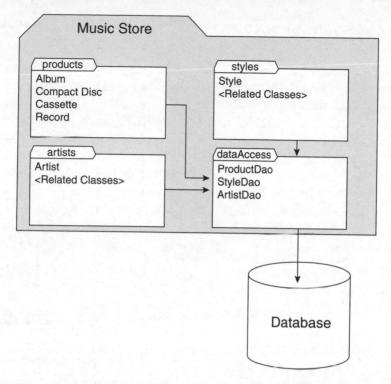

Figure 3.3 The structure of MusicStore business Object packages in relation to the dataAccess package and database.

In order to fulfill many of the product (MusicStore) requirements, good database connectivity will be essential. Many requirements and use cases will depend on the application's ability to retrieve a product from the database given its ID (though there will probably be no specified use case quite that granular). So it is essential that this functionality be repeatedly unit-tested throughout development and deployment. For the MusicStore application, a repeatable test will be necessary to ensure that products in the package can successfully be retrieved and persisted to the database (see Figure 3.4). This is a prime example of testing integrated units located in different packages. This is known as strict collaboration testing.

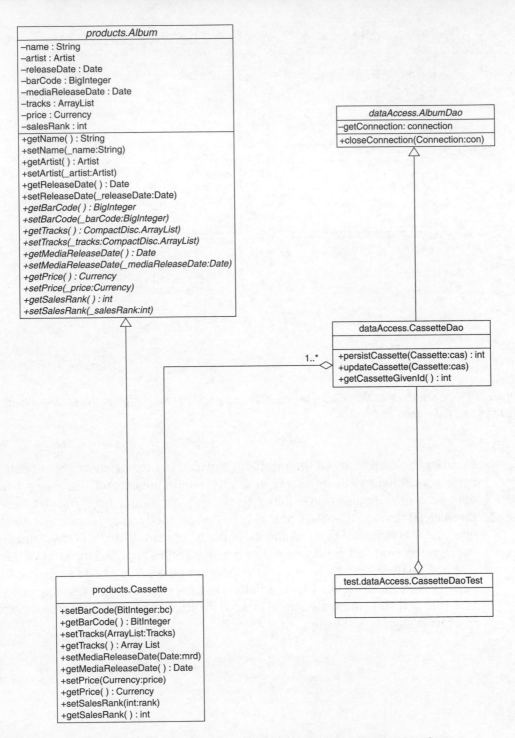

Figure 3.4 Object model for collaboration test for data access for the Cassette class.

Functional Testing and Collaboration Testing

As we stated earlier, functional testing is use case or specification driven. Structurally the tests are exactly the same. The only difference is the logic by which the integrations are assembled. A *use case* driven test may be more comprehensive than a strict collaboration test and will be based on the sum total required to achieve a use case.

In the UML specification, a use case is defined as a "coherent unit of functionality provided by a system (subsystem class) class as manifested by sequences of messages exchanged among the system and one or more interactors (called actors)."

To break this down more simply:

- One or more interactors = a user or users
- Sequence of messages = method calls
- Unit of functionality provided by the system = something measureable that the system is specified to do

So simply put, a use case is the number of method calls required within a system to perform a specific function for a user.

For our MusicStore example, we might have a series of use cases defined as follows:

A customer looks up a CD for Gary Wright's Greatest Hits. She finds the CD in the system. She then adds the CD to her shopping cart and returns to browse the store.

These use cases could be documented in UML as shown in Figure 3.5.

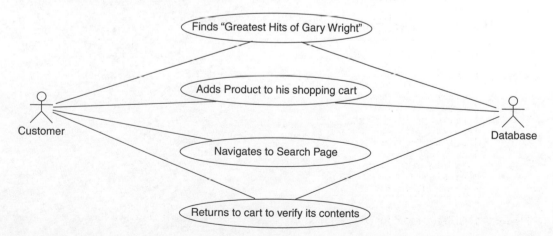

Figure 3.5 Use case diagram for a functional test.

The units involved in establishing this test would be as follows:

- products.CompactDisc
- products.artists.Artist
- products.styles.Style
- ordering.ShoppingCart
- users.Userinfo
- dataAccess.ProductDAO
- dataAccess.ShoppingCartDAO
- dataAccess.UserDAO

Figure 3.6 shows the flowchart for the use case.

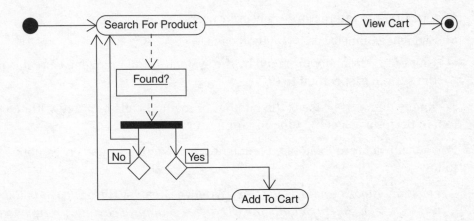

Figure 3.6 Use case flowchart.

And finally, the structure of this test is shown in Figure 3.7.

The sequence to be evaluated is shown in Figure 3.8.

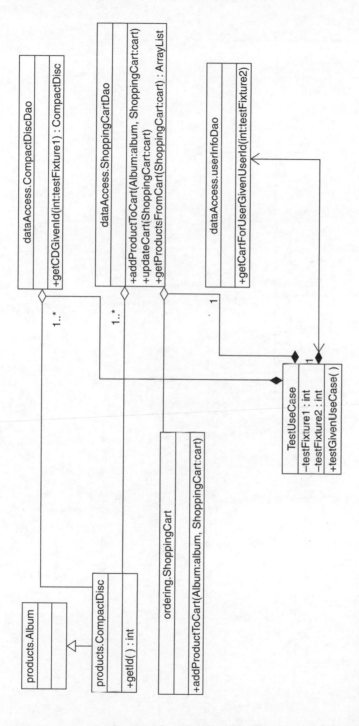

Figure 3.7 Functional test structure.

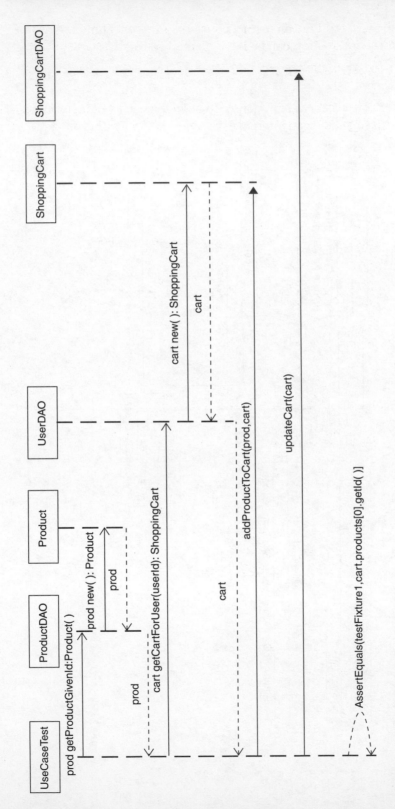

Figure 3.8 The sequence to be evaluated.

So in summary, integration testing consists of logical combinations of units of code. Integration testing can be implemented as follows:

Package testing: The aggregation of all classes within a package into a Test-Suite

Collaboration testing: The aggregation of a logical set of units (classes and interfaces) to achieve an internally testable function within an application

Functional testing: The aggregation of units into a TestSuite for the purpose of a function outlined specifically in a product specification or use case

End-to-End Testing

It is possible to fail in many ways...while to succeed is possible only in one way.

—*Aristotle*

End-to-end testing is also known as *system testing*. The goal is to evaluate all the components and/or collaborations within a system or an application. This can be done in one of two ways:

- Aggregated package testing
- Aggregated collaboration testing

These two approaches are not mutually exclusive. They each have their own benefits and can be used together or concurrently.

Aggregated Package Testing

In Chapter 3 we looked at the concept of package testing. The idea is that each package will contain test cases for the unit tests included within it. Each package will also feature a TestSuite composed of all the test cases, which enables us to run them all sequentially. Package tests can be structured in one of two ways: by integrating the tests directly in the packages with their classes under test (see Figure 4.1) or by letting the tests stand alone in a package structure resembling that of the application (see Figure 4.2).

The advantage of integrating the tests with the source (in the same package) is that the tests have the same class path as the objects they test, which means you don't need to worry about importing packages. However, the disadvantage to this approach is that unless you specifically design your build script to ignore TestCases and TestSuites they will be archived and shipped with your application, leaving your test implementations indecipherable to clients and customers.

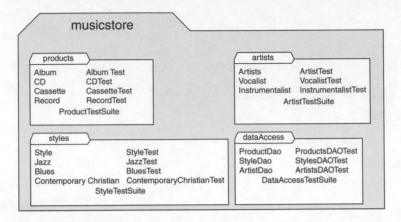

Figure 4.1 In-source package testing.

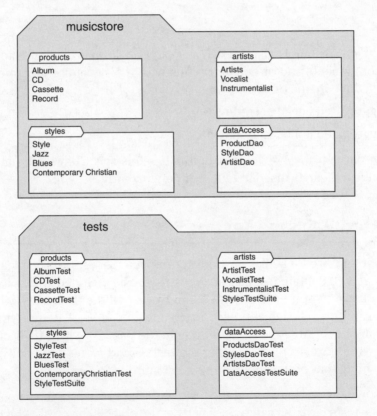

Figure 4.2 Standalone package testing.

However, that is an acceptable risk to many developers because it creates the ability to run aggregated unit tests at the client site, which can be invaluable in integration testing. Keep in mind, though, that it also adds a dependency to your application (to the testing framework) and could potentially expose implementation choices or other information to your customers that you may not have intended.

To extend the package testing concept to aggregated package testing in either of these models is quite simple, as shown in Figure 4.3.

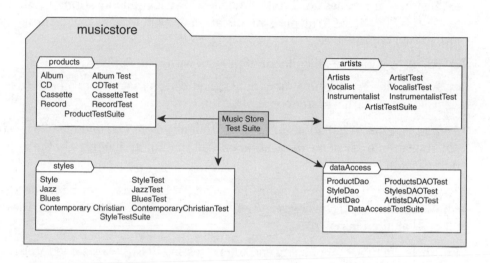

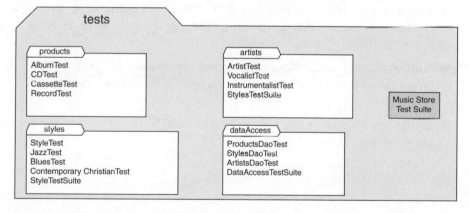

Figure 4.3 Aggregated package testing.

To run an aggregated package test within either structure, include a master test suite that aggregates and runs all the test suites in each package. For the in-source model, place the master test suite directly in the root package; for the standalone structure, it goes into the tests package.

Aggregated Collaboration Testing

Much like aggregated package testing, aggregated collaboration testing is an extension of its namesake. It takes the idea of strict collaboration or functional testing and applies it to an entire application or system. This can be done using one of two approaches:

- An aggregation of all collaboration tests within an application
- A suite designed from a functional specification that covers all use cases associated with a system or application

An aggregation of collaboration tests within a system can include all the strict collaboration tests in an application *and* all the functional tests in the application as well.

Tools like JUnit (that implement the xUnit architecture) can be made to use reflection to find all test cases and suites in an application. In that way, they can all be evaluated in one pass.

For the sake of accomplishing end-to-end testing in this way, some forethought should be given to the structure of the application and specifically where the unit tests will live. In an environment that includes both unit tests and collaboration tests, we recommend separating these tests into distinct packages using either of the two following structures:

- In the in-source approach, create a root-level package called functional-Tests (see Figure 4.4) that includes a test for each use case being aggregated.
- In the standalone model, create a functionalTests package in the root test package (see Figure 4.5).

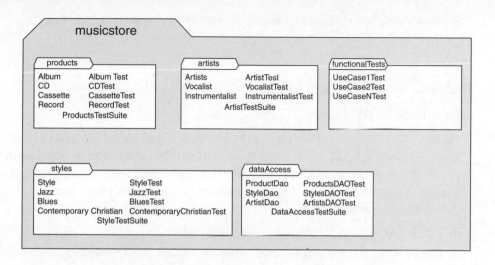

Figure 4.4 The functionalTests package in the in-source approach.

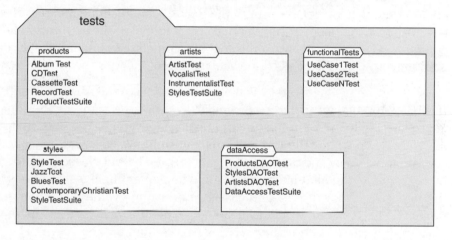

Figure 4.5 The functionalTests package in the standalone aggregated package-testing structure.

Strategies for aggregated collaboration testing include the following:

- Top-down testing
- Bottom-up testing
- Comprehensive use case testing
- Critical collaborations

The *top-down* testing strategy involves testing a system or subsystem from its most abstracted level down to its most concrete. Given the products hierarchy in our MusicStore example (Figure 4.6), a top-down test would first test the Album class and then move on to test each level (in this case, just one) below it, one class at a time.

A top-down TestSuite for the structure in Figure 4.6 would begin with AlbumTest, then run a test for each implementing class of Album, finally reporting on the results for all of the classes. The top-down strategy is highly useful for incremental development of a designed system. For example, if the Album class has been completed but the Record class has not, then the RecordTest could evaluate a Mock Object until the Record class is implemented. Having a test structure that models the eventual object model of the application helps to communicate progress toward the goal of a complete system as well as clearly pointing out what still needs to be accomplished.

The *bottom-up* testing strategy is the primary focus of the AbstractTest pattern (see Chapter 12). Its structure is similar to if not the same as the top-down approach (Figure 4.6), but the order of testing is reversed. The bottom-up strategy focuses on testing the low-level implementations first, and only once they are evaluated do we continue on to the abstracted parent classes. In our Music-Store example, the AlbumTest class would implement final test methods for all the test cases below it (CD and cassette) to use in evaluating common functionality. The TestSuite would evaluate implementing classes first and then run tests for inherited functionality deriving from Album.

Comprehensive use case testing is achieved by writing a functional test for each use case defined in the specification and running them together in a master TestSuite. This process can be highly useful in software design review.

In *critical collaboration* testing, the engineer and designer analyze the critical collaborations within the system (for example, the collaboration between business objects and database access, or the communication layer between a presentation container and an EJB container) and design tests to evaluate them specifically. The idea behind this approach is that if critical components and collaborations are continually tested, then large-scale problems will be more readily averted or recognized.

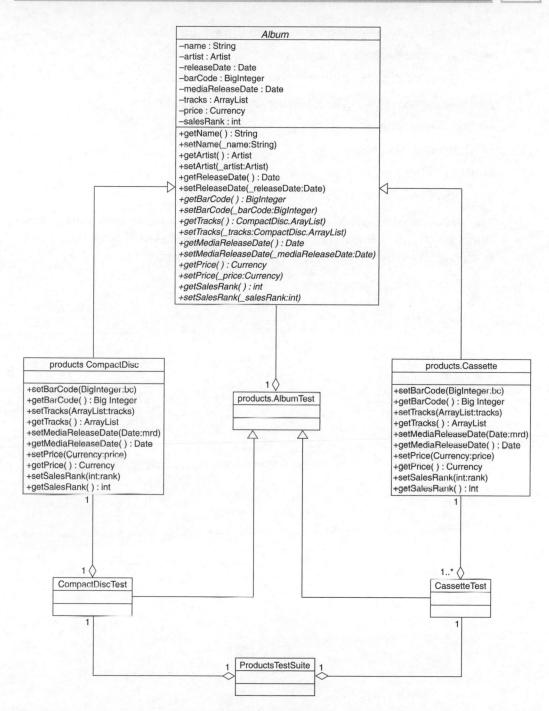

Figure 4.6 A top-down test of the products hierarchy begins with the Album class.

In summary, end-to-end testing is accomplished through

- Aggregated package testing
- Aggregated collaboration testing

And aggregated collaboration testing strategies include

- Top-down testing
- Bottom-up testing
- Comprehensive use case testing
- Critical collaboration testing

The overall goal of end-to-end testing is to provide a framework for the functional testing of a complete system or application. In every way, this type of testing is an extension of integration testing (see Chapter 3).

CHAPTER 5

Database Testing

"It is a capital mistake to theorize before one has data."

—*Sherlock Holmes*

You may wonder why this chapter is needed. After all, isn't testing database code the same as testing any other kind of Java code? The short answer is that it's not. Database testing has its own set of unique complexities and complications, necessitating the introduction of a new set of test patterns to meet those unique challenges.

So why is this true, and why should you care? Well, you should care simply because relational databases are very common in Java programming today. It's hard to imagine a program of more than a few thousand lines that doesn't interface with a relational database in some way.

In fact, we could go so far as to say that at least in enterprise (J2EE) development, relational databases are ubiquitous. Given how common they are, adequately testing the code that accesses a relational database is an obvious source of interest for developers. Prevalence alone, however, doesn't make it necessary that specific patterns should emerge to describe common elements in database testing. The reason why these patterns are necessary is that relational databases bring an added element of difficulty to Java programming.

There are many reasons why this is true. First of all, any form of persistence for Java objects, be it serialization, persistence to flat XML files, or recording information to a database, creates a set of unique challenges. Any time you change the format of information, there's a possibility of errors in mapping—this is especially true when dealing with relational databases because the mapping involves not only mapping non-Java types to Java types, but mapping a relational schema to an object graph. Secondly, when you use a relational database, you need to consider the semantics of database transactions. This means that methods that may be widely separated in a call tree may have an effect on each other. Finally, with relational databases you need to consider the fact that the database itself is external to your system and may not be under your complete control. No only may it have other programs interacting with it while you are testing, but in some cases you may not even be able to change the database schema or rules regarding relational integrity.

General Approaches to Database Testing

As with so many other parts of testing, the best approach to take towards testing your database code is to begin by considering the layering of your application, and develop tests that progressively test each layer independently. This is the basic approach taken by two of the patterns presented later in this book, Mock DAO and Test Database.

Mock DAO is an extension of the idea behind Mock objects in that it replaces the Data Access layer (DAO) objects with corresponding objects that do not directly access a relational database. In this way, you can isolate the testing of the rest of your program from dependencies on a relational database. By removing the mapping layer you make it possible to test your applications without having a relational database available at all.

Test Database is specifically concerned with making it possible to test code that directly accesses a relational database, even when the relational database the program is targeted at cannot be changed, or is not available to the developer. By removing dependencies on a specific database, the developer has more flexibility in controlling the contents of the database tables, making it easier to verify when tests pass or fail.

Ideally, you should be able to employ both patterns in most projects. They address different parts of your program, and when combined together allow you to be assured that both your code functions independently of its persistence mechanism, and that your persistence code works as planned.

Database Testing Strategies and Complications

While the patterns presented later in this book cover the most common problems in database testing, there are still several remaining issues that must be planned for and dealt with. Most of these issues stem from properties of a relational database that you need in a production system but that make testing difficult.

Some of the most important features like this are the ACID properties of relational database transactions. The acronym ACID stands for Atomic, Consistent, Isolated, and Durable. They refer to the fact that transactions in a relational database need to be able to "stay out of each others way" and only affect other transactions in specific, well-defined ways. These properties all bear upon the fact that relational databases are designed to be concurrent; that is, that multiple, simultaneous threads of execution can (and will) query and update the database at the same time. However, while nearly anyone using a database knows that this is true, the fact is that few projects actually test for situations where those properties would need to hold true.

Multithreaded testing is one of the most important parts of the database testing process. However, the tools most commonly used to test Java code (JUnit and its derivatives like dbUnit) are by nature single-threaded. Because of this limitation, few development teams even think to test any multithreaded scenarios, even though these are the types that often cause production problems. Fortunately, there are ways to develop JUnit tests for multithreaded test cases, although the topic lies outside the scope of this patterns book. For more information, we recommend an article by N. Alex Rupp on Java.net (http://today.java.net/pub/a/today/2003/08/06/multithreadedTests.html), an article by Andy Schneider on JavaWorld (http://today.java.net/pub/a/today/2003/08/06/multithreadedTests.html), and GroboUtils (http://groboutils.sourceforge.net/testing-junit/using_mtt.html) for help with multithreaded testing in JUnit.

In particular, there are a few kinds of tests that need to be performed that examine the following issues stemming from the multithreaded nature of database programming:

- **Database Locks:** The key to keeping transactions well isolated from each other is the ability of databases to lock rows and tables to keep concurrent threads from overwriting each other's data, or from reading data in an inconsistent state. To be able to test how well a locking strategy works, you need to be able to run tests simultaneously. There are several ways that you can accomplish this: you can run multiple copies of your tests in different JVMs, or you could start threads in your tests to run multiple copies of your tests. However, the first solution requires you to have additional hardware and to be able to synchronize running tests on two programs simultaneously; something that's not trivial to do. The second option is more easily implemented.

- **Long-term interactions:** Another issue that is common in enterprise systems is that individual methods that are widely separated in time may have a close link to each other. For instance, consider the following interaction common in many enterprise systems. A user makes a request that consists of reading rows from a database, for instance a list of purchase orders and then displaying them. The user then selects one of the purchase orders and modifies it and submits the modified order. If several users could be modifying the same purchase order, then there is a need for optimistic concurrency. To properly test an optimistic concurrency scheme you need composite tests, executed in different orders, to demonstrate what happens when the timestamp or optimistic predicate either matches or does not match.

- **Load Testing:** One of the other aspects of locking that needs to be considered is how locking affects the performance of the overall system. Thus, another type of testing that you will need to perform is load testing. Often only after a system is placed under load will subtle interactions stemming from locking arise. For instance, a lock held in a critical section of an application can drastically degrade the performance of an application. Likewise, if several simultaneous locks are held, databases will often upgrade the lock from a row lock to a table rock, or an even larger-grained lock that can affect otherwise unrelated parts of an application.

While not an exhaustive list, this set of concerns at least begins to introduce the kind of attention that you need to pay to testing your database code. The patterns in this book should help you begin to understand how to test your persistence layer, but there are many more complexities that real projects will encounter. Your best bet is to proceed methodically, try to anticipate the common cases described above, and don't be too surprised when unanticipated bugs show themselves.

CHAPTER 6

Assertion Pattern

So, first of all, let me assert my firm belief that the only thing we have to fear is fear itself.

—*Franklin Delano Roosevelt*

So often in famous quotes the meaning of the individual words become like so much noise to us, lost in the morass of what we perceive the meaning to be. In this particular case, why did FDR choose specifically to use the word "assert" in what would become one of the most historic statements of our time? Besides drawing our attention to the fact that this was a much more literate generation, what does his usage of the word "assert" mean to us? Let's start with Webster's definition of assert:

Assert-(v) To state or express positively. To affirm. To declare with assurance.

So what Roosevelt was saying, then, was that he wanted to state a belief—and he wanted to state it in such a way that left no margin for doubt. He wanted anyone who heard this statement to have absolute confidence in it. When we unit-test our code, we assert that we want to feel and inspire confidence in it. We must *assert* that our code will behave exactly the way it is intended to.

1. Name

Assertion pattern *(Origin:* public domain)

2. Intent

Assertion is not new. It exists in the very framework of Java (J2SE 1.4), and it has existed in the testing framework employed throughout this book (JUnit) for significantly longer.

An assertion is critical to good unit testing, and it is not enough to know and see that it exists. A good developer should understand why it exists, why it is important, and how it can be implemented in any situation.

Boris Beizer defined an assertion this way: "A programming language statement that is evaluated at runtime. If the predicate is satisfied the processing continues uninterrupted." (See Beizer's *Black-Box Testing: Techniques for Functional Testing of Software and Systems*, John Wiley & Sons, 1995.) The idea is simple: As a developer running a test, you need to assert that something is true.

For example, say you create a test fixture that is passed into a method under test (MUT) as an argument. The MUT is not supposed to make any changes to the test fixture during its run. At the end of the run , you will want to assert that the state of the test fixture is exactly the same as it was before calling the MUT.

If after the application is integrated the MUT makes some change to the state of the argument passed in (for example, it assigned null to the argument or changed some values), you might not notice until later in the scope of the application, when an error appears at runtime. The value of assertion is that if (at a unit level) you can identify the different parameters that should be asserted upon completion at a certain unit of code, then you can test them before integration and maintain those tests throughout the development cycle and into deployment. Now if at some point the method under test seems to be mishandling the argument passed to it, you can use the unit test to assert that this is not the case (saving you a great deal of time during the debug cycle).

If for some reason the assertion fails, then the test is halted with a message indicating which assertion failed and, if possible, why it failed.

3. Also Known As

- Assert
- Verification Testing

4. Motivation

Many Java developers like to use System.out.println("") from a static main method to unit-test their code. Usually this is written with some extremely useful message like this:

```
System.out.println("\n\n\n Hey there! I'm here and it worked!");.
```

or

```
System.out.println("\n\n\n Try again!");.
```

This is admittedly a very attractive prospect when you are in a hurry and want to know something has worked. I can honestly say that I don't know a single Java developer who has not done this at some point, but these messages communicate nothing unless a person is looking at the console output of the application and knows exactly what to expect to see printed out. Assertion offers a way of identifying a specific condition and communicating its success or failure. By using a consistent pattern, we can make testing code more useful across a developer team and even layers of a development organization (engineering, testing, and deployment).

Additionally, as a developer you may find it easy to get caught up in the drama of a deadline and design tests that are useful only for a short period of time (specifically that period before the code seems to work). Tests should always be designed to be useful throughout the full life cycle of a software system. By using assertions that clearly state the expectations placed on the software under given circumstances, we have an opportunity to create a self-documenting test suite that will describe exactly how the system components should behave.

Creating assertions should be very simple, and we should be able to create a framework in which the goals of the software under test, as well as the test itself, are clear to anyone inspecting the code or the output of the test. The design pattern describing assertions should fulfill these goals of simplicity and clear design.

5. Applicability

Use an assertion pattern when you want to check values for some relationship. Examples include:

- Asserting that two object references are to the same pointer. Object A should point to the exact same space in the stack as Object B.
- Asserting that two primitive values are equal.

- Asserting that one primitive value is greater than another.
- Asserting that one primitive value is less than another.
- Asserting that one object reference exists.
- Asserting that a collection contains at least one value or object.

6. Structure

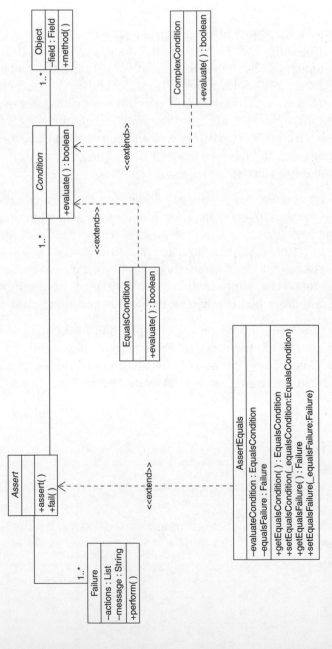

Figure 6.1 Assertion structure.

7. Participants

1. Assert

This is the container class for the whole process. An assertion is the representation for that set of conditions you want to evaluate. It contains one or more conditions and a failure. The conditions represent those evaluations that make up the Assertion itself.

2. Condition (Assert[1]←→[..]Condition)

A *condition* is the representation of some evaluation that makes up the overall assertion. If an assertion is designated by the developer to evaluate that some object is not null and that it has a numeric value greater than 1,000, then the condition would contain one object and some code to evaluate the logic. The condition will generally return a true or false value to the Assertion.

3. EqualsCondition(example realization)

This is an example of a realization of a condition that would be designed to evaluate that two object references (or two primitive values) are equal in nature.

4. ComplexCondition(example realization)

This is an example implementation that may evaluate different states or values on different sets of objects; these may be encapsulated into subconditions or sets of business logic.

5. Failure (Assert[1]←→[..]Failure)

The Failure represents the steps to undertake if the conditions of the assertion are not met.

6. Object (Condition[1]←→[..]Object)

The object is a focus of one or more conditions. It can be any class based on java.lang.Object, and its evaluation will probably be related to some intrinsic attribute or value of it.

7. AssertEquals (Assert realization)

This is the class that will implement an assertion. It extends Assert so it inherits at least one condition (in the case of the implementation of an EqualsCondition) and at least one failure. In a more complex realization, it could import multiple conditions and failures as a Collection.

8. Collaborations

Collaboration (Assert (imp) – Condition(imp))

An implementation of Assert will (in its assert() method) call the evaluate() method on each of its conditions. If the evaluate() method returns true, then the assertion will be complete.

Collaboration (Assert (imp) – Failure(imp))

If assert() fails, then it will use its fail() method. The fail() method will execute a default action (System.err.println) or create its own implementation of fail() to determine what to do.

9. Consequences

The greatest consequence in utilizing an assertion pattern is to commit as a developer and an organization to using it consistently and then optimizing it. As long as debugging code stays out of these tests, and the tests are used consistently, they will be effective for both repeatable build and integration processes as well as regression testing.

10. Implementation

As we have already stated, the purpose of an assertion pattern is to clearly and consistently identify the success of an interface in meeting its contract. So before implementing this pattern, you need to make some effort to document use cases for the unit under test (UUT), whether that unit be a method, a class, or a function of an application. It is very beneficial to document the expected behavior of the UUT at runtime. As a developer, make these assumptions intelligently, using your ability to recognize potential problem areas in your application.

In this section, we'll look at two example implementations, one rather small in scale and dependent only on Java itself (and the laws of mathematics), and the other more complex in nature and depending on business rules specific to the healthcare industry.

A simple example of an assertion pattern involves the MathUtils class we first implemented in Chapter 2. Revisiting the divideBy() method, we can see some assumptions that are ripe for assertions in unit testing:

1. Any divisor passed in must fall in value between Integer.MAX_VALUE and Integer.MIN_VALUE.

2. Any dividend passed in must be between (Integer.MIN_VALUE and –1) and (1 and Integer.MAX_VALUE).

3. Any combination of Divisor and Dividend where both are greater than one or where both are less than zero should result in a quotient greater than zero.

4. Any combination of Divisor and Dividend with mixed signs should result in a quotient less than zero.

5. Any quotient returned should be verifiable (e.g., Divisor/Dividend = Quotient AND Quotient * Dividend = Divisor).

In preparing to document our implementation of the pattern, we can list these assertions as the following:

- AssertValidIntegerValue
- AssertValidNonZeroIntegerValue
- AssertPositiveInteger
- AssertNegativeInteger
- AssertQuotientIsAccurate

More often than not, the code you are testing may be bound to complex rules and complicated business objects. Consider a medical application designed to submit surgery authorization requests from a doctor's office to an insurance company. Let's take a couple of minutes here to go over how an assertion pattern could be used for a situation like this.

If you have written (or are writing) this application, there may be some test cases that you want to assert that are not as simple as an object reference or value comparison—following is an example.

Data Flow

A doctor's office puts in a request to perform surgery on a patient. In the software system, the AuthorizationTransport class will expose a method called transportRequest, which takes an Authorization Request object and sends it to the insurance company for approval.

Based on insurance company business rules, the request is responded to with an AuthorizationResponse object (embedded into the original Authorization-Request).

To avoid confusion, AuthorizationResponse objects should have certain fields filled in consistently for each appropriate response to an AuthorizationRequest, as Figure 6.2 shows.

The Authorization object requirements are as follows:

1. If a request is approved, the Authorization object should contain a valid start and end date for the surgery to be performed, as well as an authorization number

2. If the request is pending but critical, there should be a follow-up action listed as well as a start and stop date but no authorization number.

3. If the request is not critical but the response is pending, the Authorization object should contain a follow-up action but no start and stop date or authorization number.

4. If the request is rejected, there should be a "reject reason code" in the approval but neither an approval number nor start and end dates.

So, in terms of labeling the assertions that need to be implemented here, we could list them as follows:

- AssertApproved
- AssertPendingCritical
- AssertPendingNonCritical
- AssertRejected

It's easy to imagine how important it is for the insurance company, the doctor, and the patient that communication on this issue be handled consistently and clearly; consequently, having a way of testing that these rules are successfully handled every time is critical in the scope of unit testing. When an Authorization object is returned from the insurance company, it must be approved according to these rules *without variance*. By using an assertion pattern to test this process, we can be confident that, given the right input, our application will approve and disapprove these authorization requests to specification.

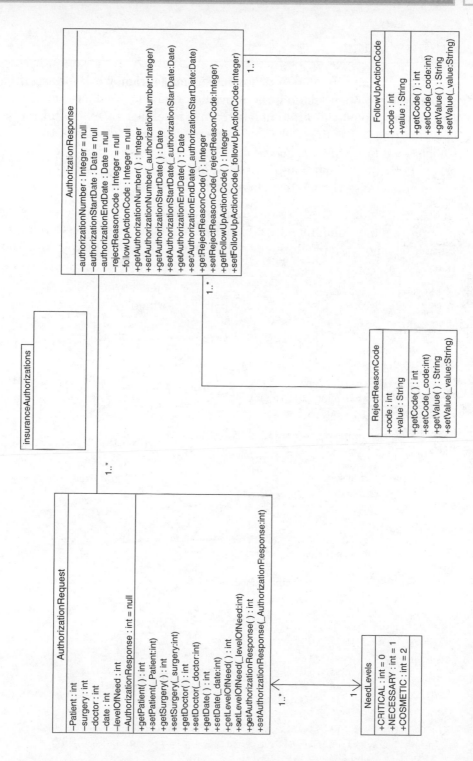

Figure 6.2 AuthorizationResponse objects respond to an AuthorizationRequest.

11. Sample Code

The example implementation will create a simple framework for asserting the equality of two object references or primitive values. It will also include a test case to run through the different test fixtures it defines. By extending the Assert class (Listing 6.1) with AssertEquals (Listing 6.2) and the Condition class with EqualsCondition, this was achievable. These two classes could be extended to assert both simple and complex conditions rather easily. Listing 6.3 contains our example AssertEqualsTest class.

In the next set of listings, a more complex set of conditions are asserted. Listing 6.4 presents the Condition class, Listing 6.5 contains the EqualsCondition, and Listing 6.6 shows the Failure class. Listing 6.7 shows the output from all our tests.

```java
import java.util.*;

public abstract class Assert {

    public Collection failure = new ArrayList(); // of type Failure
    public Collection condition = new ArrayList(); // of type Condition
    public abstract void assert();
    public abstract void fail();

} // end Assert
```

Listing 6.1 Example class Assert.

```java
import java.util.*;

public class AssertEquals extends Assert{

    private ArrayList equalsConditions;

    private ArrayList equalsFailures;



    public EqualsCondition getEqualsConditionAt(int index) {
        return (EqualsCondition)equalsConditions.get(index);
    } // end getEqualsCondition

    public void addEqualsCondition(EqualsCondition condition) {
        equalsConditions.add(condition);
    } // end setEqualsCondition
```

Listing 6.2 Example implementation AssertEquals. (continues)

```java
        public Failure getEqualsFailureAt(int index) {
            return (Failure)equalsFailures.get(index);
        } // end getEqualsFailure

        public void addEqualsFailure(Failure failure) {
            equalsFailures.add(failure);
        } // end setEqualsFailure

    public ArrayList getEqualsConditions() {
        return equalsConditions;
    }

        public ArrayList getEqualsFailures() {
            return equalsFailures;
        }

    public void setEqualsConditions(ArrayList equalsConditions) {
        this.equalsConditions = equalsConditions;
    }

        public void setEqualsFailures(ArrayList equalsFailures) {
            this.equalsFailures = equalsFailures;
        }

        public void assert() {
            for(int i=0; i<getEqualsConditions().size();i++){
                EqualsCondition thisEqC = getEqualsConditionAt(i);
                if(thisEqC.evaluate()){
                    System.out.println("\nEqualsCondition Evaluate test
number " + (i+1) + " passed");
                }else{
                    System.err.println("\nEqualsCondition Evaluate test
number " + (i+1) + " failed");
                    Failure thisFail = getEqualsFailureAt(i);
                    thisFail.perform();
                }
            }

        }

        public void fail() {
            // TODO Auto-generated method stub
        }

} // end AssertEquals
```

Listing 6.2 Example implementation AssertEquals. (continued)

```java
import java.util.ArrayList;

public class AssertEqualsTest {

    private String String1;
    private String String2;
    private Boolean bool1;

    private Boolean bool2;
    private Integer int1;
    private Integer int2;
    private Object obj1;
    private Object obj2;


    private AssertEquals assert;

    public void setAssert(AssertEquals setMe){
        assert = setMe;
    }

    public static AssertEqualsTest getInstance(){
        return new AssertEqualsTest();
    }

    public AssertEqualsTest(){
        String1 = "Jon";
        String2 = "John";
        bool1 = Boolean.valueOf("true");
        bool2=Boolean.valueOf("true");
        int1=new Integer(Integer.MAX_VALUE);
        int2=new Integer(Integer.MAX_VALUE-1);
        obj1=new Object();
        obj2=obj1;
    }

    private AssertEquals setAssertForTest(){
        AssertEquals theReturn = new AssertEquals();
        ArrayList al = new ArrayList();
        ArrayList failAl = new ArrayList();

        //set strings
        EqualsCondition eq = new EqualsCondition();
        eq.setObj1(String1);
        eq.setObj2(String2);
        al.add(eq);
        Failure fail = new Failure();
```

Listing 6.3 Example class AssertEqualsTest. (continues)

```
            fail.setMessage("The two STRING VALUES you are comparing do not
    have equal values.");
            failAl.add(fail);

            //set bools
            eq = new EqualsCondition();
            eq.setObj1(bool1);
            eq.setObj2(bool2);
             al.add(eq);
            fail = new Failure();

            fail.setMessage("The two BOOLEAN VALUES you are comparing do not
    have equal values.");
            failAl.add(fail);

            //set ints
            eq = new EqualsCondition();
            eq.setObj1(int1);
            eq.setObj2(int2);
            al.add(eq);
            fail = new Failure();
            fail.setMessage("The two INTEGER VALUES you are comparing do not
    have equal values.");
            failAl.add(fail);

            //set objects
            eq = new EqualsCondition();
            eq.setObj1(obj1);
            eq.setObj2(obj2);
            al.add(eq);
            fail = new Failure();
            fail.setMessage("The two OBJECT REFERENCES you are comparing do
    not have equal values.");
            failAl.add(fail);

            theReturn.setEqualsConditions(al);
            theReturn.setEqualsFailures(failAl);
            return theReturn;
        }


    public static void main (String args[]){
        AssertEqualsTest myThis = AssertEqualsTest.getInstance();
        myThis.setAssert(myThis.setAssertForTest());
        myThis.assert.assert();
        }
    }
```

Listing 6.3 Example class AssertEqualsTest. (continued)

```
public abstract class Condition {

    private Object obj1;
    private Object obj2;


    public void setObj1(Object setMe){
        obj1 = setMe;
    }

    public void setObj2(Object setMe){
        obj2 = setMe;
    }

    public Object getObj1(){
        return obj1;
    }

    public Object getObj2(){
        return obj2;
    }


    public abstract boolean evaluate();

} // end Condition
```

Listing 6.4 Example class Condition.

```
public class EqualsCondition extends Condition{

    public boolean evaluate() {
        if(getObj1() instanceof String  && getObj2() instanceof String
){
            String string1= (String) getObj1();
            String string2= (String) getObj2();
            if(string1.equalsIgnoreCase(string2)){
                return true;
            }else{
                return false;
            }
        }else if(getObj1() instanceof Boolean && getObj2() instanceof
Boolean){
            boolean bool1=((Boolean)getObj1()).booleanValue();
            boolean bool2=((Boolean)getObj2()).booleanValue();
            if( bool1 == bool2){
```

Listing 6.5 Example class EqualsCondition. (continues)

```
                        return true;
                  }else{
                        return false;
                  }
            }else if(getObj1() instanceof Integer && getObj2() instanceof
      Integer){
                  int int1 = ((Integer)getObj1()).intValue();
                  int int2 = ((Integer)getObj2()).intValue();
                  if( int1 == int2){
                        return true;
                  }else{

                        return false;
                  }
            /**
             * TODO Implement more types here
             */
            }else{
                  if(getObj1().hashCode() == getObj2() hashCode()){
                        return true;
                  }else{
                        return false;
                  }
            }
      } // end evaluate

} // end EqualsCondition
```

Listing 6.5 Example class EqualsCondition. (continued)

```
      import java.util.List;

      public class Failure {

            private List actions;

            private String message;

            public Assert assert;


            public void perform() {
                  System.out.println(this.message);
                  //implement custom functionality here by extending
                  //this class and overwriting this method.
            } // end perform
```

Listing 6.6 Example class Failure. (continues)

```
        public List getActions() {
            return actions;
        }

        public Assert getAssert() {
            return assert;
        }

        public String getMessage() {
            return message;
        }

        public void setActions(List actions) {
            this.actions = actions;
        }

        public void setAssert(Assert assert) {
            this.assert = assert;
        }

        public void setMessage(String message) {
            this.message = message;
        }

    } // end Failure
```

Listing 6.6 Example class Failure. (continued)

```
EqualsCondition Evaluate test number 1 failed
The two STRING VALUES you are comparing do not have equal values.

EqualsCondition Evaluate test number 2 passed

EqualsCondition Evaluate test number 3 failed
The two INTEGER VALUES you are comparing do not have equal values.

EqualsCondition Evaluate test number 4 passed
```

Listing 6.7 Output of test run with sample classes.

12. Known Uses

junit.framework.Assert (includes)

- assertEquals
- assertFalse
- assertNotNull

- assertNotSame

- assertNull

- assertSame

- assertTrue

- fail

- failNotEquals

- failNotSame

- format

For a deeper description of these methods, see Appendix A (the JUnit reference).

In March 2002 David Flanigan, author of O'Reilly's *Java in a Nutshell*, recognized the J2SE 1.4+ assertion keyword as the number-one cool new thing in Java:

The assert keyword in the Java language provides great advantages in unit-testing code as well as ternery-like conditional statements within implementation code. Its usage is much simpler:

```
assert || some conditional statement || failure message
```

13. Known Abuses

Assertions should be used to test measurable expectations of a program. It is very important in unit testing to avoid coupling the testing and debugging process. Carrying assertions (in the scope of unit testing) into debugging mode is easy to do. While useful, this approach would be an abuse in terms of the scope of this pattern. So when asserting that some value exists, avoid the temptation to put more code into assertion failures. For example:

```
If(!AssertAIsNotNull){
    If(database is up){
        Fail;
    }else{
        pass anyway 'cause it goes down a lot;
    }
}
```

14. Related Patterns

None

CHAPTER 7

Mock Object Pattern

How have you made division of yourself?
An apple cleft in two is not more twin than these two creatures.

—*Antonio, Shakespeare's "Twelfth Night"*

1. Name

Mock Object pattern—MacKinnon, Freeman, Craig (2000)

2. Intent

This pattern is useful in two areas that are difficult to completely implement in unit tests (especially when following a test-first methodology). These problems are:

1. How to test code that is coupled to implementations or servers that may not be fully developed or that may be in the midst of refactoring

2. Testing on objects with unexposed interfaces coupled to an independent system

3. Also Known As

- Endo-Testing
- Server Stub (Binder, 1999)
- Test Stub, Test Messages, and Exception (Firesmith, 1996)

4. Motivation

1. Testing Undeveloped or Unimplemented Servers or Services

Often as software developers we are asked to write applications at the view or control layer (in an MVC architecture) when the next layer up the chain has not yet been developed. For instance, you may be asked to write a middle tier to grab a set of queries from an Oracle database that will be complete two weeks from your code freeze; or you may have to build a JSP taglibrary to talk to a set of 15 DAOs which will expose these 33 methods returning the data to fill the screens in your specification. At this point, you are faced with how to write the guts of an application for which a skeleton does not yet exist. You can tackle this problem by using the Mock Object pattern.

2. Unexposed Interfaces to an Independent System

Anyone who has developed under JavaServer Pages (JSP)—pre-mock object implementations like Cactus—will appreciate this example. As a developer, you are building JSP pages that pass values into a servlet or tag that will take those values (directly from the JSP) and implement some logic using them (for example, a form is submitted with registration information for a new user on your system). In JSP the information submitted via an HTML form is available through a Java 2 Enterprise Edition (J2EE) interface known as HttpServletRequest.

Now the problem for unit testing is simple. HttpServletRequest has a method called getParameter() that gets values out of the requesting form, but it does not have a corresponding setParameter() method available to it. Your tag is coupled to HttpServletRequest in that it expects to accept arguments from the request, but those arguments are set deep in the implementation of the J2EE server used to serve the JSPs. Here again is a prime example of unit testing with mock objects. HttpServletRequest is an interface. For your test, write a simple class that meets the interface requirements and implement your own set Parameter() method. Then call the getParameter() method of the interface in your unit test and voilà!

5. Applicability

It can sometimes be difficult during use case–driven application development to maintain a focus on unit testing independent of functional testing, but this is critical to creating an environment that can depend on reusable, well-documented, and encapsulated software components. Each component has a specific purpose in design and should be testable to ensure it is meeting its interface requirements. Mock objects allow us to reinforce the purpose of each module of code by writing tests that evaluate only the implementation in focus, and not those upon which it depends.

6. Structure

1. Testing Undeveloped or Unimplemented Servers or Services

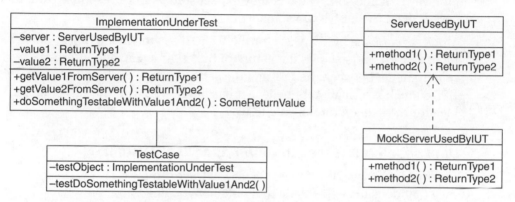

Figure 7.1 UnimplementedInterface structure.

2. Unexposed Interfaces to an Independent System

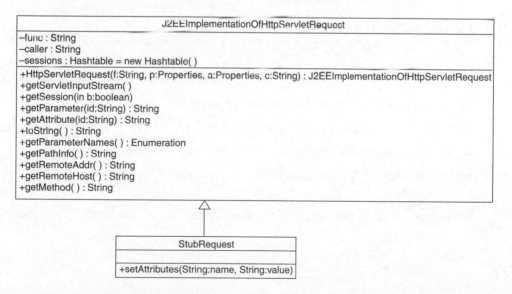

Figure 7.2 UnexposedInterface structure.

7. Participants

1. Testing Undeveloped or Unimplemented Servers or Services

- Implementation under test (IUT): This is the unit being tested. It will connect to some form of server to do some of its work.

- Server used by the IUT: This is the server or service depended on by the IUT. It could be an RDBMS, a mail server, a Data Access Object, or an EDI gateway of some sort. The IUT may expect some sort of response from this server that it will use to do some work.

- Mock server used by TestCase for the IUT: This is the mock object implementation. It understands the nature of the relationship and interface requirements between the IUT and the server or service. It will give the IUT enough information to believe it has interacted with the server or service for the sake of running a unit test.

2. Unexposed Interfaces to an Independent System

- Original interface (HttpServletRequest in the example): This is the interface that does not expose the functionality you need.

- Mock interface (StubRequest in the example): This is an interface extending the original interface and implementing some stub allowing you to mock the functionality.

8. Collaborations

1. Testing Undeveloped or Unimplemented Servers or Services

In this implementation, mock objects will usually

- Return a value within the predefined structure of the server being stubbed.

- Return values from persistence mechanisms, like properties files.

- Send a message indicating that a non-returning function has successfully completed.

- Report an error based on the state of the IUT when the mock object is called.

2. Unexposed Interfaces to an Independent System

In this implementation, mock objects will usually

- Prepare the state of some object whose state is usually coupled to unexposed functionality at the layer of the application being tested.

9. Consequences

1. Testing Undeveloped or Unimplemented Servers or Services

Some due diligence is required here to ensure that your stub continues to meet the interface requirements of the system being developed or refactored.

2. Unexposed Interfaces to an Independent System

This pattern has not been defined fully and will require some creativity on your part in order to expose functionality and meet the interface requirements of the IUT. As tempting as it may seem, do not implement *all* the functionality of the original business objects. Merely stub the data just enough to meet the needs of the IUT.

10. Implementation

1. Testing Undeveloped or Unimplemented Servers or Services

Given an implementation to test (IUT) that uses some form of server object (examples: MailServer, DataAccessObject [DAO], objectCreationFactory), extend the server interface used by the IUT (MockServerUsedByIUT), overriding methods that do some work for and/or return values to the IUT (MockServerUsedByIUT.method1() = testObject.value1). Have them return predefined data. By creating a state of return acceptable to the IUT, you avoid any irregularities created by interacting with the server. The IUT is then free to proceed with its testable functionality (ImplementationUnderTest.doSomethingTestable WithValue1And2()).

The test case for the IUT should dynamically determine whether to use the mock object or the real one based on some parameter determined at runtime (our example will use a properties file).

2. Unexposed Interfaces to an Independent System

Given an IUT that is coupled to the state of a service or object that is defined at another layer of the application (or, in Java terms, in another container), and thus can be tested at the container running the test, create an implementation of the interface of the object in the same container as the test, allowing you to stub the data being passed into your IUT in your unit test.

11. Sample Code

1. Testing Undeveloped or Unimplemented Servers or Services

```java
import java.util.Properties;
import javax.mail.*;

public class JavaxMailServer {

    public String[] getMessages(String server, String user, String pass-
word){
        Folder folder = null;
        Store store = null;
        String[] mails = null;
        try{
          //     Create empty properties
           Properties props = new Properties();
          //     Get session
           Session session = Session.getDefaultInstance(props, null);
          //     Get the store
           store = session.getStore("pop3");
           store.connect(server, user, password);
          //     Get folder
           folder = store.getFolder("INBOX");
           folder.open(Folder.READ_ONLY);
          //      Get directory
           Message message[] = folder.getMessages();
           mails = new String[message.length];
           String nextMessage = null;
           for (int i=0, n=message.length; i<n; i++) {
              nextMessage = i + ": " + message[i].getFrom()[0]  + "\t" +
message[i].getSubject();
                  mails[i]=nextMessage;
              }
           folder.close(false);
           store.close();
```

Listing 7.1 Class JavaxMailServer (ServerUsedByIUT). (continues)

```
        }catch(Exception e){
            e.printStackTrace();
        }
        return mails;
        }
    }
```

Listing 7.1 Class JavaxMailServer (ServerUsedByIUT). (continued)

```
    import java.util.HashMap;

    public class MailNotifierForZachsDaddy {

        public MailNotifierForZachsDaddy() {
            super();
        }

        private HashMap mailInfo;

        private void getMailInfo(){
            mailInfo = new HashMap();
            mailInfo.put("server","blah.west.cox.net");
            mailInfo.put("user","whatever");
            mailInfo.put("password","asIf");
        }

        public  void checkAndNotify() {
            getMailInfo();
            JavaxMailServer srv = new JavaxMailServer();
            String[] theMail =
    srv.getMessages((String)mailInfo.get("server"),
                    (String)mailInfo.get("user"),
                    (String)mailInfo.get("password"));
            for(int i=0;i<theMail.length;i++){
            /*here we would send some notification or persist each message
    for the sake of clarity in our example we will simply write out to the
    console*/
                System.out.println("To:"
                                    + mailInfo.get("user")
                                    + "@" + mailInfo.get("server")
                                    + " it was " + theMail[i]);
            }
        }
    }
```

Listing 7.2 Class MailNotifierForZachsDaddy (IUT).

```
public class StubNotifier extends MailNotifierForZachsDaddy{
    public void checkAndNotify(){
        System.out.println("0:   <nigerianPrincess@land.ru>    Check out
our low term life rates");
        System.out.println("1:   <bubbleBoy@itsTrue.net>     FW:This really
touched my heart");
    }
}
```

Listing 7.3 Class StubNotifier(MockServerUsedByIUT).

```
import java.io.FileInputStream;
import java.io.IOException;
import java.util.Properties;

import junit.framework.TestCase;


public class MailNotifierForZachsDaddyTest extends TestCase {

    private MailNotifierForZachsDaddy notifier;
    private Properties testEnvironment;

    private Properties getTestProps() throws IOException{
    //        create and load default properties
     Properties testProps = new Properties();
     FileInputStream in = new FileInputStream("testEnvironment.
properties");
     testProps.load(in);
     in.close();
    return testProps;
    }

    public void setUp(){
        try{
            testEnvironment = getTestProps();
        if(!testEnvironment.getProperty("SERVER_UNAVAILABLE").
equalsIgnoreCase("true")){
                notifier = new MailNotifierForZachsDaddy();
            }else{
                    notifier = new StubNotifier();
            }
        }catch(IOException ioe){
            fail("Could not read the properties file");
        }
    }
```

Listing 7.4 Class MailNotifierForZachsDaddyTest (TestCase). (continues)

```
        public MailNotifierForZachsDaddyTest() {
            super();
        }

        public void testCheckAndNotify(){
            notifier.checkAndNotify();
        }
    }
```

Listing 7.4 Class MailNotifierForZachsDaddyTest (TestCase).(continued)

```
        SERVER_UNAVAILABLE=true;
        // Or
        SERVER_UNAVAILABLE=false;
```

Listing 7.5 Properties File(testEnvironment.properties).

```
0:  <nigerianPrincess@land.ru>      Check out our low term life rates
1:  <bubbleBoy@itsTrue.net>      FW:This really touched my heart
```

Listing 7.6 TestCase Output where PropertiesFile is true.

```
To:whatever@blah.west.cox.net it was 0:   <muffininvestigenvious1@land.ru>
Check out our low term life rates
To:whatever@blah.west.cox.net it was 1: Ginny <Ginny@foo-net.com> Re. dresses
To:whatever@blah.west.cox.net it was 2: Apple Developer Connection
<noreply@adc.apple.com>    ADC News #345
To:whatever@blah.west.cox.net it was 3: Ken Bah <konweller@cox.net>
To:whatever@blah.west.cox.net it was 4: ddyTag <nnw123@456.com>     Make lots
of MONEY with only $25 twsgj
To:whatever@blah.west.cox.net it was 5: The Netscape Network <netscape-net-
work@dms.netscape.com>    What's Hot on Netscape in April?
...
```

Listing 7.7 TestCase Output where PropertiesFile is false (live email lookup).

2. Unexposed Interfaces to an Independent System

```
    import java.util.*;
    import javax.servlet.http.HttpServletRequest;

    public class StubRequest extends J2EEImplementationOfHttpServletRequest
    implements HttpServletRequest{
```

Listing 7.8 Class StubRequest. (continues)

```
        public StubRequest(){
            super();
            this.pars = new Properties();
        }

        /**
          * Only one thing matters in this class and that is this method
          * The class extends your appservers implementation of
            HttpServletRequest
          * Adding this method which adds to the collection of parameters
          * available to the Servlet.  Then when making a call to the
            servlet you
          * can use
          * servlet(StubRequest, Response)
          * @param name
          * @param value
          */
        public void setParameter( String name,  String value) {
            this.pars.put(name,value);
        } // end setAttribute

} // end StubRequest
```

Listing 7.8 Class StubRequest. (continued)

```
import javax.servlet.http.HttpServlet;
import javax.servlet.http.HttpServletRequest;
import javax.servlet.http.HttpServletResponse;

/*
 * Created on Apr 17, 2003
 *
 * To change this generated comment go to
 * Window>Preferences>Java>Code Generation>Code and Comments
 */

public class TestServlet extends HttpServlet {


    protected void doGet(HttpServletRequest req, HttpServletResponse
resp){
        doPost(req,resp);
    }

    protected void doPost(HttpServletRequest req, HttpServletResponse
resp){
```

Listing 7.9 Class TestServlet. (continues)

```
            System.out.println("Hello " + req.getParameter("firstName"));
            System.out.println("It is " + req.getParameter("servletTime"));
            System.out.println("Would you like to play a game of chess?");
        }
    }
```

Listing 7.9 Class TestServlet. (continued)

```
import junit.framework.*;

/*
 * Created on Apr 17, 2003
 *
 * To change this generated comment go to
 * Window>Preferences>Java>Code Generation>Code and Comments
 */

/**
 * @author ua01422
 *
 * To change this generated comment go to
 * Window>Preferences>Java>Code Generation>Code and Comments
 */
public class TestServletTest extends TestCase{

    StubRequest req;
    J2eeImplementationOfHttpServletResponse resp;
    TestServlet srv;

    public void setUp(){
        req = new StubRequest();
        resp = new J2eeImplementationOfHttpServletResponse();
        srv = new TestServlet();
    }

    public void testDoPost(){
        req.setParameter("firstName","Jon");
        req.setParameter("servletTime", String.valueOf(new
java.util.Date(System.currentTimeMillis())));
        srv.doPost(req,resp);
    }

}
```

Listing 7.10 Class TestServletTest.

```
Hello Jon
It is Thu Apr 17 23:18:17 MST 2003
Would you like to play a game of chess?
```

Listing 7.11 TestCase Output.

12. Known Uses

1. Testing Undeveloped or Unimplemented Servers or Services

Factory Method design patterns

2. Unexposed Interfaces to an Independent System

Jakarta Cactus

13. Known Abuses

Mock objects need to be simple. They should neither duplicate (even with some minor changes) the implementation of existing objects, nor should they be coupled to other mock objects.

14. Related Patterns

- Mock Database Pattern
- Factory Method

Mock Data Access Objects (DAOs)

Errors using inadequate data are much less than those using no data at all.

—*Charles Babbage*

1. Name

Mock Data Access Objects

2. Intent

Simulate a backend data store in order to be able to test code depending on objects derived from a database (e.g., business logic and GUI) without having to have a database in place.

3. Also Known As

Simulated Data Access Objects

4. Motivation

Software developers often find themselves in the position of building an application based on components not yet built, or based on external interfaces that are not available. But a good developer will nonetheless find a way of influencing the overall system design and documenting the validity of his or her work. The Data Access Object pattern shows one approach for accomplishing this end.

The DAO pattern is a common way of providing a single, common "point of contact" to a particular data source. The Data Access Object pattern provides a separation of concerns in your designs–keeping your business logic independent from your database persistence code. Data Access Objects are responsible for operating on objects that hold data stored in a relational database–these objects are referred to by Deepak Alur as "Value Objects," although Data Transfer Object (DTO) (as referred to by Martin Fowler) is a more meaningful term. Most commonly, these DAO classes will contain methods that are collectively known as CRUD (for Create, Read, Update, Delete) that operate on these DTO's. For instance, let's assume that we are building a system to register conference attendees. Our Data Access Object class could have the following interface:

```
public interface AttendeeDAO {
    public void createAttendee(Attendee person) throws DAOException;
    public void updateAttendee(Attendee person) throws DAOException;
    public Collection getAllAttendees() throws DAOException;
    public void deleteAttendee(Attendee person) throws DAOException;
public Attendee findAttendeeForPrimaryKey(int primaryKey) throws
DAOException;

}
```

Declaring this interface is a standard part of implementing the Data Access Object Pattern. For example, Alur shows the use of such an interface in nearly all of the design diagrams that illustrate the pattern. A concrete DAO implementation for our design would implement this interface, as shown in Figure 8.1.

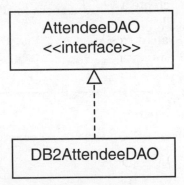

Figure 8.1 Attendee DAO Interface.

As you would expect, the Db2AttendeeDAO would implement the messages in the interface above by using the facilities of JDBC. For instance, in the case of the "getAllAttendees()" method, the class would obtain a connection to a DB2 database, query the database for the list of rows in the Attendee table, iterate through the ResultSet returned from the query, and then construct Attendee objects for each of the rows in the ResultSet filled with the information in that row. Alur provides plenty of examples of how this works for queries as well as updates, so we refer the interested reader there for more information.

While this pattern is useful, and nearly ubiquitous in J2EE applications, when implemented as described it does not help at all when you are in any of the following situations:

- If you are building an application where the database schema has not yet been implemented, then you cannot implement a DAO because you do not know the structure or contents of the database. This creates a time dependency in the project where the rest of the project code would need to wait until the DAO implementation is complete before the program can be tested as a whole.

- In many cases, not every developer will have ready access to the database. If a developer is working remotely, then access to the database over the network may be prohibitively slow. Or, the developer may have only intermittent network access, and may need to test code without having a database connection at all.

At this point it becomes apparent why the DAO interface is important. In Alur, the DAO Interface is declared in order to allow for the creation of additional Data Access Objects that sit on top of other data sources. This is important for solving the problems described above. You can create different, interchangeable DAOs for other data sources that are more easily applicable to the problems at hand. For instance, you can build a DAO that retrieves its records from a local XML file, or even create a DAO that sits on no external data source, but instead an in-memory collection. In this way, you can continue to develop and test your remaining code apart from the presence or absence of a database, and maintain a strict isolation of layers so that you can execute tests independently either with, or without the database.

5. Applicability

When you build a Mock DAO you can test your code without having a database available. Of course, this assumes that your code uses the DAO pattern to encapsulate database access; if you do not use this pattern, then Mock DAOs will not be applicable. However, if you are employing DAOs, you should use Mock Data Access Objects in the following circumstances:

- In situations where the database is either inaccessible or does not perform adequately for reasons of network capacity.

- In situations where the database schema is not completely known.

- In situations where there is a time dependency of other layers on the DAO layer; implementing Mock DAOs allows the other layers to proceed independently of the development of the persistence layer.

Mock Database can aid in performance profiling and load testing as well. By eliminating dependency on a database you can more easily isolate many performance and multi-threading problems. While some classes of performance problems (stemming from database deadlock, for example) still require the database to resolve, you can obtain useful measurements of domain and GUI performance, and more easily resolve problems in those layers, by using this technique.

When building an application using Servlets, JSP's and EJBs you have enough to worry about without having to deal with database errors too. The concept of layered testing as implemented in the Mock DAO pattern allows you to work out the problems with your presentation and business logic without simultaneously dealing with database issues.

6. Structure

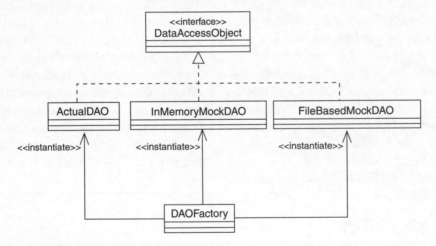

Figure 8.2 Mock Data Access Object Structure.

7. Participants

- **DataAccessObject:** This interface defines the set of methods for all DAO types, and defines the standard CRUD interfaces for creating, retrieving, updating, and deleting objects from a persistent store.

- **ActualDataAccessObject:** This class works against a relational database and facilitates the running of SQL queries and updates against the database (using JDBC facilities).

- **InMemoryMockDataAccessObject:** This class would return stub data in the form of business objects from the methods defined in the DataAccess-Object interface from an in-memory collection.

- **FileBasedMockDataAccessObject:** This class would return stub data in the form of business objects from the methods defined in the DataAccess-Object interface from a disk file containing serialized Java objects or XML.

- **DataAccessObjectFactory:** This class is a FactoryMethod implementation that uses a properties file (or other mechanism) to determine which type of DAO to return. The DAOFactory determines whether to return a DAO with a live data connection or a Mock DAO containing stub data.

8. Collaborations

The DataAccessObjectFactory must be configured to return the proper DataAccessObject subtype when a DAO is requested. Thus, the DataAccessObjectFactory must know about all of the subtypes of DataAccessObject. It may be either hard-coded to return the appropriate subtype, or it may use reflection to do so.

9. Consequences

The simplest implementation of this pattern is one where results are simply fetched from an in-memory Singleton collection that must be populated during the test. Another common extension of this idea is to "prefill" the collection with default values in the constructor of the class. The major disadvantage of using a Singleton is that you must "clear" the singleton between each test—if you miss it in one test, it can cause a failure in a later test. Fortunately, most unit test frameworks (like JUnit) provide facilities to make this easy. For instance, in JUnit, you can put code to "clear" the Singleton in the "teardown()" method of your test class, and put any "prefill" code in the "setUp()" method of the test class.

A second approach, which is slightly more complicated, but also provides for more realistic tests, is to use Java Serialization to read a set of objects from a file or to use XML for the same purpose. The advantage of this is that it is possible to use several files to represent different initial conditions for the test. The disadvantage of this approach is that you then need to maintain the different XML data files as part of your tests. Since they are outside of the JUnit test classes, they can become a source of test failures as the underlying assumptions in the code change.

10. Implementation

In order to realize the benefits of this pattern, your DAO interface should not introduce any external dependencies on classes in the java.sql package. For instance, a DAO should never return a java.sql.ResultSet from a public method, or accept a java.sql.PreparedStatement as a method argument. Instead, your DAO interface should be defined entirely in terms of business objects (DTOs), primitive types and classes from the collection framework. If your DAO interface relied upon classes from the java.sql package then you would need to implement Mock versions of those classes as well, significantly complicating the resulting Mock DAOs.

11. Sample Code

The sample code is a simple implementation of an In-Memory Mock DAO. First, examine the classes persisted by this DAO (Listings 8.1 and 8.2).

```
package com.ibm.examples.DAO;

/**
 * This is a simple Data Transfer Object representing
 * a conference attendee.
 *
 * @author kbrown
 */
public class Attendee {

    private int attendeeId;
    private String name;
    private Address address;

    /**
```

Listing 8.1 Attendee class. (continues)

```
 * Class Constructor for an Attendee
   */
  public Attendee(int attendeeId, String name, Address address ) {
      super();

   this.attendeeId = attendeeId;
      this.name = name;
      this.address = address;
  }

  /**
   * Getter for the primary key (attendeeId)
   *
   * @return int
   */
  public int getAttendeeKey() {
      return attendeeId;
  }

  /**
   * Getter for the name
   *
   * @return String
   */
  public String getName() {
      return name;
  }

  /**
   * Setter for the name
   *
   * @param name the name of the Attendee
   */
  public void setName(String string) {
      name = string;
  }

  /**
   * Getter for the Attendee's Address
   *
   * @return Address
   */
  public Address getAddress() {
      return address;
  }

  /**
```

Listing 8.1 Attendee class. (continues)

```
 * Setter for the Attendee's Address
 *
 * @param address the {@link Address} for this Attendee
 */
public void setAddress(Address address) {
    this.address = address;
}


}
```

Listing 8.1 Attendee class. (continued)

```
package com.ibm.examples.DAO;

/**
 * A simple Address Data Transfer Object.
 *
 * @author kbrown
 */
public class Address {

    private String street;
    private String city;
    private String state;
    private String zip;

    /**
     * Class constructor for Address
     */
    public Address(String street, String city, String state, String zip)
{
        super();
        this.street = street;
        this.city = city;
        this.state = state;
        this.zip = zip;
    }

    /**
     * Getter for the City
     *
     * @return String
     */
    public String getCity() {
        return city;
    }
```

Listing 8.2 Address Class. (continues)

```
/**
 * Getter for the State
 *
 * @return String
 */
public String getState() {
    return state;
}

/**
 * Getter for the Street Address
 *
 * @return String
 */
public String getStreet() {
    return street;
}

/**
 * Getter for the Zip Code
 *
 * @return String
 */
public String getZip() {
    return zip;
}

/**
 * Setter for the City
 *
 * @param string the City to be set
 */
public void setCity(String string) {
    city = string;
}

/**
 * Setter for the State
 *
 * @param string the State name to be set
 */
public void setState(String string) {
    state = string;
}

/**
 * Setter for the Street Address
 *
```

Listing 8.2 Address Class. (continues)

```
     * @param string the Street Address to be set
     */
    public void setStreet(String string) {
        street = string;
    }

    /**
     * Setter for the Zip code
     *
     * @param string the zip code to be set
     */
    public void setZip(String string) {
        zip = string;
    }

}
```

Listing 8.2 Address Class. (continued)

Next you can see how the Mock DAO pattern is implemented to simulate persisting Attendee objects (Listing 8.3). Note that it implements the interface described earlier in the pattern.

```
package com.ibm.examples.DAO;

import java.util.Collection;
import java.util.Enumeration;
import java.util.Vector;

/**
 * InMemoryDAO is an implementation of the Mock DAO pattern.  It can
 * replace a "real" database-backed DAO by substituting values from a
 * static collection.
 *
 * @author kbrown
 */
public class InMemoryDAO implements AttendeeDAO {

    private static InMemoryDAO instance = new InMemoryDAO();
    private Vector attendees = new Vector();

    /**
     * Creates a new Attendee person.
     * In this implementation it simply inserts it into the
       * static collection.
```

Listing 8.3 Mock DAO Implementation. (continues)

```
         *
         * @param person the {@link Attendee} being inserted
         * @see AttendeeDAO#createAttendee(Attendee)
         */
        public void createAttendee(Attendee person) throws DAOException {
            getAllAttendees().add(person);
        }

        /**
         * Update a persisted Attendee.
         * In this implementation it removes the previous
     * {@link Attendee}
         * matching the input Attendee primary key and then
           * adds the input Attendee into the static collection.
         *
         * @param person the {@link Attendee} being updated
         * @see AttendeeDAO#updateAttendee(Attendee)
         */
        public void updateAttendee(Attendee person) throws DAOException {
            Attendee match =
    findAttendeeForPrimaryKey(person.getAttendeeKey());
            attendees.remove(match);
            attendees.add(person);
        }

        /**
         * Return the entire set of {@link Attendee} objects.
         * This implementation simply returns the contents of the static
         * collection of Attendees.
         *
         * @return java.util.Collection
         * @see AttendeeDAO#getAllAttendees()
         */
        public Collection getAllAttendees() throws DAOException {
            return getAttendees();
        }

        /**
         * Remove a persisted {@link Attendee}.
         * This implementation finds the current Attendee having
           * the primary key of the Attendee object being
         * passed in and removes it from the list.
         *
         * @param person the Attendee being deleted
         * @see AttendeeDAO#deleteAttendee(Attendee)
         */
```

Listing 8.3 Mock DAO Implementation. (continues)

```
        public void deleteAttendee(Attendee person) throws DAOException {
Attendee match =
            findAttendeeForPrimaryKey(person.getAttendeeKey());
        attendees.remove(match);
    }

    /**
     * Gets the attendees
     * @return Returns a Vector
     */
    private Vector getAttendees() {
        return attendees;
    }
    /**
     * Sets the attendees
     * @param attendees The attendees to set
     */
    private void setAttendees(Vector attendees) {
        this.attendees = attendees;
    }

    /**
     * Gets the Singleton InMemoryDAO instance
     * @return Returns a DefaultDAO
     */
    public static InMemoryDAO getInstance() {
        return instance;
    }

    /**
     * Sets the Singleton instance
     * @param instance The instance to set
     */
    public static void setInstance(InMemoryDAO anInstance) {
        instance = anInstance;
    }

    /**
     * Return the single {@link Attendee} instance matching
 * this primary key
     * @param primaryKey the integer primary key
     * @return Attendee
     */
    public Attendee findAttendeeForPrimaryKey(int primaryKey)
throws DAOException {
        Enumeration enum = attendees.elements();
        while (enum.hasMoreElements()) {
```

Listing 8.3 Mock DAO Implementation. (continues)

```
            Attendee current = (Attendee) enum.nextElement();
            if (current.getAttendeeKey() == primaryKey)
                return current;
        }
        throw new
    DAOException("Primary Key not found " + primaryKey);
        }


    }
```

Listing 8.3 Mock DAO Implementation. (continued)

All this class does is to store an instance of itself as a Singleton (see Gamma for more information) in the static variable "instance", and allow access to that through the getInstance() method (more on this later). Users of the class can then add and remove Attendee elements from the collection the singleton instance holds, or replace the elements in the collection.

To make this work in our program, there must be an easy way to replace the "real" DAO class with our new Mock DAO class that polymophically substitutes for the original class. The solution for this is provided by Alur in their discussion of the use of object factories in the implementation of the DAO pattern. If the client code avoids references to either the concrete Db2AttendeeDAO class or the new In-Memory DefaultDAO class but only refers to the interface, then using an object factory will allow you to provide the client code with instances of the concrete class when one is necessary.

In this case, an even simpler object factory than in any of the examples given in Alur can be used. Here the object factory will use a software "switch" that allows it to return an instance of either the "real" DAO class, or the "simulated" DAO class as necessary. This switch can check the value of a System property, or examine some other globally settable value, as shown in the following code (Listing 8.4).

```
    package com.ibm.examples.DAO;


    /**
     * AttendeeDAOFactory is a simple factory object for DAO's as
     * described in the book Core J2EE Patterns.  This version simply
     * chooses between a mock {@link InMemoryDAO} and a Database-backed DAO
     * {@link DbAttendeeDAO} based on the value of the
     * <code>book.testmode</code> System property.
     *
```

Listing 8.4 DAO Factory Implementation. (continues)

```
   * @author kbrown
   */

public class AttendeeDAOFactory {

    /**
     * Return an instance of an {@link AttendeeDAO} based on
        * the value of the <code> book.testmode </code>
     * System property.  If the value of the
     * property is set to "Simulated" it returns a mock DAO.  If
     * it is set to any other value (or not set) it returns a
     * {@link DbAttendeeDAO}.
     *
     * @return AttendeeDAO
     */

    public static AttendeeDAO getAttendeeDAO() {
        String mode = (String) System.getProperty("book.testmode");
        if ("Simulated".equals(mode))
            return InMemoryDAO.getInstance();
        else
            return new DbAttendeeDAO();
    }
}
```

Listing 8.4 DAO Factory Implementation.

As you run your tests, you will often begin by setting this switch to return the simulated class so that you can test the remainder of the system in isolation from the database. Only in later tests will you ever set the switch to return the "real" database-backed DAO.

12. Known Uses

None

13. Known Abuses

None

14. Related Patterns

- Mock Objects
- Test Database
- Factory Method (GOF)

Test Database Pattern

Let men in office substitute the midnight oil for the limelight.

—*Calvin Coolige*

1. Name

Test Database pattern

2. Intent

Provide a lightweight relational testing database as a replacement for a database that cannot be accessed in unit or integration tests.

3. Also Known As

- Mock DB

4. Motivation

The relational database aspects of many enterprise systems are often the trickiest and hardest to test. Not the least of the reasons why this is true is that full-blown RDBMS systems are not generally part of developer's desktop tool set. The most popular commercial relational databases are large, complex, and expensive beasts that require large amounts of disk space, CPU, and memory to run. What's more, Oracle, Sybase, or DB2 administration is usually not a skill that the typical Java developer has.

As a result, many development shops take a sub-optimal approach to testing the relational access portions of their systems. In some cases, several developers share a single relational database that they use to test their code. However, this causes its own problems. The particular question that often makes developers tear out their hair is how to set up the appropriate initial conditions for their tests. In order to obtain repeatable, consistent results in your tests, you need stable test data. Thus, you need to be able to populate the database tables with appropriate test data and clear the database tables between test runs—something that's not normally possible with a shared database. Running simultaneous tests on shared database tables can easily interfere with each other and create test failures that can be difficult to reproduce. Even if you separate developers from each other by allowing multiple copies of tables under different schema names, this will have an impact on your code because you must be able to configure each SQL statement to work against different schemas—this is sometimes challenging for generated SQL of the type that is common in JDO and Container-Managed Persistence EJBs.

Since sharing a commercial database is problematic, and installing a commercial database on each developer's desktop is also problematic, consider instead a solution that avoids each of these problems. Install a lightweight, but still SQL-compliant database on each developer's desktop for unit testing, and then perform integration testing on a full-fledged commercial database.

Development teams have several choices today when looking for such a lightweight database for testing use. Some very good options include Cloudscape, PointBase, and MySQL. Cloudscape is a lightweight all-Java database that is currently a product of IBM (a trial version can be downloaded from IBM's Web site). It is included in WebSphere Application Server and the WebSphere Studio Application Developer (WSAD) from IBM. In the past, BEA has also included Cloudscape with versions of WebLogic Server and Sun included Cloudscape as part of the J2EE 1.3 SDK from Sun. Currently, Sun includes a copy of PointBase (from DataMirror) as part of the J2EE 1.4 SDK. BEA includes PointBase with WebLogic 7.0

Likewise, MySQL is a lightweight open-source database that can be purchased in a commercial form from MySQL AB, or downloaded from MySQL AB and used under the GNU public license. MySQL is a full-featured database but one with the distinct advantage that its entire installation package is less than 25 MB, while its JDBC driver install package is less than 2 MB. While these three databases are certainly the most popular options, there are other cheap or free lightweight options as well. There are other pure-Java databases that you can choose, such as JDataStore from Borland, and Daffodil DB from Daffodil Software Limited; or you could use other simple single-user databases like MS Access.

However, the key to this pattern is that the two databases (the test database and the production database) have to be closely compatible. At the very least, they should both be SQL-92 capable. You are liable to create additional problems if the two databases are not compatible; for instance, some versions of MS Access will give you problems in this regard, since they are not SQL-92 compatible. Also, there are certain types of tests that it will be difficult to run on some databases (for instance multi-user tests or multithreaded tests).

5. Applicability

While there are alternative testing measures (see the Mock DAO pattern) that make it possible to remove database code entirely from a larger program, when the code under test directly accesses the database (e.g., uses JDBC), there is no other way to test that code except against a database. Use the Test Database pattern whenever:

You have complex data access logic (involving joins, SQL functions, or other SQL features) and application of Mock DAO would leave large portions of your code untested.

You do not have complete control of the target database schema your code relates to.

There is the possibility of interference from other applications (or other ongoing tests) with the data contained in the database you are using for testing.

6. Structure

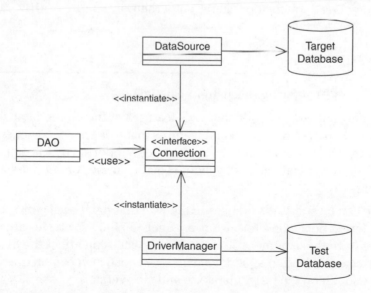

Figure 9.1 Test Database structure.

7. Participants

There are three major participants in this pattern:

- The DAO (or other persistence layer object) will use a java.sql.Connection on either a Target Database or a Test Database.

- The Target Database is the "final" database that will be used within the program being developed. It will not be used during the testing phase being considered here, but will be replaced by the Test Database.

- The Test Database is the lightweight, local database that is used during testing.

  The DAO may choose to use a J2EE DataSource or a java.sql.DriverManager to instantiate connections to either the Test Database or Target Database as appropriate.

8. Collaborations

Clients make requests of the DAO, which obtains java.sql.Statements and java.sql.PreparedStatements against a Connection.

The DAO obtains the connections from a DriverManager or DataSource.

The Connections operate either against the Test Database or the Target database, depending upon the configuration of the DataSource or DriverManager.

9. Consequences

Consequences of applying this pattern can include:

- Not being able to test code that uses features of the target database, such as stored procedures, or special features (such as sequence generators). The way around this is to only use features supported by the standard JDBC interfaces and not use vendor-specific classes or vendor-specific features.

- There can be subtle differences in the way that databases act that can lead to different behavior—for instance, Oracle locking strategies are quite different from those of most other databases. This can affect the outcome of your tests and lead to situations where tests can succeed on the test database and fail on the target database and vice-versa.

- Databases can differ in the SQL syntax they support. To mitigate this risk, ensure that your code only uses SQL-92 compliant SQL syntax.

10. Implementation

In most cases, applying the Test Database pattern is as simple as installing a lightweight database and then changing your program to point to that database. In J2SE this can be achieved through parameterizing the program such that it reads the Class name and Driver information for a database driver from a properties file. In J2EE this can be done by creating a new J2EE DataSource that points at the new database, and then updating the deployment descriptor of the J2EE modules to refer to the new data source rather than the old one, or by parameterizing a JNDI lookup to find a differently named data source. An example of this in J2EE follows:

```java
public Connection getConnection() {
    Connection connection = null;
    InputStream stream =
        this.getClass().getClassLoader().getResourceAsStream(
            "myprops.properties");
    Properties newProps = new Properties();
    try {
        newProps.load(stream);
        String jndiName = newProps.getProperty(
                "Datasource-Name");
        InitialContext initialContext;
        initialContext = new InitialContext();
        DataSource ds = (DataSource)
                initialContext.lookup(jndiName);
        connection = ds.getConnection();
    } catch (NamingException e1) {
        e1.printStackTrace();
    } catch (IOException e) {
        e.printStackTrace();
    } catch (SQLException e) {
        e.printStackTrace();
    }
    return connection;
}
```

In this case, if the File "myprops.properties" is on the classpath, it will load the contents of the file and look for the property named "Datasource-Name", which presumably will contain the JNDI name of the DataSource.

In J2EE, you can even avoid the if condition altogether by deploying the application to different application server instances. In J2EE, a DataSource is bound to a specific JNDI name within an application server. If you configure an application server instance (perhaps on a developer's desktop) to refer to a Test Database with a particular JNDI name (such as "jdbc/MyDataSource") you can then configure a production application server instance to refer to the Target Database with the same JNDI name. In this way, you never have to change code at all, and the code only needs to reference a single JNDI name.

The more interesting problem, though, is not how you can change the database that the program refers to, but instead, how you set up the data within the database so that your tests will run correctly. Executing tests against unstable data or system setup can result in mysterious failures which can be very challenging to debug. The worst situations are when a test case does not properly cleanup after itself, leaving changed data which then results in unrelated test cases failing later in the test suite execution. The worst part of this is that since JUnit tests are not guaranteed to run in any particular order, that in some cases different tests can fail due to the improper cleanup of an earlier test, leading the developer on a wild goose chase for the real problem.

A common approach to solving this problem is to use the setup() and tear-down() methods of the JUnit TestCase subclasses to insert and delete data into the database. A data repository helper class which provides methods to insert the related data into the database is often used in this situation. The repository class would have different methods to support different types of situations, for example, it would have methods for setupOverdrawnAccount, setupShared-OverdrawnAccount, etc. The creation methods on the repository maybe called in the testcase's setup() method or from the testXXX methods. Likewise the repository would need to contain a cleanup method which clears the dynamic data from the database and the repository, so the data is set back to an initial state. This cleanup method is called from the testcase's tearDown() method.

Probably the best implementation of this general population/depopulation approach is found in the open source dbUnit extension to JUnit. dbUnit is an open source effort (originally authored by Manuel LaFlamme) that allows you to control the contents of your database tables during your tests by automating the setup and removal of sample data. dbUnit is capable of reading information from XML files (and other datasources) to seed a database with information at the beginning of a test, and then remove the information from the database at the end of the test. Likewise, it contains methods for comparing the contents of a table to an external XML file, making it simpler to verify that database updates have functioned correctly.

11. Sample Code

In this example we'll describe a DAO and demonstrate how you can test it against a lightweight Test Database using dbUnit. First you need to examine the DAO that will be tested against a replacement Database. This example is an extension of the example in the Mock DAO pattern. Note that this class (Listing 9.1) implements the same AttendeeDAO interface as the Mock DAO in that pattern.

```java
package com.ibm.examples.DAO;

import java.sql.Connection;
import java.sql.PreparedStatement;
import java.sql.ResultSet;
import java.sql.SQLException;
import java.util.Collection;
import java.util.Vector;

import javax.naming.InitialContext;
import javax.naming.NamingException;
import javax.sql.DataSource;

import org.dbunit.database.DatabaseConnection;

/**
 * DbAttendeeDAO is a Data Access Object (implementing the
 * {@link AttendeeDAO} interface) that is capable of
 * performing simple CRUD operations for the
 * {@link Attendee} class.
 *
 * @author kbrown
 */
public class DbAttendeeDAO implements AttendeeDAO {

  private static final String UPDATE_STRING =
          "UPDATE ATTENDEE SET NAME = ?, " +
        "STREET = ?, CITY = ?, STATE = ?, ZIP = ? WHERE ID = ?";
  private static final String FULL_SELECT_STRING =
      "SELECT * FROM ATTENDEE";
  private static final String DELETE_STRING =
      "DELETE FROM ATTENDEE WHERE ID = ?";
  private static final String SELECT_STRING =
      "SELECT * FROM ATTENDEE WHERE ID = ?";
  private static final String LOCAL_DATABASE_REFERENCE =
      "java:comp/env/jdbc/AttendeeDatasource";
  private static final String INSERT_STRING =
      "INSERT INTO ATTENDEE (ID,NAME,STREET,CITY,STATE,ZIP) " +
          " VALUES (?,?,?,?,?,?)";

  /**
   * Default constructor for the DbAttendeeDAO class
   */
  public DbAttendeeDAO() {
      super();
  }
```

Listing 9.1 Attendee Data Access Object. (continues)

```java
/**
 * Persists an {@link Attendee} object by inserting a new
   * row mapping to that object in the database.
 *
 * @param person an Attendee object to be persisted
 * @return void
 */
public void createAttendee(Attendee person) throws DAOException {
    Connection conn = null;
    PreparedStatement stmt = null;
    try {
        conn = getConnection();
        stmt = conn.prepareStatement(INSERT_STRING);
        stmt.setInt(1, person.getAttendeeKey());
        stmt.setString(2, person.getName());
        stmt.setString(3, person.getAddress().getStreet());
        stmt.setString(4, person.getAddress().getCity());
        stmt.setString(5, person.getAddress().getState());
        stmt.setString(6, person.getAddress().getZip());
        boolean result = stmt.execute();
    } catch (SQLException e) {
        e.printStackTrace();
        throw new DAOException(e);
    } finally {
        try {
            if (stmt != null)
                stmt.close();
            if (conn != null)
                conn.close();
        } catch (SQLException e1) {
            e1.printStackTrace();
        }
    }

}

/**
 * Obtain a {@link java.sql.Connection} for use in executing SQL
 * @return java.sql.Connection
 */
private Connection getConnection() throws DAOException {
    String mode = (String)
            System.getProperty("dbunit.test.mode");
    if (mode != null && mode.equals("TestMode"))
        return getNonJ2EEConnection();
    else
        return getJ2EEConnection();
```

Listing 9.1 Attendee Data Access Object. (continues)

```
        }

        /**
         * Obtain a {@link java.sql.Connection} for use in executing SQL
         * This method uses a {@link java.sql.DriverManager} to obtain
           * the connection and is thus not compatible with J2EE.  It is,
           * however useful for testing within JUnit.
         *
         * @return java.sql.Connection
         */
        private Connection getNonJ2EEConnection() throws DAOException {
            java.sql.Connection conn;
            try {
                System.setProperty("cloudscape.system.home",
                                     "C:\\Cloudscape\\");
                conn = java.sql.DriverManager.getConnection(
                                     "jdbc:db2j:sample_book");
            } catch (SQLException e) {
                e.printStackTrace();
                throw new DAOException(e);
            }
            return conn;

        }

        /**
         * Obtain a {@link java.sql.Connection} for use in executing SQL.
         * This method is compatible with J2EE and relies on the value of
           * the LOCAL_DATABASE_REFERENCE local reference for obtaining
           * its Datasource.
         *
         * @return java.sql.Connection
         */
        private Connection getJ2EEConnection() throws DAOException {
            try {
                InitialContext initContext = new InitialContext();
                DataSource ds =
(DataSource)
 initContext.lookup(LOCAL_DATABASE_REFERENCE);
                return ds.getConnection();
            } catch (NamingException e) {
                e.printStackTrace();
                throw new DAOException(e);
            } catch (SQLException e) {
                e.printStackTrace();
                throw new DAOException(e);
            }
        }
```

Listing 9.1 Attendee Data Access Object. (continues)

```
    /**
     * Update the row representing a {@link Attendee} in the
      * database.
      *
     * @param person the {@link Attendee} to be updated
     * @return java.sql.Connection
     */
    public void updateAttendee(Attendee person) throws DAOException {
        Connection conn = null;
        PreparedStatement stmt = null;
        try {
            conn = getConnection();
            stmt = conn.prepareStatement(UPDATE_STRING);
            stmt.setString(1, person.getName());
            stmt.setString(2, person.getAddress().getStreet());
            stmt.setString(3, person.getAddress().getCity());
            stmt.setString(4, person.getAddress().getState());
            stmt.setString(5, person.getAddress().getZip());
            stmt.setInt(6, person.getAttendeeKey());
            boolean result = stmt.execute();
        } catch (SQLException e) {
            e.printStackTrace();
            throw new DAOException(e);
        } finally {
            try {
                if (stmt != null)
                    stmt.close();
                if (conn != null)
                    conn.close();
            } catch (SQLException e1) {
                e1.printStackTrace();
            }
        }

    }

    /**
     * Return the set of all {@link Attendee} objects.
     * This method maps all rows found in the database table to
      * {@link Attendee} instances.
     *
     * @return java.util.Collection
     * @see com.ibm.examples.DAO.AttendeeDAO#getAllAttendees()
     */
    public Collection getAllAttendees() throws DAOException {
        Connection conn = null;
        PreparedStatement stmt = null;
```

Listing 9.1 Attendee Data Access Object. (continues)

```
              Vector vect = new Vector();
              try {
                  conn = getConnection();
                  stmt = conn.prepareStatement(FULL_SELECT_STRING);
                  ResultSet result = stmt.executeQuery();
                  while (result.next()) {
                      Attendee person = null;
                      person = mapFrom(result);
                      vect.addElement(person);
                  }
              } catch (SQLException e) {
                  e.printStackTrace();
                  throw new DAOException(e);
              } finally {
                  try {
                      if (stmt != null)
                          stmt.close();
                      if (conn != null)
                          conn.close();
                  } catch (SQLException e1) {
                      e1.printStackTrace();
                  }
              }
              return vect;
      }

      /**
       * Remove the row representing an {@link Attendee} from
       * the database.
       * This method executes a SQL DELETE statement, removing a
       * row corresponding to the {@link Attendee} provided as a
       * parameter.  Note that this method uses the getAttendeeKey()
       * method of {@link Attendee} to determine what row to remove.
       * If there are multiple rows matching that key, it will
       * delete all of them (of course, this should not happen,
       * since the primary keys should be unique).
       *
       * @param person the {@link Attendee} to be removed
       * @return void
       */
      public void deleteAttendee(Attendee person) throws DAOException {
          Connection conn = null;
          PreparedStatement stmt = null;
          try {
              conn = getConnection();
              stmt = conn.prepareStatement(DELETE_STRING);
              stmt.setInt(1, person.getAttendeeKey());
              boolean result = stmt.execute();
```

Listing 9.1 Attendee Data Access Object. (continues)

```
        } catch (SQLException e) {
            e.printStackTrace();
            throw new DAOException(e);
        } finally {
            try {
                if (stmt != null)
                    stmt.close();
                if (conn != null)
                    conn.close();
            } catch (SQLException e1) {
                e1.printStackTrace();
            }
        }
    }


    /**
     * Return the single {@link Attendee} represented by this
     * primary key.
     * This method returns one {@link Attendee} mapped to the
     * first row whose primary key matches the input integer.
     * Note that if there are several rows matching the primary
     * key it will only return the value of the first.  In any
     * case, a multiple match should never happen.
     *
     * @param primaryKey an int representing the primary key
     * @return Attendee
     */
    public Attendee findAttendeeForPrimaryKey(int primaryKey)
        throws DAOException {
        Connection conn = null;
        PreparedStatement stmt = null;
        Attendee person = null;
        try {
            conn = getConnection();
            stmt = conn.prepareStatement(SELECT_STRING);
            stmt.setInt(1, primaryKey);
            ResultSet result = stmt.executeQuery();
            if (result.next())
                person = mapFrom(result);
        } catch (SQLException e) {
            e.printStackTrace();
            throw new DAOException(e);
        } finally {
            try {
                if (stmt != null)
                    stmt.close();
                if (conn != null)
                    conn.close();
```

Listing 9.1 Attendee Data Access Object. (continues)

```
                      } catch (SQLException e1) {
                          e1.printStackTrace();
                      }
              }
          return person;

      }


      /**
       * Create an {@link Attendee} containing the information in
        * the current row pointed to by this result set.
       *
       * @param result a {@link java.sql.ResultSet}
       * @return Attendee
       */

      private Attendee mapFrom(ResultSet result) throws SQLException {
          String name = result.getString("NAME");
          int key = result.getInt("ID");
          String street = result.getString("STREET");
          String city = result.getString("CITY");
          String state = result.getString("STATE");
          String zip = result.getString("ZIP");
          Address address = new Address(street, city, state, zip);
          Attendee person = new Attendee(key, name, address);
          return person;
      }

  }
```

Listing 9.1 Attendee Data Access Object. (continued)

Now that you've seen the DAO (the object under test) you should go back and note the implementation of the getConnection() method. That method is the heart of this implementation of the Test Database pattern. It can be configured (by setting a System property) to either return a connection against a Database configured through a J2EE Local reference (which would presumably be the target database), or against a Test Database (in this case a local Cloudscape database). The next class to examine is the JUnit test case (which extends the DatabaseTestCase class from dbUnit) that tests the DbAttendeeDAO (Listing 9.2).

```java
package com.ibm.examples.DAO.tests;

import java.io.File;
import java.io.FileInputStream;
import java.sql.SQLException;
import java.util.Collection;

import org.dbunit.Assertion;
import org.dbunit.DatabaseTestCase;
import org.dbunit.database.DatabaseConnection;
import org.dbunit.database.IDatabaseConnection;
import org.dbunit.dataset.IDataSet;
import org.dbunit.dataset.ITable;
import org.dbunit.dataset.xml.FlatXmlDataSet;

import com.ibm.examples.DAO.Address;
import com.ibm.examples.DAO.Attendee;
import com.ibm.examples.DAO.DAOException;
import com.ibm.examples.DAO.DbAttendeeDAO;

/**
 * DbAttendeeDAOTest is a JUnit test for the DbAttendee DAO class.
 * It uses the dbUnit extension to JUnit to populate a Test Database
 * and compare the contents of the database against an expected result.
 *
 * @author kbrown
 */
public class DbAttendeeDAOTest extends DatabaseTestCase {

    /**
     * Constructor for DbAttendeeDAOTest.
     * @param arg0
     */
    public DbAttendeeDAOTest(String arg0) {
        super(arg0);
    }

    /**
     * main method for the DbAttendeeDAOTest.
     * This method invokes the JUnit text TestRunner.
     *
     * @param args an array of Strings containing program arguments
     */
    public static void main(String[] args) {
        junit.textui.TestRunner.run(DbAttendeeDAOTest.class);
    }
```

Listing 9.2 Attendee Data Access Object Testcase. (continues)

```java
/**
 * Set up the test fixtures
 * @see DatabaseTestCase#setUp()
 */
protected void setUp() throws Exception {
    super.setUp();
}

/**
 * Remove the test fixtures
 * @see DatabaseTestCase#tearDown()
 */
protected void tearDown() throws Exception {
    super.tearDown();
}

/**
 * Test the updateAttendee method of the DbAttendeeDAO class.
 * This test changes the name of an Attendee in the database
 * and then compares the resulting rows against rows held
 * in an XML file named updated.xml.
 *
 * @see DatabaseTestCase#tearDown()
 */
public void testUpdateAttendee() {
    DbAttendeeDAO dao = new DbAttendeeDAO();
    Address address =
        new Address("33 Maiden Lane", "NY", "NY", "11111");
    Attendee person = new Attendee(42, "Kyle Gene Brown",
                                            address);
    try {
        dao.updateAttendee(person);
    } catch (DAOException e) {
        e.printStackTrace();
        fail();
    }
    // Need to look for the row and validate the update
    IDataSet databaseContents;
    try {
        databaseContents = getConnection().createDataSet();
        ITable actualTable =
                    databaseContents.getTable("ATTENDEE");

        IDataSet expectedDataSet = new FlatXmlDataSet(
                        new File("updated.xml"));
        ITable expectedTable =
                        expectedDataSet.getTable("ATTENDEE");
```

Listing 9.2 Attendee Data Access Object Testcase. (continues)

```
                        Assertion.assertEquals(expectedTable, actualTable);
            } catch (SQLException e1) {
                e1.printStackTrace();
                fail("Database Exception thrown");
            } catch (Exception e1) {
                e1.printStackTrace();
                fail("Exception thrown");
            }

    }

    /**
     * Test the deleteAttendee method of the DbAttendeeDAO class.
     * This test removes the sole row in the database (which was
     * placed there in the test setup method) and then examines
     * the database contents to determine that the number
     * of rows is zero.
     *
     */
    public void testDeleteAttendee() {
        DbAttendeeDAO dao = new DbAttendeeDAO();
        Address address =
            new Address("210 Spring Hill Ln", "Cary",
                                       "NC", "22222");
        Attendee person = new Attendee(42, "Kyle Brown", address);
        try {
            dao.deleteAttendee(person);
        } catch (DAOException e) {
            e.printStackTrace();
            fail();
        }
        // Need to look for the row and validate it's not there.
        IDataSet databaseContents;
        try {
            databaseContents = getConnection().createDataSet();
            ITable actualTable =
                        databaseContents.getTable("ATTENDEE");
            int rowCount = actualTable.getRowCount();
            assertEquals("Row Count not Zero", rowCount, 0);
        } catch (SQLException e1) {
            e1.printStackTrace();
            fail("Database Exception thrown");
        } catch (Exception e1) {
            e1.printStackTrace();
            fail("Exception thrown");
        }
```

Listing 9.2 Attendee Data Access Object Testcase. (continues)

```
        }

        /**
         * Test the selectAllAttendees method of the DbAttendeeDAO class.
         * This test retrieves all the Attendees and then asserts that
         * the size of the remaining collection to determine is 1
         * (since only one row is inserted in the test setup method).
         */
        public void testSelectAllAttendees() {
            Collection coll = null;
            DbAttendeeDAO dao = new DbAttendeeDAO();
            try {
                coll = dao.getAllAttendees();
            } catch (DAOException e) {
                e.printStackTrace();
                fail();
            }
            assertEquals("Size not 1", coll.size(), 1);
        }

        /**
         * Test the createAttendee method of the DbAttendeeDAO class.
         * This test creates a new Attendee (not previously added in
         * the test setup method) and then examines the database
         * contents and asserts that the new row count is 2.
         */
        public void testCreateAttendee() {
            DbAttendeeDAO dao = new DbAttendeeDAO();
            Address address =
                new Address("33 Maiden Ln", "NY", "NY", "11111");
            Attendee person = new Attendee(45, "John Smith", address);
            try {
                dao.createAttendee(person);
            } catch (DAOException e) {
                e.printStackTrace();
                fail();
            }

            // Need to look for the row and validate that it is there

            IDataSet databaseContents;
            try {
                databaseContents = getConnection().createDataSet();
                ITable actualTable =
                            databaseContents.getTable("ATTENDEE");
                int rowCount = actualTable.getRowCount();
                assertEquals("Row Count not Two", rowCount, 2);
```

Listing 9.2 Attendee Data Access Object Testcase. (continues)

```
                    } catch (SQLException e1) {
                        e1.printStackTrace();
                        fail("Database Exception thrown");
                    } catch (Exception e1) {
                        e1.printStackTrace();
                        fail("Exception thrown");
                    }
            }


            /**
             * Test the findAttendee method of the DbAttendeeDAO class.
             * This test obtains the Attendee previously inserted in the
             * test setup method and then asserts that the Attendee was
             * found, and that the retrieved name matches what was inserted.
             */
            public void testFindAttendee() {
                DbAttendeeDAO dao = new DbAttendeeDAO();
                Address address =
                    new Address("210 Spring Hill Ln", "Cary",
                                        "NC", "22222");
                Attendee person = new Attendee(42, "Kyle Brown", address);
                try {
                    Attendee found = dao.findAttendeeForPrimaryKey(42);
                    assertNotNull("No attendee found", found);
                    assertEquals(
                        "Names don't match",
                        person.getName(),
                        found.getName());
                } catch (DAOException e) {
                    e.printStackTrace();
                    fail("Exception caught");
                }

            }


            /**
             * Return an IDatabaseConnection on a new java.sql.Connection
             * on a local Cloudscape database.  This database needs to be
             * the same database as the one used by the DAO.
             *
             * @return IDatabaseConnection
             * @see org.dbunit.DatabaseTestCase#getConnection()
             */
            protected IDatabaseConnection getConnection() throws Exception {
                Class.forName("com.ibm.db2j.jdbc.DB2jDriver");
                System.setProperty("db2j.system.home", "C:\\Cloudscape\\");
                java.sql.Connection conn =
```

Listing 9.2 Attendee Data Access Object Testcase. (continues)

```
              java.sql.DriverManager.getConnection(
                    "jdbc:db2j:sample_book;create=true");
            return new DatabaseConnection(conn);
        }


    /**
     * Return a new IDataSet consisting of the data held in the
     * XML file named full.xml
     *
     * @return IDataSet
     * @see org.dbunit.DatabaseTestCase#getDataSet()
     */
    protected IDataSet getDataSet() throws Exception {
        return new FlatXmlDataSet(new FileInputStream("full.xml"));
    }


}
```

Listing 9.2 Attendee Data Access Object Testcase. (continued)

The dbUnit framework is quite easy to use. The first part of this test that you need to understand is how the data is populated in the Test Database. The way this works is that (by default) in a DatabaseTest subclass, dbUnit executes the method getDataSet() to return an IDataSet containing the information to be inserted in the database. In the setup() method of DatabaseTest, that IDataSet is inserted into the database using what dbUnit refers to as a clean insert. This operation performs a DELETE_ALL operation (which removes all row from the affected tables) followed by an INSERT operation of the information in the IDataSet. This approach ensures that the database is in a known state prior to the beginning of each test method. The IDataSet is read from an XML file (here named full.xml, Listing 9.3) which contains the following information:

```
<?xml version='1.0' encoding='UTF-8'?>
<dataset>
  <ATTENDEE ID="42" NAME="Kyle Brown"
      STATE="NC" CITY="Apex" ZIP="27502"
      STREET="214 Rushing Wind Way"/>
</dataset>
```

Listing 9.3 full.xml.

At this point, a little explanation about the structure of the dbUnit data file format is in order. In this format, each XML element corresponds to a table row. Each XML element name corresponds to a table name. The XML attributes correspond to table columns. So in our case, the table name is ATTENDEE, while the columns are named ID, NAME, STATE, CITY, ZIP and STREET. An XML file can contain as many elements (referring to as many tables) as it needs.

This approach allows us to easily test methods which run SELECT statements, such as getAllAttendees(), since we can compare the results that are returned from the DAO methods with the expected results that are contained in the seed IDataSet. Testing methods that simply insert or delete rows are easy as well. We can perform a "reverse" operation on a connection and obtain an IDataSet from the database, then make assertions against that object. For instance, consider the following excerpt from the testInsertAttendee method.

```
// Need to look for the row and validate that it is there

    IDataSet databaseContents;
    try {
        databaseContents = getConnection().createDataSet();
        ITable actualTable =
                    databaseContents.getTable("ATTENDEE");
        int rowCount = actualTable.getRowCount();
        assertEquals("Row Count not Two", rowCount, 2);
    } catch (SQLException e1) {
        e1.printStackTrace();
        fail("Database Exception thrown");
    } catch (Exception e1) {
        e1.printStackTrace();
        fail("Exception thrown");
    }
```

This code uses the createDataSet() method of IDatabaseConnection (see getConnection() discussed previously) to obtain an IDataSet and then fetches the table named ATTENDEE from that DataSet. Finally, it gets the row count from the table and makes an assertion about the number of rows.

However, this doesn't yet fully explain how to test methods that update the data in the database. We still would need to compare the changed database contents against an expected state. Luckily, dbUnit provides this for us as well through the Assertion class. As you see in Listing 9.4 from the testUpdateAttendee method, Assertions can be used to compare two Data Sets.

```
               // Need to look for the row and validate the update

               IDataSet databaseContents;
               try {
                   databaseContents = getConnection().createDataSet();
                   ITable actualTable =
                           databaseContents.getTable("ATTENDEE");

                   IDataSet expectedDataSet = new FlatXmlDataSet(
                           new File("updated.xml"));
                   ITable expectedTable =
                           expectedDataSet.getTable("ATTENDEE");

                   Assertion.assertEquals(expectedTable, actualTable);
               } catch (SQLException e1) {
                   e1.printStackTrace();
                   fail("Database Exception thrown");
               } catch (Exception e1) {
                   e1.printStackTrace();
                   fail("Exception thrown");
               }
```
In this case, we compare the entire contents of the ATTENDEE table drawn
from the database with a corresponding ATTENDEE table drawn from a Flat
file named updated.xml (Listing 9.4). The updated.xml file is shown
below, and as you can see, matches what is in the method.
```
<?xml version='1.0' encoding='UTF-8'?>
<dataset>
  <ATTENDEE ID="42" NAME="Kyle Gene Brown" STATE="NY" CITY="NY"
ZIP="11111" STREET="33 Maiden Lane"/>
</dataset>
```

Listing 9.4 updated.xml.

12. Known Uses

In one sense, this is a problem that is well known and supported by all the major
J2EE vendors. The reason that IBM, Sun, and BEA include lightweight databases like Cloudscape and PointBase in their products is that not everyone
developing code using their product will have access to a database like Oracle
or DB2.

13. Known Abuses

None

14. Related Patterns

- Mock DAO

CHAPTER 10

Controlled Exception Pattern

Try as hard as we may for perfection, the net result of our labors is an amazing variety of imperfectness. We are surprised at our own versatility in being able to fail in so many different ways.

—*Samuel McChord Crothers*

1. Name

Controlled Exception pattern

2. Intent

Any implementation under test (IUT) can be expected to receive or handle certain exceptions. *Exceptions* are known problems that a designer or developer can reasonably anticipate occurring during some unit of work. *Exception handling* refers to recognizing (at the time of design and development) which exceptions might occur and planning how the application would respond if and when they do.

The ability to handle unexpected circumstances is referred to as *robustness*. Handling all types of exceptions in a single application can be daunting. The point of the Controlled Exception pattern is to automate that process to ensure that the IUT will consistently handle the variety of exceptions it could receive. This pattern was originally penned by Robert V. Binder in *Testing Object-Oriented Systems: Models, Patterns, and Tools* (Addison-Wesley, 1994).

3. Also Known As

- Exception Testing
- Raised Exception Testing
- Exception Handling Validation
- Robustness Testing

4. Motivation

In building client/server or "N"-tiered systems, the designer may find an application bogged down by many types of exceptions that may or may not have been considered at design time. To illustrate some of these exceptions in a J2EE environment, let's consider the high-level architecture for a typical catalog borrowing/purchasing application, as shown in Figure 10.1.

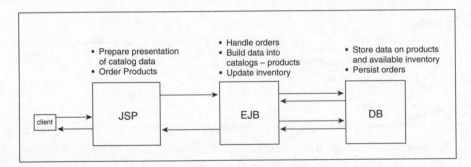

Figure 10.1 A typical catalog browsing/purchasing application.

The design of this application will handle many application-level exceptions. These errors will include such events as:

- Bad credit card information
- Expected data does not exist
- Invalid query parameters passed in
- Access violations

These errors are valid and can be tested with this pattern. However, putting these exceptions aside for a moment, let's consider the non-application exceptions that can be thrown in this application:

- The database is unavailable.
- An IO exception is thrown while the EJB container attempts to talk to the DB server.

- An IO exception is thrown while the JSP container attempts to talk to the EJB container.
- The EJB container runs out of available memory.
- The EJB container cannot be found through JNDJ.
- The JSP container runs out of available memory.

As an application developer, you will frequently run into these types of errors—especially after deployment of an application—and they can happen in almost any unit of code.

Now imagine testing an application (at a functional scope) and trying to provide adequate coverage for all these different exceptions. It would be a Herculean task just trying to document them all. At the unit level, however, this task can actually be manageable. For example, in the middle layer of our sample application discussed previously, we have a limited set of each of these types of exceptions, as shown in Figure 10.2.

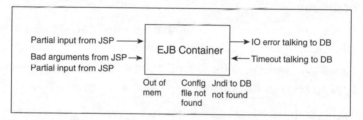

Figure 10.2 Exceptions in the middle layer of the sample application.

This is the beauty of this pattern at the unit level. If this pattern is applied to each unit of code being developed in the application, then we can automate adequate coverage testing and assert consistent exception handling across the application.

5. Applicability

1. Identify Exceptions for the Unit Under Test

The first step in applying the Controlled Exception pattern is to identify and categorize the various combinations of different types of exceptions that should be handled by the unit under test (UUT). As stated earlier, for the EJB container layer in our example application (category borrowing/purchasing), there are two types of errors to consider:

- **Application errors:** Errors that occur as a result of using the implementation under test in a way in which it was not designed to be used. These can include exceptions raised by usage that meets the interface requirements of the UUT but does so with inconsistent or invalid arguments. Note: These types of exceptions are best handled by applying the Category Partition Test pattern.

- **System errors:** These can include I/O errors, file errors, memory management errors, communication errors, configuration errors, and exception management errors. Since these errors are a little more cryptic, let's look at an example for each one:

  - I/O errors: The EJB receives a malformed request from the JSP.

  - File errors: The EJB tries to read in a properties file that is not where it is expected to exist.

  - Memory management errors: The EJB container runs out of memory.

  - Communication errors: The database is not taking connections or times out.

  - Configuration errors: The database is configured to a JNDI name that cannot be found in the EJB container.

  - Exception management errors: The UUT catches an exception and tries to recover but throws itself into an unrecoverable loop.

From these examples, we could document the known exceptions for our example application as shown in Table 10.1.

Table 10.1 Known Exceptions for the Example Application (continues)

EVENT	TYPE	EXCEPTION	EXPECTED RESULT
Invalid argument from JSP	APP Exception	Throw Invalid Argument w/msg	Redirect to error page
Access violation	APP Exception	Throw Access Violation w/msg	Redirect to error page
EJB container out of memory	SYS	Catch out of memory error	System.exit (1)
Config file not found	SYS	Catch IO Exception	Read props from DB
Config file access violation	SYS	Catch IO Exception	Read props from DB
DB not taking connection	SYS	Java.net.Connection error	Try alternate DB
Catch loop receives same problem infinitely	SYS	Runaway Process/ Memory Leak	Catch exception after fourth time; reduce to error page w/message

Table 10.1 Known Exceptions for the Example Application (continued)

EVENT	TYPE	EXCEPTION	EXPECTED RESULT
DB times out	SYS	Java.socket.timeout Exception	While 1 2 3 try again; then reduce to error page w/msg
DB cannot be found through Jndi	SYS	Javax.naming.Name Not Found Exception	Reduce to error page w/msg and e-mail admin

2. Identify Means for Creating These Exceptions

In his exploration of the pattern, the original author outlined three ways to generate the exceptions to test. They are:

- **Exception activation:** Use test fixtures to create the problem that will generate the exception in the UUT. Example: Given the model below, creating a new person object and trying to set the father ID attribute to a value equal to the child_ID will throw an invalid argument exception. We can test this by setting up a test case with the necessary TestFixture and parameters, as shown in Figure 10.3.

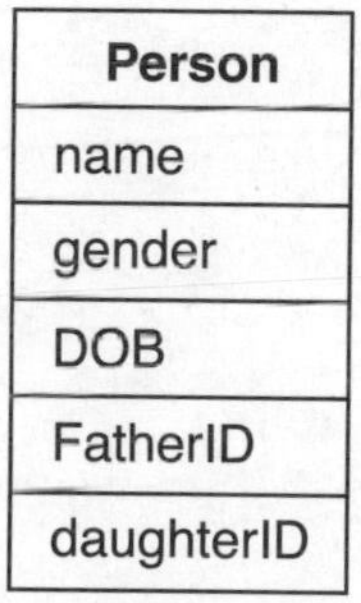

Person
name
gender
DOB
FatherID
daughterID

```
public voidsetFatherId (int id) {
     if (this.daughterId:==id) {
          throw new Exception(;);
     }else{
          fatherId = Id;
     }
}
```

Figure 10.3 TestFixture and parameters for the test case.

- **Exception inducement:** Create an environment in which the desired exception will occur. This can be done in the following ways:
    - Taking the DB offline
    - Using up all available memory in EJB container
    - Referring to a bad JNDI name to look up a database

For the purposes of automated testing, the test case should make these changes programmatically.

- **Exception simulation:** This is an implementation of the Mock Object pattern that extends the API of the target system and simulates a situation that will result in the desired exception. When testing software, it may not be advisable to induce an exception that could affect your operating environment. For example, if you are testing a satellite, you will not want to expose it to its upper threshold of operating temperatures just to evaluate the performance of an exception. In this case you would use exception simulation to drive the exception forward without risking damage to your multi-million-dollar equipment.

6. Structure

1. Exception Activation

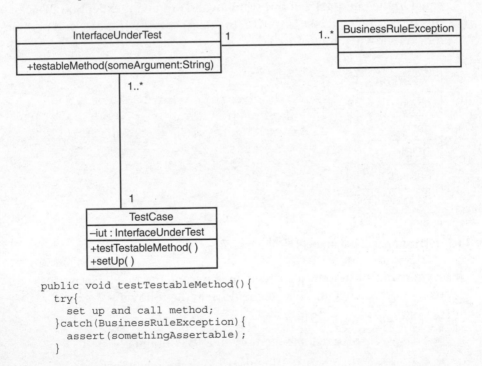

```
public void testTestableMethod(){
  try{
    set up and call method;
  }catch(BusinessRuleException){
    assert(somethingAssertable);
  }
}
```

Figure 10.4 Exception activation structure.

2. Exception Inducement

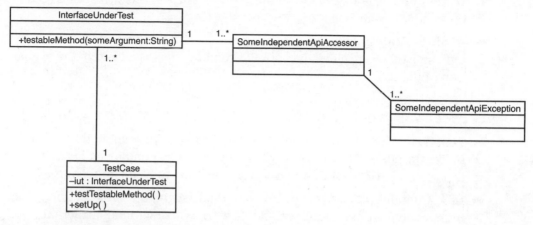

Figure 10.5 Exception inducement structure.

3. Exception Simulation

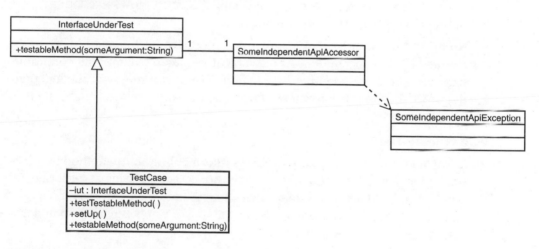

Figure 10.6 Exception simulation structure.

7. Participants

1. Exception Activation

- **TestCase:** Contains one or more IUTs. Sets up some condition in the IUT to fail on a specified business rule upon activation of the test method. Possesses knowledge of the exception that should be thrown by this condition and asserts that the exception is caught or that the IUT behaves in such a way as to indicate that the exception occurred.

- **IUT:** Contains at least one testable method. Throws BusinessRuleException under certain conditions.

- **BusinessRuleException:** Inherits from java.lang.exception. Its presence indicates that a specified exceptional condition has occurred in the evaluation of the IUT.

2. Exception Inducement

- **TestCase:** Contains one or more IUTs. Has a public setup method to initialize the state of the necessary test fixtures. Also contains at least one test method and possibly a teardown ( ) method to clean up resources.

- **IUT:** Contains at least one testable method. Aggregates connections to an independent API that it uses to do its work and meet its contractual obligations.

- **Some Independent API Accessor:** A class used by the IUT to access data or perform work. Implementation might be an RDBMS, a J2EE container, a directory service, or a mainframe system. Throws exceptions defined by its own API implementation.

- **Some Independent API Exception:** Inherits from java.lang.Exception. Defined by the independent API. It indicates that an exceptional condition has been encountered either in connecting to or working with the independent API. This exception can be thrown all the way to (or through) the IUT.

3. Exception Simulation

- **TestCase:** Contains one or more IUTs. Has a public setup method to initialize the state of the necessary test fixtures. Also contains at least one test method and possibly a teardown ( ) method to clean up resources. Extends the implementation under test and overwrites the method under test to throw an exception.

- **IUT:** Contains at least one testable method. Aggregates connections to an independent API that it uses to do its work and meet its contractual obligations.

- **Some Independent API Accessor:** A class used by the IUT to access data or perform work. Implementation might be an RDBMS, a J2EE container, a directory service, or a mainframe system. Throws exceptions defined by its own API implementation.

- **Some Independent API Exception:** Inherits from java.lang.Exception. Defined by the independent API. It indicates that an exceptional condition has been encountered either in connecting to or working with the independent API. This exception can be thrown all the way to (or through) the IUT.

■ **Mock Some Independent API Accessor:** Meets interface requirements of SomeIndependent API Accessor either through inheritance and overriding or by façade. Throws some exception that would be too difficult to dependably reproduce through exception inducement.

8. Collaborations

TestCase → IUT

TestCase evaluates the results of running method(s) in the IUT.

In ExceptionSimulation TestCase inherits from the IUT.

IUT → BusinessRuleException

IUT throws BusinessRuleException when prespecified exceptional conditions occur.

IUT → Some Independent API (API)

IUT uses a connection to API to connect and do some unit(s) of work.

Some Independent API (API) → Some Independent API Exception (Exception)

API throws an exception when some prespecified exception (within the scope of the API) occurs. Example: connection error, connection time-out, configuration error.

IUT → Some Independent API Exception (Exception)

IUT catches or passes through the exception to its clients.

TestCase → Some Independent API Exception (Exception)

TestCase "might" catch the exception or evaluate that the IUT has appropriately handled it.

9. Consequences

You should use exception simulation only when the exception under test cannot be reproduced through activation or inducement. Extending and implementing independent APIs such as RDBMS or vender-specific J2EE implementations can be both complicated and risky. Using this method to produce an exception can result in an environment that does not consider all the intricacies of the original API, resulting in tests that evaluate what would never happen in the original environment under test.

10. Implementation

1. Exception Activation

Write a unit test for person.setID() to ensure that it meets the assumptions outlined in Tables 7.2 and 7.3. For each entry assert that the value exists after the value is entered or that the expected exception is thrown by the IUT. Implement this test using Category Partition.

Table 7.2 Class Person

ID	INT
Name	String
DOB	Date
Gender	char
FatherID	int
MotherID	int
Eyecolor	char
Haircolor	char
distinguishing marks	array list

Table 7.3 Category Partition Person (setters)

FIELD	VALUE	EXPECTED RESULT
ID	Integer.min_value −1	InvalidID Exception
	Integer.min_value	OK
	0	OK
	1	OK
	Integer.max_value	OK
	Integer.max_value +1	InvalidID Exception
	"foo"	NumberFormatException

2. Exception Inducement

Given the model shown in Figure 10.7, attempt to add a new person record to the database while the database is unavailable. Ensure that the result is a java.sql.SqlException with a nested java.net.ConnectException.

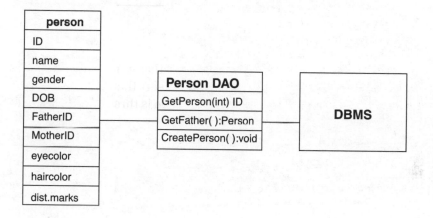

Figure 10.7 Database model.

3. Exception Simulation

Has the same requirements as exception inducement, except that you may *not* take the database down. It must be alive and accessible 24x7.

11. Sample Code

1. Exception Activation

Person class (Note: Methods are shown to get a sense of the class. The only necessary method in here is setId(String).) Listing 10.1 shows the Person class, and Listing 10.2 shows the PersonTest class. Listing 10.3 provides the output of TestCase.

```
import java.util.ArrayList;
import java.util.Date;

public class Person {

    private int id;
```

Listing 10.1 Person class. (continues)

```java
        private String name;
        private Date dob;
        private int fatherId;

        private int motherId;
        private char gender;
        private char eyeColor;
        private char hairColor;
        private ArrayList distinguishingMarks;

        public Person() {
            super();
        }

        public Date getDob() {
            return dob;
        }

        public char getEyeColor() {
            return eyeColor;
        }

        public int getFatherId() {
            return fatherId;
        }

        public char getGender() {
            return gender;
        }

        public char getHairColor() {
            return hairColor;
        }

        public int getId() {
            return id;
        }

        public int getMotherId() {
            return motherId;
        }

        public String getName() {
            return name;
        }

        public void setDob(Date dob) {
            this.dob = dob;
        }
```

Listing 10.1 Person class. (continues)

```java
    public void setEyeColor(char eyeColor) {
        this.eyeColor = eyeColor;
    }

    public void setFatherId(int fatherId) {
        this.fatherId = fatherId;
    }

    public void setGender(char gender) {
        this.gender = gender;
    }

    public void setHairColor(char hairColor) {
        this.hairColor = hairColor;
    }

    public void setId(String id) throws InvalidIdException{
        int newId = Integer.parseInt(id);
        if(newId >= Integer.MIN_VALUE && newId <= Integer.MAX_VALUE){
            this.id = newId;
        }else{
            throw new InvalidIdException("The id being passed must be
between 2^31 -1 and -2^31");
        }
    }

    public void setMotherId(int motherId) {
        this.motherId = motherId;
    }

    public void setName(String name) {
        this.name = name;
    }


    public ArrayList getDistinguishingMarks() {
        return distinguishingMarks;
    }

    public void setDistinguishingMarks(ArrayList distinguishingMarks) {
        this.distinguishingMarks = distinguishingMarks;
    }

}

    public char getEyeColor() {
        return eyeColor;
    }
```

Listing 10.1 Person class. (continues)

```java
        public int getFatherId() {
            return fatherId;
        }

        public char getGender() {
            return gender;
        }

        public char getHairColor() {
            return hairColor;
        }

        public int getId() {
            return id;
        }

        public int getMotherId() {
            return motherId;
        }

        public String getName() {
            return name;
        }

        public void setDob(Date dob) {
            this.dob = dob;
        }

        public void setEyeColor(char eyeColor) {
            this.eyeColor = eyeColor;
        }

        public void setFatherId(int fatherId) {
            this.fatherId = fatherId;
        }

        public void setGender(char gender) {
            this.gender = gender;
        }

        public void setHairColor(char hairColor) {
            this.hairColor = hairColor;
        }

        public void setId(String id) throws InvalidIdException{
            int newId = Integer.parseInt(id);
            if(newId >= Integer.MIN_VALUE && newId <= Integer.MAX_VALUE){
                this.id = newId;
            }else{
```

Listing 10.1 Person class. (continues)

```
                        throw new InvalidIdException("The id being passed must be
    between 2^31 -1 and -2^31");
            }
        }

        public void setMotherId(int motherId) {
            this.motherId = motherId;
        }

        public void setName(String name) {
            this.name = name;
        }

        public ArrayList getDistinguishingMarks() {
            return distinguishingMarks;
        }

        public void setDistinguishingMarks(ArrayList distinguishingMarks) {
            this.distinguishingMarks = distinguishingMarks;
        }

    }
```

Listing 10.1 Person class. (continued)

```
    import junit.framework.TestCase;

    public class PersonTest extends TestCase {

        private Person person;
        private String[] ids;

        public void setUp(){
            person = new Person();
            ids = new String[7];
            ids[0]=String.valueOf(Double.MIN_VALUE);
            ids[1]=String.valueOf(Integer.MIN_VALUE);
            ids[2]=String.valueOf(0);
            ids[3]=String.valueOf(1);
            ids[4]=String.valueOf(Integer.MAX_VALUE);
            ids[5]=String.valueOf(Double.MAX_VALUE);
            ids[6]="foo";
        }

        public void testSetId(){
            int i = 0;
            while(i<7){
                try{
                    person.setId(ids[i]);
```

Listing 10.2 PersonTest class. (continues)

```
                    assertEquals("The Id was not the value it Should have
        been after mutation ",person.getId() , Integer.parseInt(ids[i]));

                    System.out.println("Asserted that Lhe values were equal
        for the " + i + "nth element and were (" + person.getId() + ").");
                }catch(InvalidIdException e){
                    System.out.println("Asserted that the failure at the " +
        i + "nth element was as it should have been.");
                    if(i!=0 || i!=5){
                        fail("The value at element " + i + " was not
                        expected to fail.");
                    }
                }catch(NumberFormatException n){
                    System.out.println("Asserted that the failure at the " +
        i + "nth element was as it should have been.");
                    if(i!=6){
                        fail("The value at element " + i + " was not
                        expected to fail with a NumberFormatException.");
                    }
                }finally{
                    i++;
                    continue;
                }
            }
        }

    }
```

Listing 10.2 PersonTest class. (continued)

```
Asserted that the failure at the 0nth element was as it should have been.
Asserted that the values were equal for the 1nth element and were
(-2147483648).
Asserted that the values were equal for the 2nth element and were (0).
Asserted that the values were equal for the 3nth element and were (1).
Asserted that the values were equal for the 4nth element and were
(2147483647).
Asserted that the failure at the 5nth element was as it should have been.
Asserted that the failure at the 6nth element was as it should have been.
```

Listing 10.3 Output of TestCase.

2. Exception Inducement

Person class (see Person class in the "Exception Activation" section, above). Listing 10.4 shows the PersonDao class, and Listing 10.5 shows the Person-DaoTest class.

```
        package exceptionInducement;

        import java.sql.Connection;
        import java.sql.DriverManager;
        import java.sql.PreparedStatement;
        import java.sql.SQLException;
        import java.util.ArrayList;
        import java.util.Date;

        public class PersonDao {

            public PersonDao() {
                super();
            }

            public Person getPerson(int personId){
                //implement lookup here
                return null;
            }

            public Person getFather(int childId){
                //implement lookup here
                return null;
            }

            private Connection getConnection() throws SQLException{
                Connection con = null;
                try{
                    Class.forName( "org.gjt.mm.mysql.Driver" ) ;
                    String userName = "jdbc";
                    String password = "jdbc";
                    String url = "jdbc:mysql://192.168.72.13/person";
                    con = DriverManager.getConnection( url,userName,password) ;
                }catch(ClassNotFoundException cnfe){
                    cnfe.printStackTrace();
                    throw new RuntimeException("Error while attempting to access
        the database");
                }
                return con;
            }


            public void createPerson(String name, int fatherId,
                                int motherId, char eyeColor,char gender,
                                char hairColor, Date dob,
                                ArrayList distinguishingMarks) throws
                                SQLException{
                char comma = ',';
                char tick = 39;
                String sql = "INSERT INTO person (name,gender,father_id,
```

Listing 10.4 PersonDao Class. (continues)

```
               mother_id, eye_color, hair_color,date_of_birth) "
                             +"VALUES (" + tick + name + tick + comma
                             + tick + gender + tick + comma + fatherId + comma +
       motherId
                             + tick + eyeColor + tick + comma + tick + hairColor
       + tick + comma
                             + tick + dob + tick;
             Connection con = null;
             try{
                 con = getConnection();
                 PreparedStatement ps = con.prepareStatement(sql);
                 ps.execute();
                 //              insert distiguishing marks code here...
             }finally{
                 con.close();
             }
         }
       }
```

Listing 10.4 PersonDao Class. (continued)

```
       package exceptionInducement;

       import java.util.ArrayList;
       import java.util.Date;

       import junit.framework.TestCase;

       public class PersonDaoTest extends TestCase {

           private PersonDao dao;
           private String name;
           private int fatherId, motherId;
           private char hairColor, eyeColor, gender;
           private Date dob;
           private ArrayList marks;


           public void setUp(){
               dao = new PersonDao();
               name = "Zachary";
               fatherId = 777;
               motherId = 888;
               hairColor = 'R';
               eyeColor = 'H';
               gender = 'M';
               dob = new Date();
               marks = new ArrayList();
```

Listing 10.5 PersonDaoTest class. (continues)

```
                marks.add("scar under chin");
        }

        public PersonDaoTest() {
            super();
        }

        public PersonDaoTest(String arg0) {
            super(arg0);
        }

        public void testCreatePersonControlledException(){
            try{
                DatabaseUtility.stopDatabaseServices();

dao.createPerson(name,fatherId,motherId,eyeColor,gender,hairColor,dob,
marks);
                DatabaseUtility.startDatabaseServices();
            }catch(Exception e){
                assertEquals(e.getClass().getName(),"java.sql.Sql
                Exception");

assertEquals(e.getCause().getClass().getName(),"java.net.Connect
Exception");
            }
        }
}
```

Listing 10.5 PersonDaoTest class. (continued)

3. Exception Simulation

- Person Class (same as in the "Exception Activation" and "Exception Inducement" sections)
- PersonDao Class (same as in the "Exception Inducement" section)

Listing 10.6 provides the code for the PersonDaoTest class.

```
package exceptionSimulation;

import java.net.ConnectException;
import java.sql.SQLException;
import java.util.ArrayList;
import java.util.Date;

import junit.framework.*;
```

Listing 10.6 PersonDaoTest class. (continues)

```
public class PersonDaoTest extends PersonDao{

    private PersonDao dao;
    private String name;
    private int fatherId, motherId;
    private char hairColor, eyeColor, gender;
    private Date dob;
    private ArrayList marks;


    public void setUp(){
        dao = this;
        name = "Zachary";
        fatherId = 777;
        motherId = 888;
        hairColor = 'R';
        eyeColor = 'H';
        gender = 'M';
        dob = new Date();
        marks = new ArrayList();
        marks.add("scar under chin");
    }

    public void testCreatePersonControlledException(){
        try{

dao.createPerson(name,fatherId,motherId,eyeColor,gender,hairColor,dob,
marks);
        }catch(Exception e){
            Assert.assertEquals(e.getClass().getName(),"java.sql.Sql
Exception");

Assert.assertEquals(e.getCause().getClass().getName(),"java.net.
ConnectException");
        }
    }

    public void createPerson(String name, int fatherId,
                             int motherId, char eyeColor,char gender,
                             char hairColor, Date dob,
                             ArrayList distinguishingMarks) throws
SQLException{
        ConnectException ex = new ConnectException();
        SQLException se = new SQLException();
        se.initCause(ex);
        throw se;
    }
```

Listing 10.6 PersonDaoTest class. (continues)

```
        public static void main(String[] args){
            PersonDaoTest test = new PersonDaoTest();
            test.setUp();
            test.testCreatePersonControlledException();
        }

        public PersonDaoTest(){
    }
}
```

Listing 10.6 PersonDaoTest class. (continued)

12. Known Uses

The controlled exception process is common in environments that test applications for robustness.

13. Known Abuses

Over-designing the exception simulation process, or extensively modifying the IUT, can create a situation in which the code being evaluated has been altered so significantly that the value of testing it is greatly diminished. Consequently, you should use exception simulation only in areas where it makes sense and there is an existing mechanism in the architecture to facilitate it.

14. Related Patterns

- **Category Partition:** Exception Activation pattern
- **Mock Objects:** Exception Simulation pattern

Self-Shunt Pattern

We are what we pretend to be—most of the time.

—*Kurt Vonnegut Jr.*

1. Name

Self-Shunt pattern—Originally proposed by Michael Feathers, of Object Mentor Inc.

2. Intent

The Self-Shunt pattern provides a way for your tests to observe states and conditions that may not otherwise be presented to other (external) objects.

The goal of the Self-Shunt pattern is to enable us to become one of the collaborators in the test. But if we can't become a collaborator, we can at least *pretend* to be. You'll see what we mean in a moment.

3. Also Known As

None

4. Motivation

Let's face it: We have a lot of information that we'd prefer to keep to ourselves. Even though we may interact with our friends during the day, we'd rather not expose (or subject) them to our dirty laundry. A good object-oriented design is no different. Through the principles of information hiding and abstraction, we keep the internal workings of our systems to ourselves. But what happens at integration time, when we need confirmation that those actions have been taken? Sure, we've unit-tested the individual components, but now we want to confirm that when Object A calls Object B, Object B does exactly what it is supposed to do. Yet if Object B doesn't expose the details, what are we to do?

Self-Shunt can provide the answer by (presto, chango!) becoming the collaborating object. Like a good stage magician, we have to have a little more than our arm up our sleeve to fool our class under test. But with help from our lovely assistants (and some practice) you too can have your objects standing up and applauding your efforts.

5. Applicability

Self-Shunt provides a way for your testing classes to gain valuable information about collaborating objects without compromising the information-hiding capabilities and abstraction of your design. While there are several ways to implement this pattern that serve to make your job easier, the basic idea is the same—you become the collaborator.

6. Structure

There are numerous ways to implement the self-shunt pattern, but the basic ideas remain the same. The Basic Structure (Figure 8.1) is useful in situations where the Collaborator object has few methods to implement, whereas the Self-Shunt with Delegation (Figure 8.2) allows you to implement larger object structures without having to reinvent the wheel.

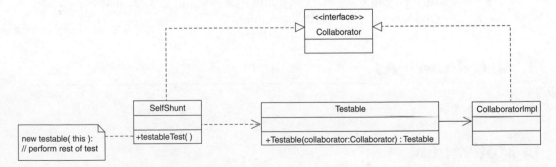

Figure 8.1 Self-Shunt Basic Structure.

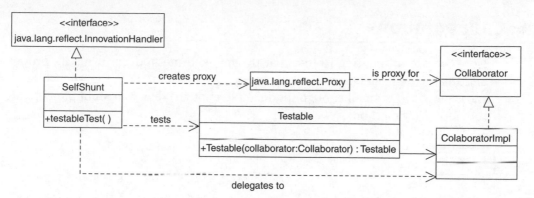

Figure 8.2 Self-Shunt with Delegation.

7. Participants

Basic Structure

- **Testable:** The class under test. It is associated with a Collaborator object, which contains some information that we want to observe for the test.

- **Collaborator:** An interface that implements the methods that Testable will call in its interactions.

- **CollaboratorImpl:** The actual implementation that Testable will use.

- **SelfShunt:** The testing utility. It also implements the Collaborator interface and will pretend to be the CollaboratorImpl object.

Self-Shunt with Delegation

- **Testable:** The class under test. It is associated with a Collaborator object that contains some information that we want to observe for the test.

- **Collaborator:** An interface that implements the methods that Testable will call in its interactions.

- **CollaboratorImpl:** The actual implementation that Testable will use.

- **SelfShunt**: The testing utility. It will create a Proxy object and delegate some of its responsibilities back to the CollaboratorImpl() method.

8. Collaborations

Here we are attempting to test that the invoked method performs its proper actions on the Collaborator (see Figure 8.3). We assume here that the Collaborator interface is small enough (and simple enough) that we can implement all the necessary methods:

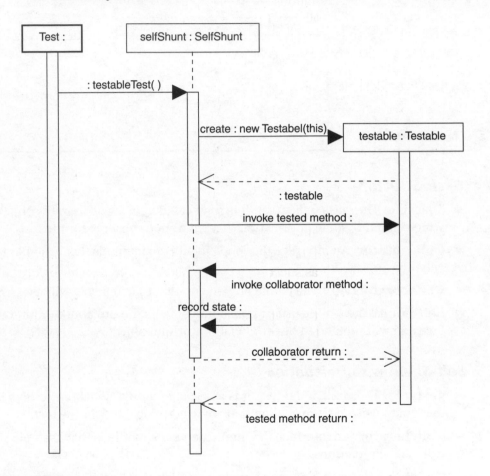

Figure 8.3 Self-Shunt basic collaboration.

- During the test, we create the new Testable object.
- We pass ourselves in as the Collaborator, pretending to be the collaborating object.

- When we invoke the method under test, the Testable object invoked the necessary methods within our test class (Self-Shunt).

  We can record internally any state information that we need.

- When we return from the test, we have information that we can use to assert that the method has performed as required.

Here again, we are attempting to test that the invoked method performs its proper actions on the Collaborator. However, this time we assume that the Collaborator interface is too large (or too critical) to implement all of the necessary methods, so we create a proxy and delegate calls to a real object, after we've gained the information we need:

- Prior to testing the method, we create a proxy for the Collaborator, setting the invocation handler for the proxy to be our test class.

- This time, when we invoke the method under test and it invokes a method on the Collaborator, the invocation handler within our test class is called.

- Again, we can record any state information that we need, but this time we dispatch the call to a real Collaborator object to finish the work.

- If we don't care about any state information, we can simply delegate the call without saving data.

- When we return from the test, we have the information that we can use to assert that the test was successful and the critical functions have done their work.

There are many different ways to implement such a delegating pattern, but the effects are the same: intercept the calls, save your information, and pass the message along for a real object to handle (see Figure 8.4).

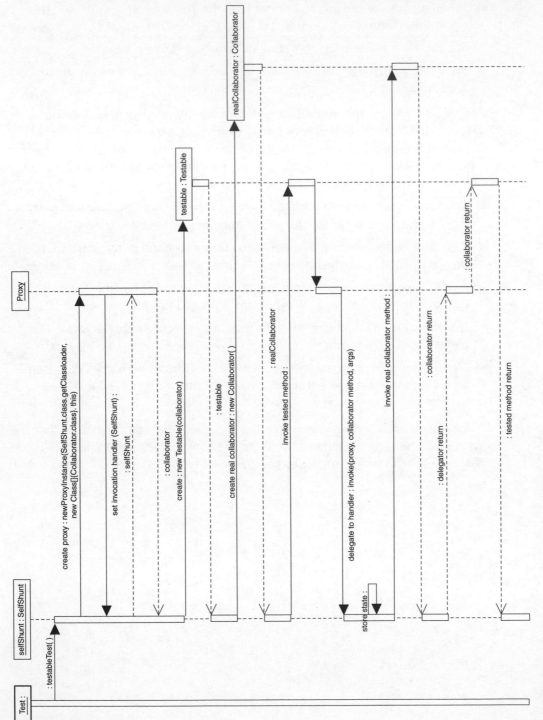

Figure 8.4 Self-Shunt with Delegation collaboration.

9. Consequences

As you can see, it is much simpler to implement the basic pattern—and simpler is always better. This becomes a problem, however, when you have critical functions or just too many functions to implement. For a simple pattern, some implementations can get out of hand. Experience will tell you when to use Self-Shunt or when other patterns, such as Mock Object (see Chapter 7), might save you some time and coding.

10. Implementation

Implementation for the Basic Structure pattern is straightforward, as Listing 8.1 shows. Your test case simply acts (and actually becomes) the Collaborator. It will implement all the methods of the Collaborator interface, and won't do anything other than store relevant state to verify that the test is successful.

```
// Test Class
public class SelfShunt implements Collaborator {

    // flag to indicate that the test has passed
    boolean testPassed = false;

    // Test method
    public testTestableMethod(){
        Testable testable = new Testable( this );
        testable.testableMethod();
        assertTrue( testPassed );
    }

    // implementation of Collaborator interface...
    public void collaboratorMethod(){
        testPassed = true;
    }
}

// Class Under Test
public class Testable{

    Collaborator collaborator;

    public Testable( Collaborator collaborator ){
        this.collaborator = collaborator;
    }
```

Listing 8.1 The Test class. (continues)

```
        // Method under test, invokes Collaborator.collaboratorMethod()
        public void testableMethod(){
            collaborator.collaboratorMethod();
        }
    }

    // Collaborator interface
    public interface Collaborator{
        // Method invoked from Testable class
        public void collaboratorMethod();
    }
```

Listing 8.1 The Test class. (continued)

For Self-Shunt with Delegation, there are a number of ways in which you might opt to implement a proxy or proxy-like pattern. Although the options are varied, the basic call structure remains the same, as you can see in Listing 8.2. Listing 8.3 shows the class under test.

```
    import java.lang.reflect.*;

    public class SelfShunt implements InvocationHandler{

        // flag to indicate that the test has passed
        boolean testPassed = false;
        Collaborator realCollaborator;

        // Test method
        public testTestableMethod(){

            // create a Collaborator proxy and redirect all method calls to
this class
            Collaborator collaborator
                = (Collaborator)Proxy.newProxyInstance(
Collaborator.class.getClassLoader(),

new Class()[]{ Collaborator.class},

this );

            // create a real collaborator
            realCollaborator = new RealCollaborator();

            // create an object of the class under test
            // and pass it the proxy
            Testable testable = new Testable( collaborator );
```

Listing 8.2 Delegation form of Self-Shunt. (continues)

```
            // invoke the testableMethod...will call Collaborator.
    criticalMethod()
            testable.testableMethod();
            assertTrue( testPassed );
        }


        // this method will "intercept" any calls to the collaborator
        public Object invoke(Object proxy,  Method method, Object[] args)
            throws Throwable {

            // we can save the state for our call to criticalMethod()
            if( "criticalMethod".equals(method.getName()) ){
                testPassed = true;
            }


          // delegate the calls to the realCollaborator
            return method.invoke( realCollaborator, args );
        }
    }
}
```

Listing 8.2 Delegation form of Self-Shunt. (continued)

```
    // Class Under Test
    public class Testable{

        Collaborator collaborator;

        public Testable( Collaborator collaborator ){
            this.collaborator = collaborator;
        }

        // Method under test, invokes Collaborator.criticalMethod() a
        // method that must complete
        public void testableMethod(){
            collaborator.criticalrMethod();
        }
    }

    // Collaborator interface
    public interface Collaborator{
        // Method invoked from Testable class
        // This method needs to complete...
        public void criticalMethod();
    }
```

Listing 8.3 Class under test.

11. Sample Code

For our example (see Figure 8.5), we'll assume that we have a Pilot Control System (PCS) package that we have received from another company. We have written the error-handling functions that will be called to correct the PCS when the code detects an anomaly. We don't have any means to change or add to the PCS package, and worse yet, it's tied to hardware that we really don't understand (and we don't want to have to reimburse the other company for it if we destroy it).

You've written the ErrorHandler class, and now you need to test that your correctSystems() method is correcting the HUD (Heads Up Display, for those who haven't watched *Top Gun* for the one-millionth time) and the Environmental-Controls. So let's write our first test case (Listing 8.4).

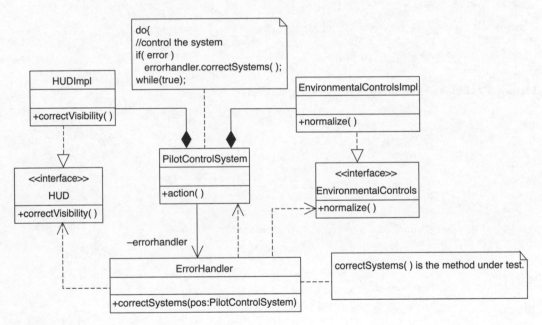

Figure 8.5 Pilot Control System basic concept.

```
       public class ErrorHandlerTest implements TestCase {

           public testCorrectSystems(){
               PilotControlSystem pcs = new PilotControlSystem();

               ErrorHandler errorhandler = new ErrorHandler();

               errorhandler.correctSystems( pcs );
           }

       }
```

Listing 8.4 TestCase.

Okay, but this is not a test. You made the call, but you're not really verifying that you did anything here. This is an excellent opportunity to employ Self-Shunt. Knowing that the PCS is critical, you opt to create a delegating pattern and capture the output of the HUD and EnvironmentalControl interfaces within the ErrorHandler (which will be acting as the proxy). With two "state" variables, you can now make the test a little more meaningful, as Listing 8.5 shows.

```
       import java.lang.reflect.*;

       public class ErrorHanderTest implements TestCase, InvocationHandler {


           HUD realHUD = new HUD();
           EnvironmentalControls realEnvironmentalControls = new Environmental
       Controls();
           boolean fixedHUD = false;
           boolean fixedEnvironment = false;

           public testCorrectSystems(){

               // create a proxy for both the HUD and EnvironmentalControls
               Object proxy = Proxy.newProxyInstance( HUD.class.
       getClassLoader(),
                       new Class[]{ HUD.class, EnvironmentalControls.class },
                       this );

               PilotControlSystem pcs = new PilotControlSystem();
               pcs.setHUD( (HUD)proxy );
               pcs.setEnvironmentalControls( (EnvironmentalControls)proxy);
```

Listing 8.5 An improved TestCase. (continues)

```
            ErrorHandler errorhandler = new ErrorHandler();
            errorhandler.correctSystems( pcs );
            assertTrue( fixedHUD );          // we fixed the HUD
            assertTrue( fixedEnvironment ); // we fixed the Environmental
Controls
    }

    // this method will "intercept" any calls to the HUD and Environmental
Controls
    public Object invoke(Object proxy, Method method, Object[] args)
        throws Throwable {

        if( HUD.class.equals(proxy.getClass()) ){
            if( "correctVisibility".equals(method.getName()) ){
                fixedHUD = true;
            }
            return method.invoke( realHUD, args );
        }
        else if( EnvironmentalControls.class.equals( proxy.getClass())){
            if( "normalize".equals( method.getName() )){
                fixedEnvironment = true;
            }
            return method.invoke( realEnvironmentalControls, args );
        }
        else
            throw new NoSuchMethodException();
    }
}
```

Listing 8.5 An improved TestCase. (continued)

12. Known Uses

Self-Shunt can be particularly useful when you need to test specialized utility class implementations (those classes that implement one or more of the java.util or Collections interface). It is also useful to test things that you would typically have to see to validate (such as video/graphics displays or physical hardware interactions).

13. Known Abuses

Of course, even with a simple pattern like this there is potential for abuse. In fact, the abuses of simple patterns may be greater than abuse of the more complex ones, and the consequences may lead to greater failures. Let's take a look.

If you begin with the Basic Structure pattern, you can quickly get in over your head with method implementation. Sure, interfaces like java.util.Iterator and java.util.Map have only a handful of methods to implement, but look at java.sql.ResultSet. Self-Shunt may cause you more work than you bargained for. You may want to reexamine your design to see if what you need from the test is information that you may want to make publicly available.

In writing the proxy object, especially with the large quantity of methods that you may be writing, you will generate a lot of code. This code has to be tested just as your main classes do. More often than not, a programmer has chased down an elusive bug only to find that the error was a simple mistake in the test class and not in the class under test. In writing the proxy code for the Self-Shunt, take care that you don't introduce an added level of complexity and testing to your system. Delegate to the real objects when you can.

14. Related Patterns

- Proxy pattern (see *Design Patterns: Elements of Reusable Object-Oriented Software*, by Erich Gamma, Richard Helm, Ralph Johnson, and John Vlissides (Gang of Four), Addison-Wesley, 1994)

CHAPTER 12

AbstractTest Pattern

The longer mathematics lives the more abstract—and therefore, possibly also the more practical—it becomes.

—*Eric Temple Bell*, The Mathematical Intelligencer *(vol. 13, no. 1)*

1. Name

AbstractTest pattern—Portland Pattern Repository

2. Intent

Inheritance is one of the core concepts of object-oriented programming (OOP). When Object or Interface A defines contractual requirements, then every object or interface inheriting from it is obliged to meet them. In Chapter 2 we talked about *deep* testing of classes to ensure that inherited functionality is preserved. The AbstractTest pattern is part of a testing framework, the purpose of which is to ensure that the structure of an interface or class (as it passed down through inheritance) is preserved.

Eric George, in his article on AbstractTest at wikiwikiweb, calls this *metric functional compliance*.

3. Also Known As

- Inheritance Testing Framework

4. Motivation

When developing a large-scale application, we establish inheritance structures during the design phase. These inheritance structures define our object model from day one. As the object model grows, these inheritance relationships define the objects within the system and describe what they do. A designer or architect will use interfaces and abstract classes to define the inheritance requirements in a system or application, but it is up to the engineer(s) implementing the system to ensure that the spirit of the design is met (and refactored as necessary).

If there is a common behavior (albeit with a different implementation) across the inheritance structure of these objects, then there should be a way to test that behavior's success uniformly for all parent and child objects. Additionally, if test suites are to become a part of our framework, then they should resemble the object structure upon which they are based. This facilitates the project in terms of clarity and documentation.

5. Applicability

1. Testing Common Functionality Across Layers of Inheritance

By using Java's integral inheritance framework (extension and implementation), we can design test cases that will define behaviors to be tested. From a single test case, designed specifically to test the class or interface under test (IUT), they will receive a roadmap of the structure and behaviors that define their testing methodology. This parent test case will also define final unalterable implementation methods for testing any functionality whose behavior should be consistent across levels of inheritance, thus enforcing functional compliance testing of the IUT.

2. Object Structure Mirroring

By utilizing inheritance in building the test cases for the object model, the test suites will more accurately resemble the model they are testing.

6. Structure

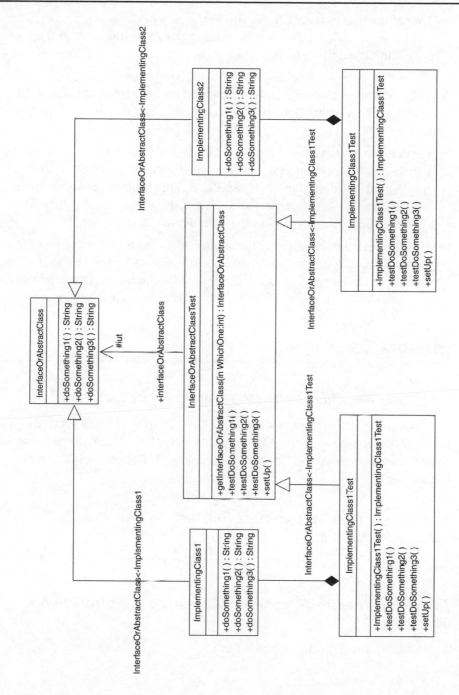

Figure 12.1 Test structure.

7. Participants

- **InterfaceOrAbstractClass:** This is the parent class in a hierarchical structure. It defines abstract methods that will be implemented by classes inheriting from it. It can be implemented as an abstract class or an interface.

- **ImplementingClass:** This is a class that inherits from InterfaceOr AbstractClass. It implements the contractual and functional requirements it inherited.

- **InterfaceOrAbstractClassTest:** This is a test case designed to define the contractual and functional requirements for test cases that will test classes implementing InterfaceOrAbstractClass. This is accomplished through abstract methods that define structural requirements and public final methods that evaluate functional compliance.

- **ImplementingClassTest:** This is the concrete implementation of a test case for the ImplementingClass class. It implements the abstract methods it inherits and runs (through inheritance) the final methods implemented in InterfaceOrAbstractClassTest. It also inherits from a JUnit test case.

8. Collaborations

ImplementingClass → Interface or Abstract Class (IAC)

ImplementingClass extends (AbstractClass) or implements (interface) InterfaceOrAbstractClass. If the IAC contains actual behavior, then it inherits or overrides that behavior. It also implements all contractual requirements defined by the IAC.

InterfaceOrAbstractClassTest (IACTest) → InterfaceOr AbstractClass (IAC)

IACTest contains at least one instance of the IAC.

InterfaceOrAbstractClassTest (IACTest) → junit.framework. TestCase

IACTest extends junit.framework.TestCase.

ImplementingClassTest (ICTest) → InterfaceOrAbstractClass Test (IACTest)

ICTest extends IACTest.

ImplementingClassTest (ICTest) → ImplementingClass

ICTest contains at least one instance of ImplementingClass.

9. Consequences

In order for AbstractTest to be effective, each developer on the team must understand it and be willing to commit to incorporating it when testing objects descending from abstract classes or interfaces and when deferring abstract classes or interfaces themselves.

Another consequence is that you have a hierarchy of classes or interfaces in the tests that must parallel the hierarchy of the classes or interfaces being tested. Having two hierarchies that must be maintained in parallel increases the difficulty of maintenance and adds a failure mode for testing.

10. Implementation

Given an abstract class that defines the functionality to be implemented by several classes, write a test that will be used to evaluate the structural and functional compliance of each test case in this branch of inheritance. In short, write a template for test cases designed to test classes that implement the class or interface under test.

11. Sample Code

Following is all the code for our test. Listing 12.1 contains the InterfaceOrAbstractClass class. Listings 12.2 and 12.3 contain ImplementingClass1 class and ImplementingClass2 class, respectively. Listing 12.4 shows the InterfaceOrAbstractClassTest class. And finally, Listings 12.5 and 12.6 contain ImplementingClass1Test class and ImplementingClass2Test class, respectively.

```
public abstract class InterfaceOrAbstractClass {

    public abstract String doSomething1();

    public abstract String doSomething2();

    public abstract String doSomething3();

    public abstract int divideBy1(int divisor);
}
```

Listing 12.1 InterfaceOrAbstractClass class.

```
public class ImplementingClass1 extends InterfaceOrAbstractClass {

    public String doSomething1() {
        return "doSomething1 in impl1";
    } // end doSomething1

    public String doSomething2() {
        return "doSomething2 in impl1";
    } // end doSomething2

    public String doSomething3() {
        return "doSomething3 in impl1";
    } // end doSomething3

    public int divideBy1(int divisor){
        return divisor/1;
    }
}
```

Listing 12.2 ImplementingClass1 class.

```java
public class ImplementingClass2 extends InterfaceOrAbstractClass {

    public String doSomething1() {
        return "doSomething1 in impl2";
    } // end doSomething1

    public String doSomething2() {
        return "doSomething2 in impl2";
    } // end doSomething2

    public String doSomething3() {
        return "doSomething3 in impl2";
    } // end doSomething3

    public int divideBy1(int divisor){
            return (divisor/(1/1));
    }
}
```

Listing 12.3 ImplementingClass2 class.

```java
import junit.framework.TestCase;

public abstract class InterfaceOrAbstractClassTest extends TestCase{

    protected InterfaceOrAbstractClass iut;

    public InterfaceOrAbstractClass interfaceOrAbstractClass;

    public final InterfaceOrAbstractClass
getInterfaceOrAbstractClass(int whichOne){
        InterfaceOrAbstractClass returnMe = null;
        switch(whichOne){
            case 1:
                returnMe = new ImplementingClass1();
                break;
            case 2:
                returnMe = new ImplementingClass2();
                break;
        }
        return returnMe;
    }

    public abstract void testDoSomething1() ;
```

Listing 12.4 InterfaceOrAbstractClassTest class. (continues)

```
    public abstract void testDoSomething2() ;


    public abstract void testDoSomething3() ;

    public final void testDivideBy1(){
        assertEquals(iut.divideBy1(777),777);
        System.out.println("The int asserted by the final method was
good.");
    }

    public abstract void setUp() ;
}
```

Listing 12.4 InterfaceOrAbstractClassTest class.(contined)

```
public class ImplementingClass1Test extends InterfaceOrAbstract-
ClassTest{


    public ImplementingClass1Test() {
        super();
    }

    public void testDoSomething1() {
        assertEquals(iut.doSomething1(),"doSomething1 in impl1");
}

    public void testDoSomething2() {
        assertEquals(iut.doSomething2(),"doSomething2 in impl1");
    }

    public void testDoSomething3() {
        assertEquals(iut.doSomething3(),"doSomething3 in impl1");
    }

    public void setUp() {
        iut = super.getInterfaceOrAbstractClass(1);
    }
}
```

Listing 12.5 ImplementingClass1Test class.

```
public class ImplementingClass2Test extends InterfaceOrAbstract-
ClassTest{


    public ImplementingClass2Test() {
        super();
    }

    public void LestDoSomething1() {
        assertEquals("Did not get the expected value from doSomething1",
iut.doSomething1(),"doSomething1 in impl2");
    }

    public void testDoSomething2() {
        assertEquals("Did not get the expected value from doSomething2",
iut.doSomething2(),"doSomething2 in impl2");
    }


    public void testDoSomething3() {
        assertEquals("Did not get the expected value from doSomething3",
iut.doSomething3(),"doSomething3 in impl2");
    }

    public void setUp() {
        iut = super.getInterfaceOrAbstractClass(2);
    }
}
```

Listing 12.6 ImplementingClass2Test class. (continued)

12. Known Uses

None

13. Known Abuses

None

14. Related Patterns

- Strategy (*Design Patterns: Elements of Reusable Object-Oriented Software*, by Erich Gamma, Richard Helm, Ralph Johnson, and John Vlissides (Gang of Four), Addison-Wesley, 1994)

- Template method

- Factory method (GoF)

- Mock Object pattern (see Chapter 7)

CHAPTER 13

Category-Partition Pattern

Keep on going and the chancesare that you will stumble on something,
perhaps when you are least expecting it.

—*Charles F. Kettering*

1. Name

Category-Partition pattern—Originally proposed by Robert Binder (author of *Testing Object-Oriented Systems: Models, Patterns, and Tools*, Addison-Wesley, 2000).

2. Intent

Category-Partition is a strategy for examining a representative sample of inputs in various combinations. This allows the tester to examine boundary and special conditions in combination, based on the premise that most errors occur due to compounded errors (in other words, two or more faults occurring simultaneously). While most tests can spot when the individual parameter is out of bounds, Category-Partition is geared toward finding special combinations of parameters that can lead to unexpected results.

The Category-Partition pattern accomplishes the following:

- Examines the input parameters to a method (black-box mode)
- Examines the output influences within a method (white-box mode)
- Determines categories for each parameter/influence
- Partitions the categories into representative choices
- Runs through all possible combinations of the choices

3. Also Known As

- Parameterized testing
- Combinational test

4. Motivation

On June 4, 1996, just 40 seconds after liftoff on her maiden flight, the Ariane 5, the newest space launch platform for the European Space Agency (ESA), was destroyed. In the days and months after the well-publicized debacle, interesting facts about the software came to light. The Ariane 5's software was not only based on the Ariane 4, but was indeed the complete source that was running on the Ariane 4. The Ariane 4 was a very successful launch platform, but it was significantly smaller in mass, propulsion, and payload than that of the Ariane 5. The engineers felt at the time that testing the software against the new parameters was unnecessary–they had adopted an "If it ain't broke, don't fix it!" philosophy. Sure, individual pieces of code were tested for the new system specification and everything checked out fine. But, on the morning of June 4, a certain combination of parameters led to disaster:

- An internal calculation of horizontal bias was larger than anticipated.
- This caused an operand error in a non-critical module (one that was used only to calculate pre-liftoff values).
- The result was that invalid data was set in the initial parameters for the launch sequence.

More often than not, it is not the individual error within a module that kills the application, but rather a special combination of parameters that leads to a fault. But what are we to do? Run our code through every possible combination of all data inputs? Even if this weren't a next-to-impossible task, who would want to write the test cases? Or review the data to make sure it was correct? No, there has to be a better way.

Enter the Category-Partition pattern. It gives us a way to break input values into categories and run through representative choices from those partitions. Although this approach will not catch every error, with a smart choice of categories and partitions and a little battle knowledge, you will be able to capture the bulk of these types of errors and feel a little better about your software "launch."

5. Applicability

Category-Partition provides a strategy for testing representative values of parameters in combinations that you may not typically encounter. This pattern is not a "real-world" test case/scenario like the ones you are probably used to writing. The intent is to examine combinations of parameters that you may not otherwise encounter to test the limits of the application. To the diehard tester, Category-Partition can be quite fun (yes, testing can be fun) when the goal is to try combinations that break the unit under test.

6. Structure

Category-Partition is more of a strategy than the typical pattern, so its structure is rather open to interpretation. Basically, it follows the strategy shown in Figure 13.1.

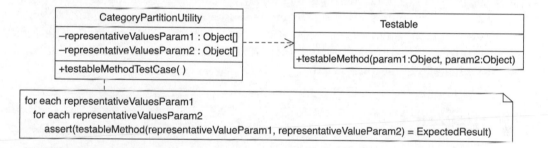

Figure 13.1 The Category-Partition strategy.

The real trick to Category-Partition is how you select the set of values to test with. While most of this will come with practice, there are some common issues that you can start with:

Integer

- Integer.MAX_VALUE/Integer.MIN_VALUE
- Double.MAX_VALUE/Double.MIN_VALUE (or any of the other constant range values
- 0 & 1– (remember those off by one errors)
- -1 (some older systems used values of -1 to indicate EOF and such)
- 1/3 (creating an irrational number can make sure you math is valid with precisional bounds)

Strings

- Null Strings

- Empty strings (" ")

- Strings containing Unicode and or special characters ("\r\a")

Dates

- Today's date/tomorrow's date (similar to the 0 & 1 test)

- Dec 31/Jan 1

- Feb 29,

- Apr 1,1918 (the start of Daylight savings time), etc.

Object Values

- Null values

- Unexpected object (especially useful to catch errors in upcasting)

In addition to the method values, you should also take care to view all the influences on a method. Methods might rely on class/object fields to hold certain values, or they might rely on system resources (time, filesystem, locations, or network) that might not be present or might be in an unknown state. The trick is to think of your method as the center of the universe and expand outward looking at all that influence it.

7. Participants

- **CategoryPartitionUtility:** Utility class that holds tests cases and representative values for the class under test.

- **Testable:** A simple class under test.

8. Collaborations

TestTestable: With this scenario (see Figure 13.2), we are trying to test the testableMethod() method within the Testable class:

- The test or some external utility (Builder, Factory, ObjectMother) creates an instance of the Testable class.

- The CategoryPartitionUtility is called upon to test an individual method.

- Representative values for each of the parameters are fetched.

- The method under test is invoked, and its expected result is measured against its actual result (error, exception thrown, normal condition, output values, etc.).

■ This fetch-test cycle is repeated until all the combinations of input values have been tested against expectations.

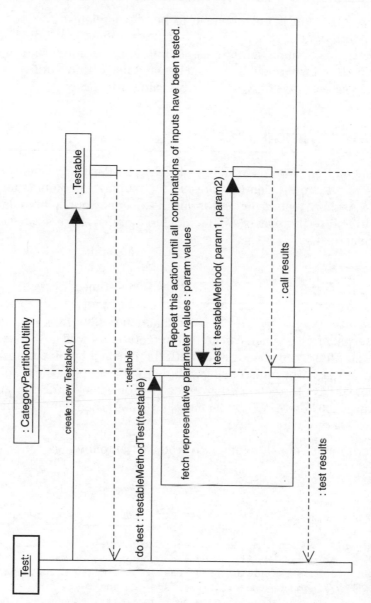

Figure 13.2 The fetch-test cycle.

9. Consequences

Category-Partition is not intended to be a "complete coverage" test case. It should test combinations of representative values and concentrate on the extremes (maximums, minimums, null, 0, etc.). As more and more tests are developed, you will find it beneficial to maintain (within a utility class) the lists, collections, or arrays of representative values for reuse.

10. Implementation

Implementation can vary widely with Category-Partition. One thing to keep in mind is a way to efficiently represent the parameter combination and results matrix. As these tests grow, and as you discover newer test boundaries, you will want to add to the matrix. We'll examine more of these strategies within the sample code.

11. Sample Code

For our test case, we will test a basic function to illustrate the dangers of both the internal factors which can affect our method, as well as the external factors which so often go undiscovered (until the finished application is delivered to the customer). Our functionality will be rather simple; calculate the absolute number of days between two given dates. For example: Between Jan 1, 2004 and Jan 3, 2004 there is 1 day (namely Jan 2, 2004) and between Mar 1, 2004 and Feb 1, 2004 there are 28 days.

For our first attempt at coding, we produce the following:

```java
public class DaysUtility {

    // Number of milliseconds in a day
    static final long MILLIS_PER_DAY = 1000 * 60 * 60 * 24;

    public static long daysBetween( Date date1, Date date2 ){
        long date1Milliseconds = date1.getTime(); // get date1 in millis
        long date2Milliseconds = date2.getTime(); // get date2 in millis
        // compute the difference and get the days.
        return (date1Milliseconds - date2Milliseconds) / MILLIS_PER_DAY;
    }
}
```

Next we write the following simple test and run it.

```java
public class DaysUtilityTest extends TestCase {

    public void testDaysBetween() {
        Date today = new Date();
```

```
        Calendar cal = Calendar.getInstance() ;
        cal.add(Calendar.DAY_OF_YEAR,1);
        Date tomorrow = cal.getTime();

        cal.add(Calendar.DAY_OF_YEAR,1);
        Date nextDay = cal.getTime();

        // there should be 0 days between today and tomorrow...
        assertEquals( 0, DaysUtility.daysBetween(today,tomorrow) );

        // there should be 1 day between today and the next day...
        assertEquals( 1, DaysUtility.daysBetween(today,nextDay) );
    }

}
```

Viewing the results, however, we see a problem right at the start:

```
testDaysBetween - DaysUtility Test

junit.framework.AssertionFailedError: expected:<-1> but was:<0>
```

Oops, we forgot a simple absolute value function in there, and now we're off by one. So we make a change: return the absolute value instead of the difference, subtract one, and we're happy. In fact we're so happy that we package up the code and ship it off to the QA department. Shockingly, we receive the code back within minutes: it failed!

Not wanting to be humiliated again (and desperately wanting to return to more "important" work) we decide to dust off that copy of *Java Testing Patterns* and apply the Category-Partition pattern. This time we'll run through a range of values to make sure everything is OK:

```
public class DaysUtilityTest extends TestCase {

    public static int DAY_RANGE_MAX = 50;

    public void testDaysBetween() {

        // start a calendar at today
        Calendar cal = Calendar.getInstance() ;

        // keep adding a day for the course of the range
        for( int daysDifference = 0; daysDifference <= DAY_RANGE_MAX;
daysDifference++ ){
            cal.add(Calendar.DAY_OF_YEAR, 1 );
            // make sure we are at an ever increasing distance
            assertEquals( daysDifference,
DaysUtility.daysBetween(cal.getTime(),new Date() ) );
        }
    }
}
```

Happy again, we package the results and send them off to QA/Testing, which certifies your results and releases them out into your company's product. Another job well done!

Later we are shocked to see errors show up in our little function. It appears that when people in NYC and London started to run the code, they were getting different results. But how could this be? We begin to write some more tests:

```
public class DaysUtilityTest extends TestCase {

    public static int DAY_RANGE_MAX = 50;

    public void testDaysBetween() {

        // start a calendar at today
        Calendar cal = Calendar.getInstance() ;

        // keep adding a day for the course of the range
        for( int daysDifference = 0; daysDifference <= DAY_RANGE_MAX;
daysDifference++ ){
            cal.add(Calendar.DAY_OF_YEAR, 1 );
            // make sure we are at an ever increasing distance
            assertEquals( daysDifference,
DaysUtility.daysBetween(cal.getTime(),new Date() ) );
        }
    }

    public void testDaysBetween_London() {

        // start a calendar at today
        Calendar cal = Calendar.getInstance( TimeZone.getTimeZone("GMT"
) );

        // keep adding a day for the course of the range
        for( int daysDifference = 0; daysDifference <= DAY_RANGE_MAX;
daysDifference++ ){
            cal.add(Calendar.DAY_OF_YEAR, 1 );
            // make sure we are at an ever increasing distance
            assertEquals( daysDifference,
DaysUtility.daysBetween(cal.getTime(),new Date() ) );
        }
    }

}
```

When we run these new tests, we are shocked to see the following results:

```
testDaysBetween_London - DaysUtilityTest


junit.framework.AssertionFailedError: expected:<36> but was:<35>
```

We forgot to allow for different locales. And upon thinking about it more, we also realize that factors such as time zone, daylight savings time, and a host of other activities are affecting our method. Now, however, we have a process for dealing with these factors; we can continue to use Category-Partition pattern to form an even better test.

Category-Partition is all about this building up of test cases through a combination of lessons learned and common mistakes. Slowly, over time, you will build up a useful collection of values to run through on your tests, helping you to catch some of these errors that aren't always obvious at first glance.

12. Known Uses

Of course, Category-Partition is good for catching errors in methods that resemble formulas, but it can find potential problems with other methods as well. From testing expected values of linked-list transversal to finding the wholes in a constructor, Category-Partition is a strategy that can help you detect some of those hard-to-find bugs that always come back to haunt you.

13. Known Abuses

Testing Too Much

Category-Partition is not the be all, end-all of testing. It gets real tempting to run through all possible values (why not just put our Integers into a big loop and...), but this, all too often, is not effective. You wind up wasting computing time, spending too much time debugging, and setting up elaborate testing structures to catch too few errors. Most of the problems occur at the boundary areas (0, 1, MAX_VALUE, MIN_VALUE, -1, etc.). Don't be tricked into thinking that Category-Partition can catch everything. Sometimes the best error catcher is someone who has been there before and made the mistake. They know that strange things happen with values of -9999 because the legacy system used to treat that as an end-of-file marker. This "tribal knowledge" is what needs to be captured in Category-Partition and not the simple blast through a series of numbers.

Testing Too Little

From the earlier example, you can see that, had you not had a diligent QA staff and you had stopped testing after your first round of Category-Partition, you would have missed a big flaw. Category-Partition is most effective when you run through the "common errors" typically found in your application. Start to compile a list of common Integer values that fail and begin to create a utility that tests all methods that take integers against that list. You may find some don't work. Maybe the method wasn't expecting a negative value, or maybe the method won't work for Integer.MAX_VALUE. Fixing the errors may be as simple as commenting the code or as involved as refactoring the method to meet the new and clearer specifications. Whatever the case, you'll be more appreciative of Category-Partition when you reach to your code draw and pull out an old routine to use in a new way and can run some tests to feel a little more confident in the dusted-off code.

14. Related Patterns

None

CHAPTER 14

Use Case Testing Pattern

But he doesn't know the territory!

—Charlie, in Meredith Willson's "The Music Man"

1. Name

Use Case Testing

2. Intent

The purpose of this pattern is to define a template usable for evaluating an application, system, or subsystem against a predefined scenario of usage (otherwise known as a *UseCase*).

What Is a UseCase?

With help from Ivar Jacobson, UseCases have become a stalwart of contemporary object-oriented analysis. The idea of UseCase-based modeling is to come up with a way to define the project in the customer's terms and the customer's expectations. Often we programmers tend to think of applications in terms of their implementation, and from this approach we can lose the perspective of the very people for whom we are building the system.

By using UseCases we can stay more focused on what the customer expects from the system and be distracted less by what we think the system should do. This helps us avoid getting trapped into working on features the customer won't care about. We can also avoid the trap of not implementing, or underimplementing, a feature that is very important to the customer. Martin Fowler talks at length about defining UseCases on index cards to keep them simple, and many, many developers use this method with great success. According to Jacobson, UseCases are defined by three simplc rules:

1. UseCases must be kept as independent of each other as possible.

2. UseCases must be described using the language of the customer.

3. Each UseCase must be structured to form a complete and intuitive specification of functionality.

Following is a clear distinction from Jacobson himself about the difference between UseCase analysis and more traditional engineering analysis:

USECASE MODEL	ANALYSIS MODEL
Described using the language of the customer	Described using the language of the developer
External view of the system	Internal view of the system
Structured by use cases; gives structure to the external view	Structured by stereotypical classes and packages; gives structure to the internal view
Used primarily as a contract between the customer and the developers on what the system should and should not do	Used primarily by developers to understand how the system should be shaped, i.e., designed and implemented
May contain redundancies, inconsistencies, etc. among requirements	Should not contain redundancies, inconsistencies, etc. among requirements
Captures the functionality of the system, including architecturally significant functionality	Outlines how to realize the functionality within the system, including architecturally significant functionality; works as a first cut at design
Defines use cases that are further analyzed in the analysis model	Defines use-case realizations, each one representing the analysis of a use case from the UseCase model

3. Also Known As

None

4. Motivation

A great deal of object-oriented programming is driven from product specifications that include UseCase. When a product is released to QC at the end of its initial development, analysts and testers often use these use cases as a map to testing the product. Thus, the engineer or development team is at a distinct advantage if the system has been pretested against the same set of requirements and its success has been documented.

This scenario is less of a traditional design pattern and more of an implementation strategy or template. It is highly valuable for any engineer or development team wanting to design TestCases or TestSuites driven from UseCases.

5. Applicability

Customers typically use graphical user interfaces (GUIs). Developers need to create unit tests that are independent of GUIs. Is there a way to unite customer use cases with unit tests that are uncoupled to any GUI by nature? Yes, there is. By identifying the units of work required to accomplish a given use case (in terms of the internal system or subsystem), we can develop a clustered unit test to evaluate the use case in terms of the customer's expectation. This way, if the end-to-end test (utilizing the GUI) does not work, the developer can run the UseCase test to see whether the problem is based on the performance of a particular class used in the use case itself or whether it is somewhere in the view layer (or the interactions between the controller and the view).

This pattern applies to any system, subsystem, application, or component that is derived from, or can be measured by, a use case. The steps taken in order to arrive at a UseCase-based test can be applied to a system, subsystem, application, or component. By following the steps in this pattern, a developer should be able to prove that the UseCase Under Test (UUT) meets the defined requirements at the level of class and object behavior. In other words, this test template will not prove that an integrated MVC system will meet its UseCase requirements. It will prove, however, that the calls to the controller layer in that system, when supplied with appropriate arguments, will perform their functions as specified. Engineering and test teams can use this test template to determine whether the errors in an application are occurring at the view layer or in the integration of the model and controller layers.

6. Structure

Classes Involved

Classes are commonly involved in a static context in the execution of UseCase-based code. The classes recognized in this structural element of the pattern are classes within the UUT's framework. For example, a static method call to get a database connection will often be made using a Factory pattern with a call similar to the following:

```
Connection con = SomeDatabaseConnectionFactory.getConnection();
```

This call is made to a class within the application's framework and is treated (for the purposes of this test pattern) differently than a call such as this:

```
Boolean trueOrFalse = Boolean.valueOf(someString);
```

The call to Boolean.valueOf is a static method call outside the scope of the application's framework (in this case it is a call to the Java Class Library itself, but it could also be a call to Log4J, JUnit, or Ant. None of these would qualify for the class element in the structure of this test pattern because they are not within the scope of the UUT.

Objects Involved

The objects involved in this pattern fall within the same nature as the classes involved. They are all the objects involved in the evaluation of this test case that fall within the scope of the UUT. They do not include objects instantiated in the evaluation of the UUT that fall within a different framework that is coupled to the UUT.

Class–Object Relationships

The relationships between the classes and objects used within the UUT are critical to the design of the TestCases and/or TestSuite. Therefore, the implementing engineer will need to know the following:

- What classes each class or object is related to
- What object references each class or object is related to
- The nature of each relationship

Class-Object Interaction Arguments

The interactions between all combinations of classes and objects in evaluation of the UUT will depend on messages being passed back and forth between them. It is important, therefore, to have foreknowledge of what each entity (class or object) expects when it initializes a relationship with another entity. For example, it is important for the sake of this test pattern that when ClassA initializes a relationship with ObjectB, and the nature of that relationship is NatureN, that ClassA expects to receive a numeric value from ObjectB to help it do its work? This will all become clearer in the "Implementation" section.

Class-Object Interaction Return Values

As stated in the last section, the interactions between all combinations of classes and objects in evaluation of the UUT will depend on messages being passed back and forth between them. It is important, therefore, to have foreknowledge of what each entity (class or object) will return as the result of its interaction with another entity. Then it is important to understand that when ObjectA has a relationship with ClassB of NatureN, ClassB will return ObjectC back to ObjectA as a result of the interaction.

7. Participants

In defining the participants of this pattern, let us consider as an example the following UseCase:

Payroll System UseCase

A clerk creates a new employee record in the database. He then enters employee tax information for the new employee and adds him into the payroll schedule, as shown in Figure 14.1.

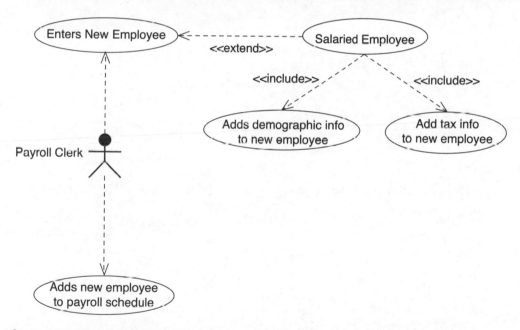

Figure 14.1 Payroll system UseCase.

The object model for the application is shown in Figure 14.2.

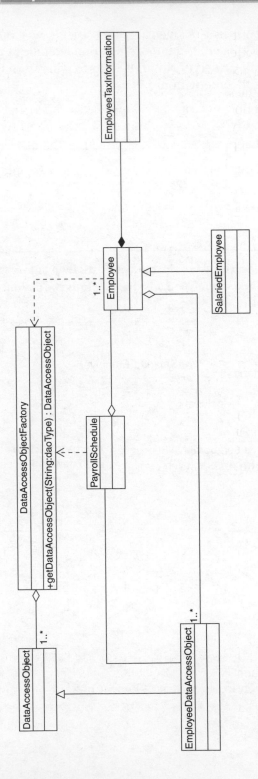

Figure 14.2 The object model for the application.

- **Entities:** In this pattern entities are the classes and objects defined previously in the "Structure" section.

- **Actors:** Actors are the entities responsible for instigating a relationship between other entities in the pattern. An actor is often one of the very entities involved in the interaction, but an actor is also responsible for passing arguments to its related entity and receiving a return value. For example, two entities in our payroll application relate as shown in Figure 14.3.

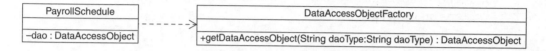

PayrollSchedule	DataAccessObjectFactory
−dao : DataAccessObject	+getDataAccessObject(String daoType:String daoType) : DataAccessObject

Figure 14.3 Relationship of two entities in the payroll application.

Here an instance of PayrollSchedule uses DataAccessObjectFactory in a static context to obtain its DAO member by calling getDataAccessFactory with an argument indicating that the DAO it wants returned is of type Employee. In this context PayrollSchedule is an actor that acts upon DataAccessObjectFactory by calling getDataAccessObject with a certain string value and expects to receive in return an instance of DataAccessObject.

- **Relationships:** It is implied by the nature of the UseCase that there are relationships between the classes and objects composing it. Identifying the relationships is extremely important in being prepared to evaluate the UseCase. In the example above, in order to add a new employee to the payroll schedule, a developer will need to understand how the payroll schedule is related to an employee in the object model.

8. Collaborations

In this pattern collaborations are essential to the very fabric of the UUT. See "Class-Object Relationships" above.

9. Consequences

While testing for UseCases is extremely useful in proving the viability of a solution, it is by no means comprehensive. A good engineer must test her software's robustness against unexpected conditions. UseCase testing is one means to the end of proving that a solution has met its requirements, but it does not in any way meet the overall testing needs of any system, subsystem, or application.

10. Implementation

The following steps should be followed for proper implementation:

1. Identify the classes and objects used in the completion of the UseCase.

2. Identify the relationships between the classes and objects identified in step one.

3. Identify the interactions between actors and the components identified in steps one and two.

4. Model TestCases and/or TestSuites to evaluate the UseCase in terms of system components and input/output.

5. Implement TestCases.

1. Identify the Classes and Objects Used in the Completion of the UseCase.

Classes

DataAccessObjectFactory

DataAccessObject (by extension)

Employee (by extension)

Objects

SalariedEmployee

EmployeeTaxInformation

PayrollSchedule

EmployeeDataAccessObject

2. Identify the Relationships between the Classes and Objects Identified in Step One

- DataAccessObjectFactory aggregates EmployeeDataAccessObject(s).

- SalariedEmployee contains one EmployeeTaxInformation.

- SalariedEmployee uses DataAccessObjectFactory (statically).

- SalariedEmployee contains at least one EmployeeDataAccessObject.

- PayrollSchedule uses DataAccessObjectFactory (statically).

- PayrollSchedule contains at least one EmployeeDataAccessObject.

- PayrollSchedule contains at least one Employee.

3. Identify the Interactions between Actors and the Components Identified in Steps One and Two

Figure 14.4 illustrates the interactions between the actors and the components previously identified.

For the purposes of this pattern, the client in the model above will be replaced by the TestCase. That being said, the interactions are as follows:

- TestCase → SalariedEmployee : new instance
- TestCase → SalariedEmployee : mutator calls
- SalariedEmployee → EmployeeTaxInformation : new Instance
- SalariedEmployee → EmployeeTaxInformation : mutator calls
- SalariedEmployee → DataAccessObjectFactory : getDataAccessObject(type) : EmployeeDataAccessObject
- SalariedEmployee → EmployeeDataAccessObject : persistEmployee(Employee) : int employeeId
- TestCase → EmployeeDataAccessObject: getPayrollSchedule : PayrollSchedule
- EmployeeDataAccessObject → PayrollSchedule : new instance
- PayrollSchedule → EmployeeDataAccessObject : load
- TestCase → PayrollSchedule : add : empId
- TestCase → EmployeeDataAccessObject : persistPayrollSchedule : isPersisted

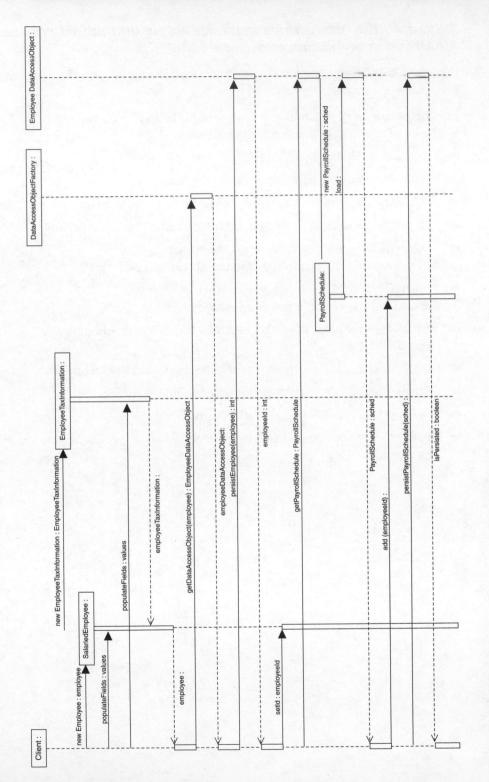

Figure 14.4 Interactions between actors and components.

4. Model TestCases and/or TestSuites to Evaluate the UseCase in Terms of System Components and Input/Output.

Figure 14.5 shows the system components and the input/output.

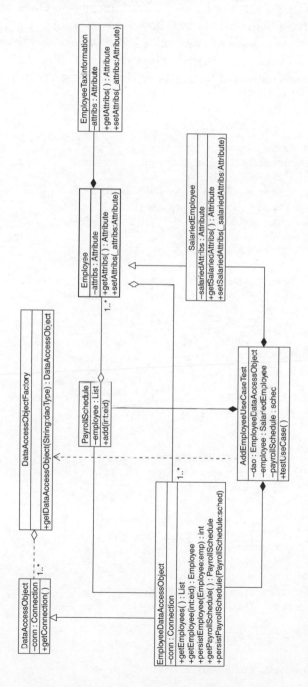

Figure 14.5 System components and input/output.

11. Sample Code

The Employee class is shown in Listing 14.1, and the SalariedEmployee class is shown in Listing 14.2. The EmployeeTaxInformation class is shown in Listing 14.3. The PayrollSchedule class is shown in Listing 14.4. The EmployeeDataAccessObject class is shown in Listing 14.5, the DataAccessObject class in Listing 14.6, and the DataAccessObjectFactory class in Listing 14.7. The ConnectionFactory class is shown in Listing 14.8. The AddEmployeeUseCaseTest class is shown in Listing 14.9.

```
public class Employee {
    private String name, department, position;
    private int age, id;
    private EmployeeTaxInformation taxInformation;
    private EmployeeDataAccessObject dao;
    private String address1;
    private String address2;

    public Employee(){
        dao = (EmployeeDataAccessObject)DataAccessObjectFactory.
getDataAccessObject(DataAccessObjectFactory.EMPLOYEE_DAO);
    }

    public int getAge() {
        return age;
    }

    public String getDepartment() {
        return department;
    }


    public EmployeeTaxInformation getTaxInformation() {
        return taxInformation;
    }

    public String getName() {
        return name;
    }

    public String getPosition() {
        return position;
    }
```

Listing 14.1 Employee class. (continues)

```java
        public void setAge(int i) {
            age = i;
        }

        public void setDepartment(String string) {
            department = string;
        }

        public void setTaxInformation(EmployeeTaxInformation information) {
            taxInformation = information;
        }

        public void setName(String string) {
            name = string;
        }

        public void setPosition(String string) {
            position = string;
        }

        public String getAddress1() {
            return address1;
        }

        public String getAddress2() {
            return address2;
        }

        public void setAddress1(String string) {
            address1 = string;
        }

        public void setAddress2(String string) {
            address2 = string;
        }

        /**
         * @return
         */
        public int getId() {
            return id;
        }

        /**
         * @param i
         */
        public void setId(int i) {
            id = i;
        }
    }
```

Listing 14.1 Employee class. (continued)

```
public class SalariedEmployee extends Employee {

    private Double yearlySalary;
    private int numberOfPayPeriods;


    public Double getSalary() {
        return yearlySalary;
    }

    public void setSalary(Double currency) {
        yearlySalary = currency;
    }

    public int getNumberOfPayPeriods() {
        return numberOfPayPeriods;
    }

    public void setNumberOfPayPeriods(int i) {
        numberOfPayPeriods = i;
    }

}
```

Listing 14.2 SalariedEmployee class.

```
public class EmployeeTaxInformation {

    private String ssn;
    private int deductions;
    private double taxRate;
    private int maritalStatus;

    public static final int MARITAL_STATUS_SINGLE = 1;
    public static final int MARITAL_STATUS_MARRIED_JOINT = 2;
    public static final int MARITAL_STATUS_MARRIED_SEPARATE = 3;
    public static final int MARITAL_STATUS_SEPARATED = 4;
    public static final int MARITAL_STATUS_DIVORCED = 5;
    public static final int MARITAL_STATUS_WIDOWED = 6;

    public int getDeductions() {
        return deductions;
    }
```

Listing 14.3 EmployeeTaxInformation class. (continues)

```
        public int getMaritalStatus() {
            return maritalStatus;
        }

        public String getSsn() {
            return ssn;
        }

        public double getTaxRate() {
            return taxRate;
        }

        public void setDeductions(int i) {
            deductions = i;
        }

        public void setMaritalStatus(int i) {
            maritalStatus = i;
        }

        public void setSsn(String string) {
            ssn = string;
        }

        public void setTaxRate(double d) {
            taxRate = d;
        }

    }
```

Listing 14.3 EmployeeTaxInformation class. (continued)

```
        import java.sql.SQLException;
        import java.util.*;

        public class PayrollSchedule {

            private Date payDate;
            private EmployeeDataAccessObject employeeDataAccessObject;
            private ArrayList employees;
            private EmployeeDataAccessObject dao;

            public PayrollSchedule(){
                dao = (EmployeeDataAccessObject)DataAccessObjectFactory.
        getDataAccessObject(DataAccessObjectFactory.EMPLOYEE_DAO);
            }
```

Listing 14.4 PayrollSchedule class. (continues)

```
        public void add(int eid) {
            try{
                Employee emp = dao.getEmployee(eid);
                employees.add(emp);

          }catch(SQLException e){

                e.printStackTrace();
            }
        }

        public void add(Employee emp) {
                try{
                    employees.add(emp);
                }catch(Exception e){
                    e.printStackTrace();
                }
            }

        public ArrayList getEmployees() {
            return employees;
        }

        public EmployeeDataAccessObject getEmployeeDataAccessObject() {
            return employeeDataAccessObject;
        }

        public Date getPayDate() {
            return payDate;
        }

        public void setEmployees(ArrayList list) {
            employees = list;
        }

        public void setEmployeeDataAccessObject(EmployeeDataAccessObject
object) {
            employeeDataAccessObject = object;
        }

        public void setPayDate(Date date) {
            payDate = date;
        }

        public HashMap processPayroll(){
            ListIterator empList = employees.listIterator();
            HashMap payroll = new HashMap();
            while(empList.hasNext()){
                SalariedEmployee emp =(SalariedEmployee)empList.next();
                payroll.put(
```

Listing 14.4 PayrollSchedule class. (continues)

```
                        emp.getTaxInformation().getSsn(),
                        new Double(emp.getSalary().doubleValue() / emp.get
        NumberOfPayPeriods() * (1-emp.getTaxInformation().getTaxRate()))
                    );
            }
            return payroll;
        }
    }
```

Listing 14.4 PayrollSchedule class. (continued)

```java
        import java.util.ArrayList;
        import java.sql.*;

        public class EmployeeDataAccessObject extends DataAccessObject {

            public void getConnection(){
                ConnectionFactory fac = new ConnectionFactory();
                if(conn==null){
                    conn=fac.getConnection();
                }
            }

            private Connection conn;
            public Employee employee;
            public PayrollSchedule payrollSchedule;

            public static final int GLOBAL_NUMBER_OF_PAY_PERIODS = 26;

            public ArrayList getEmployees() throws SQLException {
                getConnection();
                ArrayList al = null;
                try{
                    String sql = "SELECT emp.*, ti.* FROM employee emp, tax_info
        ti WHERE employee.id = tax_info.emp_id ";
                    PreparedStatement ps = conn.prepareStatement(sql);
                    ResultSet rs = ps.executeQuery();
                    while(rs.next()){
                        al = new ArrayList();
                        SalariedEmployee emp = new SalariedEmployee();
                        EmployeeTaxInformation ti = new EmployeeTax
                        Information();
                        emp.setId(rs.getInt("employee.id"));
                        emp.setNumberOfPayPeriods(EmployeeDataAccessObject
                        .GLOBAL_NUMBER_OF_PAY_PERIODS);
                        emp.setAddress1(rs.getString("emp.address_1"));
                        emp.setAddress2(rs.getString("emp.address_2"));
```

Listing 14.5 EmployeeDataAccessObject class. (continues)

```
                    emp.setAge(rs.getInt("emp.age"));
                    emp.setDepartment(rs.getString("emp.department"));
                    emp.setName(rs.getString("emp.name"));
                    emp.setPosition(rs.getString("emp.title"));
                    emp.setSalary(new Double(rs.getDouble("ti.salary")));
                    ti.setDeductions(rs.getInt("ti.deductions"));
                    ti.setMaritalStatus(rs.getInt("emp.marital_status"));
                    ti.setSsn(rs.getString("emp.ssn"));
                    ti.setTaxRate(rs.getDouble("ti.tax_rate"));
                    emp.setTaxInformation(ti);
            }

            return al;
        }finally{
            conn.close();
        }
    } // end getEmployees

    public SalariedEmployee getEmployee(int eid) throws SQLException{
        getConnection();
        try{
            SalariedEmployee emp = new SalariedEmployee();
            EmployeeTaxInformation ti = new EmployeeTaxInformation();
            String sql = "SELECT emp.*, ti.* FROM employee emp, tax_info
ti WHERE employee.id = tax_info.emp_id and employee.id = ?";
            PreparedStatement ps = conn.prepareStatement(sql);
            ps.setInt(1,eid);
            ResultSet rs = ps.executeQuery();
            if(rs.next()){
                emp.setId(eid);
                emp.setAddress1(rs.getString("emp.address_1"));
                emp.setAddress2(rs.getString("emp.address_2"));
                emp.setAge(rs.getInt("emp.age"));
                emp.setDepartment(rs.getString("emp.department"));
                emp.setName(rs.getString("emp.name"));
                emp.setPosition(rs.getString("emp.title"));
                emp.setNumberOfPayPeriods(EmployeeDataAccessObject.
                GLOBAL_NUMBER_OF_PAY_PERIODS);
                 ti.setDeductions(rs.getInt("ti.deductions"));
                ti.setMaritalStatus(rs.getInt("emp.marital_status"));
                ti.setSsn(rs.getString("emp.ssn"));
                emp.setSalary(new Double(rs.getDouble("ti.salary")));
                ti.setTaxRate(rs.getDouble("ti.tax_rate"));
                emp.setTaxInformation(ti);
            }else{
                throw new RuntimeException("The employee with the id '" +
eid + "' could not be found");
            }
```

Listing 14.5 EmployeeDataAccessObject class. (continues)

```
                    if(rs.next()){
                        throw new RuntimeException("Too many records were found
    for the employee with the id '" + eid + "'.");
                    }
                    return emp;
            }finally{
                conn.close();
            }
        } // end getEmployee


        public int persistEmployee(SalariedEmployee emp) throws
    SQLException{

            String sqlEmp = "INSERT INTO
    employee(address_1,address_2,age,department,name,title,marital_status,ss
    n) VALUES(?,?,?,?,?,?,?)";
            String sqlTi = "INSERT INTO tax_info(emp_id,deductions,tax_rate,
    salary) VALUES(?,?,?,?)";
            try{
                getConnection();
                conn.setTransactionIsolation(1);
                PreparedStatement psEmp = conn.prepareStatement(sqlEmp);
                PreparedStatement psTi = conn.prepareStatement(sqlTi);
                psEmp.setString(1,emp.getAddress1());
                psEmp.setString(2,emp.getAddress2());
                psEmp.setInt(3,emp.getAge());
                psEmp.setString(4,emp.getDepartment());
                psEmp.setString(5,emp.getName());
                psEmp.setString(6,emp.getPosition());
                psEmp.setInt(7,emp.getTaxInformation().getMaritalStatus());
                psEmp.setString(8,emp.getTaxInformation().getSsn());
                psEmp.execute();
                ResultSet rsId = conn.prepareStatement("SELECT max(id) FROM
    EMPLOYEE").executeQuery();
                if(rsId.next()){
                    psTi.setInt(1,rsId.getInt(1));
                }else{
                    throw new RuntimeException("Exception occurren inserting
    employee");
                }
                psTi.setInt(2,emp.getTaxInformation().getDeductions());
                psTi.setDouble(3,emp.getTaxInformation().getTaxRate());
                psTi.setDouble(4,emp.getSalary().doubleValue());
                psTi.execute();
                conn.commit();
            }finally{
                conn.close();
            }
```

Listing 14.5 EmployeeDataAccessObject class. (continues)

```
            return emp.getId();
        }

        public PayrollSchedule getPayrollSchedule() throws SQLException{
            PayrollSchedule sched = new PayrollSchedule();
            sched.setPayDate(new java.util.Date());
            sched.setEmployees(getEmployees());
            return sched;
        }

    }
```

Listing 14.5 EmployeeDataAccessObject class. (continued)

```
    import java.sql.*;

    public abstract class DataAccessObject {

        private Connection conn;
        public DataAccessObjectFactory dataAccessObjectFactory;
        public abstract void getConnection() ;

    }
```

Listing 14.6 DataAccessObject class.

```
    public class DataAccessObjectFactory {
        public static final int EMPLOYEE_DAO = 1;
        public static DataAccessObject getDataAccessObject(int daoType) {
            switch(daoType){
            case DataAccessObjectFactory.EMPLOYEE_DAO:
                return new EmployeeDataAccessObject();
            default :
                return null;
            }
        } // end getDataAccessObject

    }
```

Listing 14.7 DataAccessObjectFactory class.

```
import java.io.File;
import java.io.FileInputStream;
import java.io.IOException;
import java.sql.Connection;
import java.sql.DriverManager;
import java.sql.SQLException;
import java.util.Properties;

public class ConnectionFactory {

    public ConnectionFactory() {
        super();
    }

    private Properties getEnvProps() throws IOException{
        Properties envProps = new Properties();
        FileInputStream in = new FileInputStream(File.separator +
"Users"

+ File.separator + "ua01422" + File.separator + "Documents" + File.
separator + "Book" + File.separator + "chapter14" + File.separator +
"data" + File.separator + "DBEnvironment.properties");
        envProps.load(in);
        in.close();
        return envProps;
    }


    public Connection getConnection(){
        String serverName = null;
        Connection con = null;
        try{
            Properties  dbEnv = getEnvProps();
            serverName = dbEnv.getProperty("DBAvailable").equals
IgnoreCase("true")?"10.0.1.3":"127.0.0.1";
            return getConnection(serverName);
        }catch(IOException ioe){
            ioe.printStackTrace();
            throw new RuntimeException("Could not read in the database
properties");
        }catch(SQLException sqle){
            sqle.printStackTrace();
            throw new RuntimeException("Could not connect to the
database on " + serverName);
        }
    }
```

Listing 14.8 ConnectionFactory class. (continues)

```
            private Connection getConnection(String serverName) throws
        SQLException{
            Connection con = null;
            try{
                Class.forName( "org.gjt.mm.mysql.Driver" ) ;
                String dbName = "SamplePayroll";
                String userName = "jdbc";
                String password = "jdbc";
                String url = "jdbc:mysql://" + serverName + "/" + dbName;
                con = DriverManager.getConnection( url,userName,password) ;
            }catch(ClassNotFoundException cnfe){
                cnfe.printStackTrace();
                throw new RuntimeException("Error while attempting to access
                the database at " + serverName);
            }
            return con;
        }
    }
```

Listing 14.8 ConnectionFactory class. (continued)

```
        import java.sql.SQLException;
        import java.util.ListIterator;

        import junit.framework.TestCase;

        public class AddEmployeeUseCaseTest extends TestCase{

            private EmployeeDataAccessObject dao;
            private SalariedEmployee employee;
            private PayrollSchedule sched;
            private SalariedEmployee salariedEmployee;
            private EmployeeTaxInformation ti;
            private EmployeeDataAccessObject employeeDataAccessObject;
            private String employeeName;

            public void setUp(){
                dao = (EmployeeDataAccessObject)DataAccessObjectFactory.
        getDataAccessObject(DataAccessObjectFactory.EMPLOYEE_DAO);
                employeeName = "President George W Bush";
            }


            public void tearDown(){
                dao = null;
            }
```

Listing 14.9 AddEmployeeUseCaseTest class. (continues)

```
public void testUseCase() {
    //create new employee
    employee = new SalariedEmployee();
    ti = new EmployeeTaxInformation();
    employee.setAddress1("1700 Pennsylvania Ave");
    employee.setAddress2("Washington, DC 00001");
    employee.setAge(50);
    employee.setName(employeeName);
    employee.setDepartment("Executive Branch");
    employee.setPosition("POTUS");
    employee.setSalary(new Double(150000.00));

    ti.setDeductions(2);
    ti.setMaritalStatus(2);
    ti.setSsn("111111111");
    ti.setTaxRate(0.40);
    //persist new employee
    employee.setTaxInformation(ti);
    try{
        try{
            employee.setId(dao.persistEmployee(employee));
        }catch(SQLException e){
            employee.setId(1);
        }
        //getPayrollSchedule
        try{
            sched = dao.getPayrollSchedule();
        }catch(SQLException e){
            sched = new PayrollSchedule();
            sched.add(employee);
        }
        //verify employee is getting paid
        ListIterator it = sched.getEmployees().listIterator();
        boolean newEmployeeWasSuccessfullyInserted = false;
        while(it.hasNext()){
            SalariedEmployee testEmp = (SalariedEmployee)it.next();
            if(employeeName.equals(testEmp.getName())){
                newEmployeeWasSuccessfullyInserted = true;
                break;
            }
        }
        assertTrue("The new employee did not make it to the payroll
        schedule.",newEmployeeWasSuccessfullyInserted);
    }catch(Exception e){
        e.printStackTrace();
        fail(e.getMessage());
    }
} // end testUseCase

}
```

Listing 14.9 AddEmployeeUseCaseTest class. (continued)

12. Known Uses

None

13. Known Abuses

None

14. Related Patterns

None

CHAPTER 15

ObjectMother Pattern

All I am, I owe to my mother.

—*George Washington*

1. Name

ObjectMother—Originally proposed by Peter Schuh and Stephanie Punke, ThoughtWorks Inc.

2. Intent

The ObjectMother pattern provides a basic framework for object creation and modification during the testing process. It allows the tester to maintain a clean separation between the jobs of creating testable structures and the testing of those structures. ObjectMother provides a one-stop shop for testing objects, making tests more maintainable, promoting reuse, and letting the tester focus on the work of the tests and not the intricacies of setup and teardown.

The ObjectMother pattern enables us to do the following:

- Create a utility class or classes that will do all the creation and building up of business objects.
- Construct public static createXXX() methods that return valid business objects.
- Devise public static attachXXXToYYY() methods to couple business objects.
- Refactor common business object construction sequences into specialized create methods.

3. Also Known As

- Test Object Factory

4. Motivation

The motivation for this pattern is to test tests—a simple principle, but one that often becomes lost in developing software tests. All too often, the object-oriented paradigms that we have fought to maintain throughout the code base disappear when we begin to write tests. Our test cases become complex scripts that build elaborate constructs, populate them with data, and perform tests. Our objects lose their focus on testing and become do-it-all monstrosities that are difficult to understand and next to impossible to change. One change to our objects under test and we have to weed through countless lines of test code to determine if the failures (or successes) of tests are the results of the change or due to errors in the test setup. Under the extreme programming methodology this problem is amplified because the tests and objects are written at the same time, resulting in a double cost for changes to objects since the resultant tests need to be debugged and tested.

ObjectMother provides a way out of this mess. Through a separation of test building and test execution, ObjectMother allows us to:

- Create fully testable business objects, helping to reduce the errors due to incorrect setup/use of the testable objects.

- Maintain creation code in a single utility (or group of modules), reducing maintenance costs and the level of frustration when things go wrong.

- Build a repository of test cases that can take us through the testing cycle.

5. Applicability

ObjectMother, at the heart, is a Factory-like pattern that creates objects under test in various states. (The most interesting and most common ones are valid and invalid.) This allows us to maintain the principles of information hiding and encapsulation within our testing structures by abstracting the details of testable object setup and maintaining that separation between tests and test object construction.

6. Structure

The structure of the ObjectMother pattern can vary depending greatly on the size and complexity of your objects under test (see Figure 15.1). The basic concepts, however, remain the same.

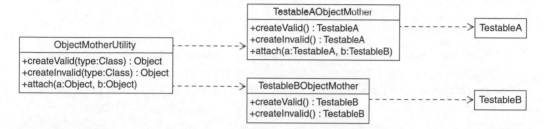

Figure 15.1 A complex ObjectMother structure.

7. Participants

1. Simple ObjectMother Structure

- **ObjectMother:** A simple utility class that creates testable business objects.

- **TestableA:** A business object under test that is a collection of TestableB objects.

- **TestableB:** A simple business object under test.

2. Complex ObjectMother Structure

- **BaseObjectMother:** The common utility for ObjectMother. It will simply invoke methods from the specialized ObjectMother utilities based on the type of class under test.

- **TestableAObjectMother:** A specialized ObjectMother for creating or modifying TestableA business objects.

- **TestableBObjectMother:** A specialized ObjectMother for creating or modifying TestableB business objects.

- **TestableA:** A business object under test that is a collection of TestableB objects.

- **TestableB:** A simple business object under test.

8. Collaborations

1. Simple ObjectMother Structure

As part of the simple ObjectMother structure we look at three testing sequences.

Test TestableA

With this sequence we are attempting to test a valid TestableA object. By default, our ObjectMother implementation will attach a TestableB object to the TestableA object (see Figure 15.2).

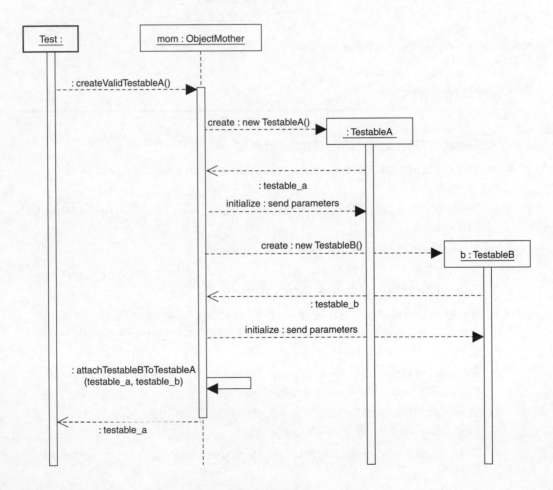

Figure 15.2 Testing a TestableA (Simple ObjectMother).

- During the test, an object of type TestableA is required.

- The ObjectMother utility is used to create a TestableA object in the desired state:

```
createValidTestableA() for a valid state
createInvalidTestableB() for an invalid state
```

- The ObjectMother creates subordinate objects for TestableA using the attach() and createTestableB() methods to build a TestableA with an attached TestableB.

Test TestableB

With this sequence we are trying to test an invalid TestableB object (Figure 15.3).

- During the test, an object of type TestableB is required.

- The ObjectMother utility is used to create a TestableB object in the desired state.

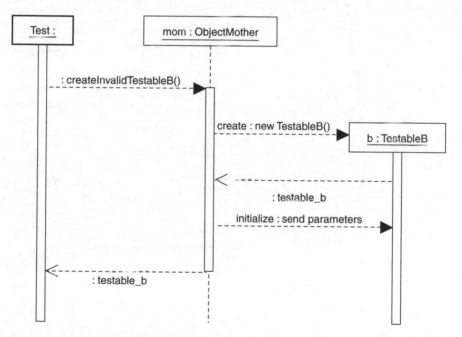

Figure 15.3 Test a TestableB (Simple ObjectMother).

Test TestableA (Attaching Additional TestableB)

With this sequence we are attempting to test a valid TestableA object. By default, our ObjectMother implementation will attach a TestableB object to the TestableA object, but we also want to test with an additional invalid TestableB object added to the collection (see Figure 15.4).

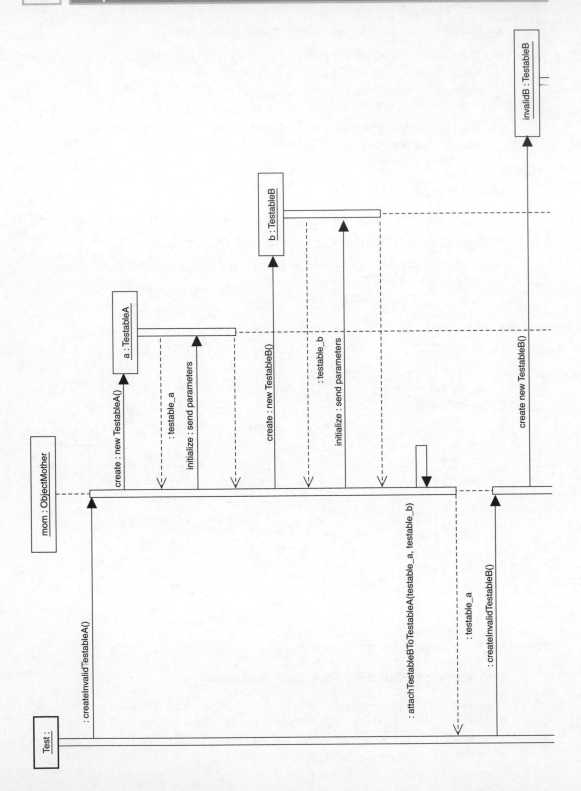

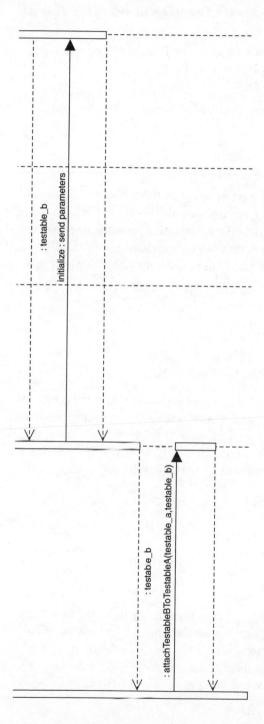

Figure 15.4 Testing a TestableA with an additional TestableB (Simple ObjectMother).

- During the test, an object of type TestableA is required.
- The ObjectMother utility is used to create a TestableA object in the desired state.
- The ObjectMother creates subordinate objects for TestableA using the attach() and createTestableB() methods to build a TestableA with an attached TestableB.
- Within the test, a new TestableB is created and attached to the TestableA.

9. Consequences

Not everything in the world breaks down so easily into valid and invalid states. You may find that additional states could and should be tested within your framework. ObjectMother should always be thought of as a work in progress. As more and more tests are written and new test cases are discovered, these object constructors should be added to the ObjectMother utility. For example, to test a String function you may create the following:

- createNullString() //returns a 'null'
- createEmptyString() //returns String.length = 0
- createBigString() //returns 'a lot' of characters
- createUnicodeString() //returns all Unicode characters

In fact, if during the test case development process you find yourself using certain attach methods over and over, you may want to consider refactoring them in a create method. For example, in the sequences we just described, the test of TestableA with two TestableB objects could be easily factored into a single createTestableAWithTwoTestableB(), or even a createTestableAWithTestableB(countOfB : int).

10. Implementation

Simple ObjectMother Structure

We implement the Simple ObjectMother by creating a utility class that contains the appropriate create and attach methods for all the objects under test. Where possible, always use ObjectMother methods to do the work, since this will result in the cleanest and most easily maintainable code. For example, the createValidTestableA() method makes use of the createValidTestableB() and attachTestableBToTestableA() methods:

```
public class ObjectMother {
    public static TestableA createValidTestableA(){
        TestableA testable_a = new TestableA();
        // set necessary fields in TestableA
        ...
        TestableB testable_b = createValidTestableB();
        attachTestableBToTestableA( testable_a, testable_b );
        return testable_a;
    }

    public static TestableB createValidTestableB(){
        TestableB testable_b = new TestableB();
        // set necessary fields in TestableB
        ...
        return testable_b;
    }

    public static void attachTestableBToTestableA( TestableA a, Testable
b ){
        // would do what is required to put b into a's collection
        ...
    }
}
```

Complex ObjectMother Structure

There are a number of ways you might choose to implement a more complex form of ObjectMother. As shown in the structures and sequences we've described, this implementation uses reflection on the class name of the object under test to determine which specialized ObjectMother to call; otherwise, the specialized ObjectMother implementations are similar to the simple structure. It would be just as easy to substitute any type of Factory/Builder pattern here to accomplish the desired effect, but the overall functionality remains the same—create methods are used to build business objects and additional associated objects are put in place using attach methods:

```
import java.lang.reflect.*;

public class ObjectMother {
    public static Object createValid( Class type ) throws Instantiation
Exception{
        try {
            Method createMethod = type.getMethod( "createValid" +
type.getName(), null );
            Object validObject = createMethod.invoke( null, null );
            return validObject;
        } catch (Exception e) {
          throw new InstantiationException();
```

```
        }
    }

    public static void attach( Object a, Object b ) throws NoSuchMethod
Exception{
        try{
            Method attachMethod = a.getClass().getMethod( "attach" +
a.getClass().getName() +

"To" + b.getClass().getName(), null );
            attachMethod.invoke( null, new Object[]{ a, b } );
        }
        catch( Exception e ){
            throw new NoSuchMethodException();
        }
    }
}
```

11. Sample Code

We'll take our example from the medical world. Let's assume that we are build-ing an application for a client to process patient referrals and determine if the referral is valid; if it not valid, then the application needs to identify the required additional information. Our object under test (let's call it ReferralAdministra-tor) will operate on the business object structure depicted in Figure 15.5.

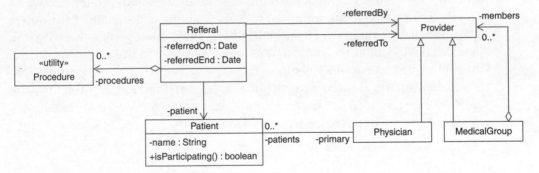

Figure 15.5 Referral business objects.

Assume, for now, that we have the following business rules to test early on in the development of our ReferralAdministrator:

■ A referral is only valid if the patient is participating.

■ A referral cannot be to the same provider.

For this example, we'll focus solely on the ParticipatingPatient business rule.

Since the administrator requires a Referral object to work on, we begin by constructing a basic ObjectMother, as shown in Listing 15.1.

```
import com.health.Patient;
import com.health.Referral;
import com.health.Provider;
import com.health.prov.Physician;

public class ObjectMother{

        public static Referral createValidReferral(){
            Referral referral = new Referral(); // create a referral
            referral.setReferredOn( new Date() ); // starting today
            referral.setReferralEnd( null ); // with no end date
            return referral;
        }


        public static Patient createParticipatingPatient(){
            // since patient would require a DB call to determine
            // participation, we'll create a specialied patient here
            return new Patient(){
                public boolean isParticipating(){
                    return true;
                }
            };
        }

        public static void attachPatientToReferral( Referral referral,
Patient patient ){
            // simply set the patient for the referral
            referral.setPatient( patient );
        }

        public static void createValidProvider(){
            // create any provider - could easily be a MedicalGroup
            return new Physician();
        }

        public static void attachReferringProviderToReferral( Referral
referral, Provider provider ){
            // attach the object
            referral.setReferredBy( provider );
        }
```

Listing 15.1 ObjectMother. (continues)

```
        public static void attachReferredProviderToReferral(Referral
referral, Provider provider) {
            // attach the object
            referral.setReferredTo(provider);
        }


}
```

Listing 15.1 ObjectMother. (continued)

We can now start to construct the test cases that we'll need using the Object-Mother utility:

```
public class ReferralAdministratorTest extends TestCase{

    public void testPatientParticipation(){
        Referral referral = ObjectMother.createValidReferral();
        Patient parPatient = ObjectMother.createParticipatingPatient();
        ObjectMother.attachPatientToReferral( referral, parPatient );

        assertTrue( ReferralAdministrator.isValid( referral ) );
    }


}
```

We soon realize that we need to test more than just success; we also need to make sure the system fails when it should. So we begin to refactor the createParticipatingPatient method to accept a Boolean flag to indicate participation. And while we're at it, we also assume that we'll need a Referral object with a Patient object for other tests, so we refactor createValidReferral(), resulting in the code shown in Listing 15.2.

```
public class ObjectMother{

    public static Referral createValidReferral(){
        Referral referral = new Referral(); // create a referral
        referral.setReferredOn( new Date() ); // starting today
        referral.setReferralEnd( null ); // with no end date


        Patient patient = ObjectMother.createParticipatingPatient(
true );
        ObjectMother.attachPatientToReferral( referral, patient );
        return referral;
    }
```

Listing 15.2 ObjectMother test case. (continues)

```
        public static Patient createParticipatingPatient( final boolean
participating ){
            // since patient would require a DB call to determine
            // participation, we'll create a specialied patient here
            return new Patient(){
                public boolean isParticipating(){
                    return participating;
                }
            };
        }

        public static void attachPatientToReferral( Referral referral,
Patient patient ){
            // simply set the patient for the referral
            referral.setPatient( patient );
        }

        public static void createValidProvider(){
            // create any provider - could easily be a MedicalGroup
            return new Physician();
        }

        public static void attachReferringProviderToReferral( Referral
referral, Provider provider ){
            // attach the object
            referral.setReferredBy( provider );
        }

        public static void attachReferredProviderToReferral(Referral
referral, Provider provider) {
            // attach the object
            referral.setReferredTo(provider);
        }

}
```

Listing 15.2 ObjectMother test case. (continued)

But why go through all of this? Wouldn't it be easier just to write a test like the following?

```
public class ReferralAdministratorTest extends TestCase{

    public void testPatientParticipation(){
        Referral referral = new Referral();
        Patient parPatient = new Patient();
        referral.setPatient( parPatient );

        assertTrue( ReferralAdministrator.isValid( referral ) );
    }
}
```

The answer is yes, for now. But what happens when you get further into the application and realize that a Patient must have a primary care provider (PCP) and that the PCP must be the referring Provider, and that the PCP might be participating or nonparticipating over time, and…well, you can see that it's not that difficult for business logic to get very complex very fast. By using the Object-Mother pattern, you provide a common, single-source location to build valid business objects. Keeping all your changes to a single method rather than hunting through a series of test cases (we're assuming that Patient, Physician, and Referral are used by other classes and therefore would be used in other test cases).

12. Known Uses

As you can see, ObjectMother is very useful in maintaining a break between setup and actual test code. While primarily a unit-test construct, ObjectMother provides a framework to build on for further levels of testing. As in the previous example, Referral, Patient, and Physician objects will be required throughout other unit tests, into integration testing, and on to regression and system testing. If constructed properly and maintained with due diligence, ObjectMother can provide a repository that will grow with your application.

13. Known Abuses

As with anything that is flexible, there is also a large potential for misuse. Since ObjectMother tends toward this "looseness," it's easy to abuse the flexibility and create even more of a mess than the one that ObjectMother is intended to save you from. Some of those abuses are as follows.

"Swiss Army" ObjectMother

From the previous example you can see how swiftly ObjectMother can grow. Create after create, attach after attach, the simple ObjectMother pattern can grow to an unwieldy beast. Care must be taken to stick strictly to the create/attach pattern and to not build in too many specialized creates. Generally, unless the business construct is going to be used in multiple cases, it's just as easy to call the create and attach methods from the test case rather than refactor them into a onetime create method. Remember, Mom can't do everything for you.

Untestable ObjectMother

Another common mistake with ObjectMother is to use it as a Factory/Builder pattern, forgetting the goal of creating valid business objects. As in the chapter example, if a valid Patient required a PCP, the ObjectMother should create and attach the PCP. ObjectMother should generate objects in their real-world use scenarios. While the PCP may not be required for the current test, the Object-Mother should (as nearly as possible) simulate the business objects that will be encountered in the working system.

14. Related Patterns

- Mock Object (Chapter 7) is similar to the ObjectMother pattern. In fact, as long as the objects being created are valid business objects, there is no reason that the "children" of the ObjectMother can't be mock objects.

- The Factory method (GoF) is really the heart of ObjectMother. A more rigorous use of this pattern could alleviate the problems of creating a "Swiss Army" ObjectMother.

CHAPTER 16

Quasi-Modal Testing Pattern

*They say that time changes things, but you
actually have to change them yourself.*

—Andy Warhol

1. Name

Quasi-Modal Testing pattern—originally proposed by Robert Binder (author of *Testing Object-Oriented Systems: Models, Patterns, and Tools*, Addison-Wesley, 2000).

2. Intent

The Quasi-Modal Testing pattern provides a mechanism for testing objects that behave differently depending on their state. Unlike traditionally modal objects, which have a clear or implied path in method firing (think of turns in a board game), quasi-modal classes have no defined pattern. How they react depends greatly on the current state, which is based on the methods and the order in which they were previously fired. (Think of a stack or a queue—what you add and remove affects what you can remove next.) The Quasi-Modal Testing pattern provides a way for you to manage the testing of these various states in a clean way, without having to bog down your code with complex if-then-else or case logic.

With the Quasi-Modal Testing pattern, you can accomplish the following:

- Analyze the states of the class under test.

- Construct an abstract class that summarizes all the states.

- Develop concrete classes that encapsulate the tests for each state.
- Call tests from a main test class, setting the state as desired.

3. Also Known As

- State Tester

4. Motivation

One of the great things about computers (from my perspective) is that they are consistent in operation. We know that, given a set of inputs, we can produce a known set of outputs. It gives us a sense of control; we can script out actions (a program) and produce the desired output. Nothing is unknown. But when we start to model more complex operations, we find that this scripted paradigm is not always useful in describing real-world operations. Sure, with small systems, we can describe them in a linear time fashion, but the more we examine complex systems, the more we see that there isn't any script. Components might be predictable and scripted, yet when we put them together into systems they become adaptive subsystems, reacting to the stimuli that they experience.

Think of your car's antilock braking system (ABS). In individual pieces, the components are scripted (i.e., given an electrical signal, calipers contract and release; sensors record speed and "control"). When we integrate all these components into a system and introduce feedback and control loops, we then have an adaptive system. How the system as a whole reacts will greatly depend on things like:

- The current situation (our speed, how much control we have, if the pavement is dry, whether the brakes are worn).
- Past performance (have we reduced speed? what action did we last perform?).
- Operator performance (are we slamming on the brakes? pumping the brakes? accelerating?).

Software is much the same. Although we can conduct scripted tests to show that individual pieces are performing according to the specified behaviors, when we start to combine units into components and systems, we create a more complex scenario that we might not be able to easily script. This is not to say that we don't know what the outcome should be—it's just that our output depends on the current and past states of the system.

Quasi-Modal Testing provides a way for us to manage these complex scenarios and generate logical testing frameworks. By building on the unit patterns that you've constructed and used thus far, you can group tests around specific scenarios and control state transitions to build confidence in your systems regardless of the ordering of operations.

5. Applicability

Pattern fans will see that, at its heart, the Quasi-Modal Testing pattern is nothing more than the State pattern. (See *Design Patterns: Elements of Reusable Object-Oriented Software*, by Erich Gamma, Richard Helm, Ralph Johnson, and John Vlissides [GoF], Addison-Wesley, 1994.) Where Quasi-Modal Testing departs from the traditional State pattern is that while State manages the states and state effects for a single class, Quasi-Modal Testing manages the states and state effects of use cases and test scenarios.

6. Structure

The structure of the Quasi-Modal Testing pattern is similar to that of the unit-based version of the State pattern, as shown in Figure 16.1.

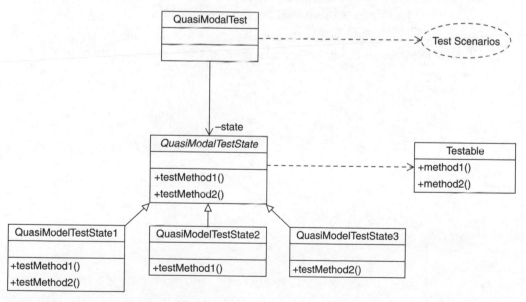

Figure 16.1 The Quasi-Modal Testing pattern.

7. Participants

- **Test Scenarios:** The collection of test scenarios you want to demonstrate.

- **QuasiModalTest:** A class for containing the tests.

- **QuasiModalTestState:** An abstract class for containing the test methods.

- **QuasiModalTestState(n):** Concrete implementations of the tests for each proposed state (for example, QuasiModalTestState1, QuasiModalTest-State2, QuasiModalTestState3).

- **Testable:** The class/interface/component under test.

8. Collaborations

With a set of test scenarios (typically based on system use cases), the outcomes of your test will vary depending on the events that have occurred (see Figure 16.2):

1. You arrange to intercept the events that you are concerned with.

2. When you receive an event (or a particular sequence), you set the state; you will create a specific instance of the state's handler and attach it to the state.

3. As you test (with the main testing class), you simply pass all the test method invocations on to the specific instance.

4. When a new event occurs that would cause a state transition, you create a new instance of the handler and save it as the wrapped state object.

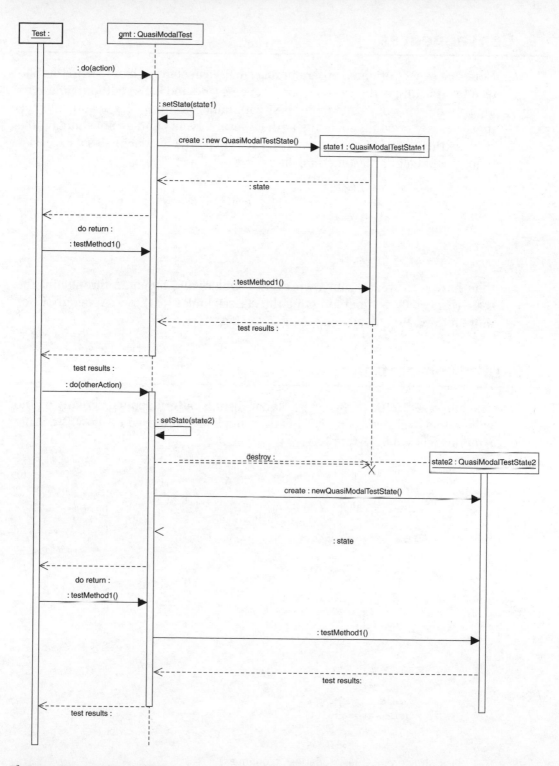

Figure 16.2 QuasiModalTest.

9. Consequences

Note that aspect-oriented programming (AOP) can come in handy with this pattern by assisting in the interception of events (method calls) without your having to muck up your code under test with unnecessary listeners and callback registries. By creating pointcuts at the relevant events and establishing up the state setting calls as advices, you can save yourself a headache. It's a lot easier to intercept calls with something like

```
public aspect QuasiModalTestApsect{
    pointcut callEvent() :  call ( public void myProject.do*(..));
        after() : callEvent(){
            QSM.setState( newState );
        }
}
```

than having to weave your own event listeners and handlers throughout the code (especially without affecting the classes under test). See Appendix E for more information about using AOP in testing.

10. Implementation

The implementation of the Quasi-Modal Testing pattern depends greatly on the events that will be driving it. However, implementation will follow the basic overview shown in Listing 16.1.

```
// Main testing class
public class QuasiModalTest {
    QuasiModalTestState state;

    // callback from performing an action
    public void doAction(){
        state = new QuasiModalTest1();
    }

    // callback from performing another action
    public void doOtherAction(){
        state = new QuasiModalTest2();
    }

    // test on method 1
    public void testMethod1(){
        state.testMethod1();
    }
```

Listing 16.1 Basic structure of QuasiModalTest. (continues)

```
                  // test on method 2
                  public void testMethod2(){
                      state.testMethod2();
                  }
              }


          // State template
          public abstract class QuasiModalTestState(){
              public abstract void testMethod1();
              public abstract void testMethod2();
          }


          // Handler for State1
          public class QuasiModalTestState1 extends QuasiModalTestState{
              public void testMethod1(){
                  // do State1 specific stuff here
              }

              public void testMethod2(){
                  // do State2 specific stuff here
              }
          }


          // Handler for State2
          public class QuasiModalTestState2  extends QuasiModalTestState{

              public void testMethod1(){
                  // do State2 specific stuff here
              }

              public void testMethod2(){
                  // do State2 specific stuff here
              }
          }
```

Listing 16.1 Basic structure of QuasiModalTest. (continued)

11. Sample Code

So your company has made the venture into Web services. Instead of writing specialized code to interface directly to your accounting system, your staff has built web service wrappers around all your legacy systems. This will leave you with more time to focus on integrating your systems because you won't be learning how the accounting, e-mail, customer relations management, (fill in your least favorite legacy system here) works. Simple, right? You just have to make a few calls to the services and pass the necessary data, and you'll get output, right? Well, it's not *that* simple. You have to create some tests and show the boss that this works. So you pull out the documentation…

WebService: UberCompanyOrderManagement

Service Methods

- **Buy(sku : String, quantity : int) : int**
  Allows the user to buy a quantity of items given a SKU; the system returns the number of items actually purchased. If a user has previously purchased or sold the item, he or she can deplete the inventory; otherwise, only one item will be shipped to the user if the amount will deplete the inventory (or 0 if there is only one item left).
- **CheckInventory(sku : String) : int**
  Checks Uber Co.'s inventory and returns the quantity of items of that SKU that a user can purchase.
- **Sell(sku : String, quantity : int) : int**
  Allows the user to sell a quantity of items of a given SKU; the system returns the number of items actually sold. If a user has previously sold the item to Uber Co., we will purchase up to either the amount of the user's immediate prior purchase or 500 units (whichever is greater). If there is no previous record of sales, Uber Co. will buy no more than 1 times its current inventory.

Simple interface, you say to yourself; integrating this will be a snap. You generate an application for a quick demonstration and fire off a memo to your management team. "Come one, come all, and see just what web services has done for the company." That afternoon, with your management team huddled around your screen you pull up your demo screen. You've coordinated with the Uber Co. team and they have set up the system with 100 units of SKU 12345 and 100 units of SKU 54321. You've got your company and Uber Co. staff as a captive audience hanging on your every keystroke.

"You test this thing?" your boss grumbles at you, just as you go to start the demonstration. Test, you think to yourself. There are only three methods here, and they aren't even yours. "Sure boss," you say, not wanting to outright lie to him, but there's no need to fill in the details either. You announce the setup and the scenario that you will run through:

Test Scenario: Buy/Sell from Uber Co. via Web Services

1. **Start with 100 units of SKU 12345 and 100 units of SKU 54321 at Uber Co.**
2. **Buy 200 units of 12345 from Uber Co. (we'll be limited to one item).**
3. **Sell 1,000 units of 12345 to Uber Co. (we'll be limited to 100).**

You launch your browser and (aside from the grumble over the colors you've chosen) everyone seems impressed that you at least have the semblance of an application in a mere three hours. You launch into the scenario (see Figure 16.3).

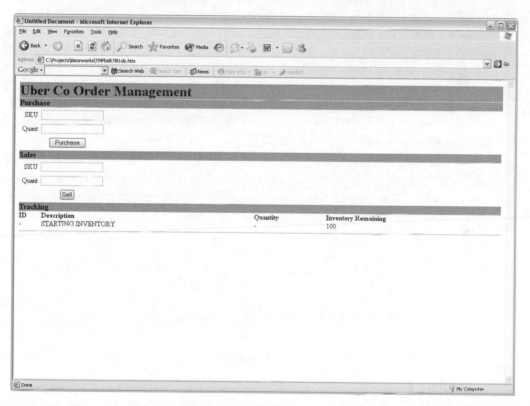

Figure 16.3 Uber Co. order management application.

"First we'll attempt to buy 200 units of SKU 12345 from Uber, even though they have only 100 units. Based on Uber Co.'s inventory and sales rules, we'll be allowed to buy only one." Just as you go to click the Purchase button, the accounts payable clerk chimes in: "My boss isn't here right now; can we skip that one?"

"Sure, not a problem," you agree. "Let's skip that one and go on to the sale. We'll sell 1,000 units to Uber, but we'll be limited to 100, their current inventory." You click the button and show that 100 units were transferred to Uber. "Okay, now getting back to the purchase…"

"Wait, Susan from marketing didn't see that," your boss says. "Let's try that again," he says as he clicks the Sell button. To everyone's amazement, including yours, the screen shows that 500 units were sold to Uber. Your boss shoots you a look that could melt steel. What is going on here?

Trying to save the show, you jump back to the Purchase transaction. "Ah, let's see the purchase," you say. "I think that might just be a glitch from clicking the button too many times." "Ah," people murmur. They've all been there—"fat-fingering" a button is a common mistake. You enter in the 200 units for purchase, telling the onlookers that with the rules, we'll be limited to buying only one. You click the button and to your horror, the screen shows that 200 units were purchased. Demo over. Your boss quickly escorts the team from the room, apologizing for the mistake. He come back to inform you that he'd like to see that test code later on today. You return to your office next to the office supply cabinet and the noisy water cooler, resigned to the fact that due to that debacle, you'll never get that window office.

So what went wrong? you muse. Must be Uber Co.'s Web services interface—after all, what did you have to do with this? You try to understand the business rules behind the scenario and sketch out the following rules for the Uber Co. interface:

```
purchase       = 0
previous_buy       = false
previous_sell      = false


BUY( x ) : purchase
     IF( previous_buy )
          purchase = x
     ELSE
          purchase = ( IF inventory_level = 1 THEN 0 ELSE 1 )

     previous_buy = true

SELL( x ) : sold
     IF (previous_sell)
          sold = MIN( MAX( 500, purchase ), x )
     ELSE
          sold = MIN( x, inventory )

     previous_sell = true

CHECK : items
     items = ( IF previous_buy THEN inventory_level
               ELSE IF inventory_level = 1 THEN 0 ELSE 1 )
```

Now you're getting somewhere. Based on what you've come up with, you can see that there are three state events you should be concerned with:

- **previous_buy state:** Have you previously bought items from Uber Co.?

- **previous_sell state:** Have you previously sold items to Uber Co.?

- **inventory_level:** Does Uber Co. have only one such item left?

This is based on examining all the decision points in the pseudo-code and finding the common expressions at those points.

Because you happen to have a copy of *Java Testing Patterns* handy, you review this chapter, quickly code the state transitions, and using AOP, intercept and maintain the state. Now with an organized test approach and a managed state pattern, you press on for that corner office.

12. Known Uses

The Quasi-Modal Testing pattern is ideal for testing event-driven systems such as graphical user interfaces and Web services. In fact, when coupled with unit-level patterns such as Object Mother and Self-Shunt, it can be an effective tool for tracking down those elusive bugs in distributed systems.

13. Known Abuses

In looking at the state transitions, people have a tendency to want to reuse what is there. After all, the developer has already coded a state engine for managing the state transitions of the class (or classes) under test—why not just piggyback on that work? Coding is all about reuse and components, right? It is tempting to think so, but keep in mind just what it is you are evaluating—you are testing the state transitions to make sure they are processing correctly. By maintaining a separate state engine, you can provide a double-check on the logic used to produce the original—and after all, that is the entire point of testing.

14. Related Patterns

- Object Mother can be a useful tool for creating the "state instances" so that you can have a consistent and working framework.

- State (GoF) is really the heart of the Quasi-Modal Testing pattern.

CHAPTER 17

Sample Application Description

Example is the school of mankind, and they will learn at no other.

—Edmund Burke

Building a TestSuite for an application is a process. By identifying the stages, we can lay out a template for designing TestSuites for almost any client/server or multitiered application. In this chapter, we will do just that by using Sun's J2EE sample application, the Java Petstore (http://java.sun.com/developer/releases/petstore/petstore1_1_2.html). First, in order to accomplish this, let's identify and discuss the steps required to create a testsuite for an entire application.

In preparation for the next few chapters we need to first outline a systematic approach to designing a TestSuite for an application. This chapter discusses those steps at a very high level.

1. Resources

This section discusses the resources we must have at hand to successfully design a TestSuite for an application.

Product Specification

The *product specification* is a document that is usually finalized prior to development of any application. It discusses the expectations of a given system in terms of the problems it is designed to solve and the approaches it (the system) will take toward solving them. The documents are usually designed in cascading levels of granularity, beginning with a high-level vision for the application and working down to implementation issues like "All of the buttons in the application need to contain our logo." The product specification is very important in building an application TestSuite because it can guide the developers toward which points in the application are most critical in the mind of the customer.

To illustrate, if the developer is looking at an application that involves a catalog-based Web site and a back-end database-driven Web site that the data administrator can use to populate the catalog, he might be tempted to build his application TestSuite to test both components with equal thoroughness. If, however, he reads in the specification that the customer really needs the catalog Web site but the back-end system is just an add-on and they have a system to populate the database already, then he is forewarned that major problems with the Web site will be considered much more critical by the customer than will problems with the back-end system.

The developer will be able to focus the majority of his effort on the catalog system so that he can ensure that it meets the customer's desires because he is able to use the product specification to determine the most critical components in the application.

UseCases

UseCases are hypothetical examples of how a system or component will likely be used. Often UseCases are included in the product specification, and they can be left up to the engineers to determine. In many cases, it can be good to have analysts and engineers come up with UseCases at different levels. (Analysts develop UseCases from the perspective of an end user and engineers develop them from the perspective of a component or application.)

For example, an analyst's UseCase for the J2EE Petstore might be as follows:

A customer using Microsoft Internet Explorer (latest) on a Macintosh 10.2.4 system enters the pet store. She searches the store for Bulldogs. *Upon finding a bulldog item, she adds it to her cart and proceeds to Checkout. She changes her mailing address to a new location and completes the sale.*

And an engineer's UseCase might be this:

A request comes into the SignOnEJB to authenticate. The requester passes a UserName of "TaylorAnn" and a password of "Coconut". The sign-on component attempts to validate this combination. Finding no match in the database it returns a "false" value to the requestor.

Both of these UseCases are invaluable when building a TestSuite for an application because they describe features of the application and how they *should* work. An integration test can be developed for each UseCase created by an analyst and the engineer's UseCases can be turned into unit tests and/or integration tests, depending on their level of granularity.

UseCases can often be strung together to create end-to-end tests as well.

The Object Model

A good object model (or a lack thereof) can make the TestSuite developer's life very easy—or very hard. Designing an application TestSuite is much like designing the application itself. The designer needs to have a high-level knowledge of each component he'll be testing and how it fits into the framework. The individual unit tests can be (and most likely will be) developed by engineers as they write the code, but the application TestSuite is a separate project with its own scope and needs to be managed as such. The only way to build integration and end-to-end tests for the application is to know how the system was architected and what components need to be tested.

If you are the owner of an application TestSuite project. you will likely need to go to different engineers who design and build the components you evaluate, but knowing the object model will help you along the way in writing the tests.

For example, if you are writing tests to evaluate the data access components for the pet store catalog, will you be looking for load methods in the business objects that manage their own JDBC connections? Or perhaps the business objects themselves are entity beans using bean-managed persistence (BMP). Again they could be stateless session beans that use the Data Access Objects (DAO) design pattern. A look at the object model will tell you which approach they use, and you will be able to plan for and design your tests accordingly.

Software Engineers

The developers writing the components will be absolutely critical in designing the TestSuite. You can infer a great deal from looking at the product specification and object model, but everything must be checked with the people who implement the solution. Code and approaches change during a development process, and a good TestSuite must be refactored along with the application it evaluates.

2. Design Steps

Given these requirements, the steps required to create the TestSuite will be as follows.

Identify Framework Components to Unit Test

Are common classes used for every database connection in the application? Do multiple components in the application use the same classes to send an e-mail? Is there a universal class in the application for data translation or String manipulation? These utility and framework classes will be used throughout the application and deserve tests of their own. The functionality of the application itself will be testable only if these components function, so these components must themselves have unit tests. If these components somehow break, there will be ripples of bad data throughout the application wherever they are depended upon.

This step is usually best done by scanning the object model for framework and utility classes and holding discussions with the engineers about which framework and utility pieces they use and for what purposes.

Identify Business Components to Unit Test

What are the widgets of this application? In a human resources application the widgets might be employees, departments, positions, and pay grades; in a pet store they might be categories, products, items, and shopping carts. Regardless, they need to be identified and their functionality must be perpetually testable. To do so, look through the product specification and the object model.

Additionally, these business classes will have dependencies that exist only to service them. In the Petstore application, an example of this is the CatalogDAO. It is a data access object that exists solely to load and persist the business objects of the catalog application. Classes like this should also be considered business objects worthy of testing at this stage.

Line up the main business components in the specification with objects in the model. Document your findings and talk to the engineers. When you are done, you will be ready to write unit tests for these components.

Identify UseCases for Integration Testing

Go through the UseCases developed by analysts as well as any walkthroughs in the product specification. Find any place that the customer or analyst may have indicated an anticipated use of the system. Next, identify which components of the application are exercised by this UseCase and whether unit tests are already available for these components. If so, then you will want to design a logical flow to these unit tests to model the UseCase. If there are no unit tests for these components, should there be? After all, the functionality being used here is identified as integral to the analysts and/or customer.

Identify Passes through the Application for End-to-End Testing

This is arguably the most difficult of the four steps outlined here (as it probably won't be defined by the specification). The goal is to identify a pass through your system (a single session of interaction with a client) that utilized all the core functionality available to that client. For example, in the J2EE Petstore application, this might include a user logging into the system, adding and removing items from her shopping cart, and finally checking out. If there various levels of authentication and consequent features are available, then one of these end-to-end tests would be desirable for each feature set.

3. Sample Overview

In the next few chapters we are going to specify an application, write a Test-Suite to cover the scope we have specified, and add that TestSuite to the automated build process for the application itself. While there is a wealth of documentation telling us that we *should* do this, there is very little that shows us *how* to actually do it. And that is why we are going to attempt to do just that, starting now:

- **Application:** The J2EE Petstore (a subset of the FrontEnd Web site)
- **Scope of testing:** Catalog browsing, some user authentication, and some shopping cart purchasing
- **Architecture:** MVC/J2EE
- **Components:** jsp/ejb/dao running in a BEA WebLogic 7.0 container connecting to PointBase RDBMS

First let's talk about the application and what we are going to try to accomplish by testing. From the Sun J2EE Blueprints book we get a description of the J2EE Petstore. The section we are testing is what the Blueprints book defines as the "front end." It is described as follows:

The Web site presents an online pet store interface to the customer. The customer shops and places orders through this interface. When a customer completes an order, the interface sends the order to the order fulfillment center. Because the Web site functional unit drives further business processing when it sends a purchase order to the fulfillment center, it can be thought of as the front end.... As discussed previously, the sample application's Web site handles customer interactions. The Web site presents the application's data—the product catalog—to the user in response to the user's requests. The Web site's primary responsibilities include handling user requests, retrieving and displaying product catalog data to a user's browser, and allowing users to select and purchase products.

In addition, the Petstore is described as follows:

The Petstore application is a typical e-commerce site. The customer selects items from a catalog, places them in a shopping cart, and, when ready, purchases the shopping cart contents. Prior to purchase, the sample application displays the order; the selected items, quantity and price for each item, and the total cost. The customer can revise or update the order. To complete the purchase the customer provides a shipping address and a credit card number.

This last paragraph describes the scope of the application we will be basing our TestSuite on. Sun describes it as the "front end" or "storefront" of the J2EE sample application. Figure 17.1 is a model of the J2EE Petstore with our portion of the application circled.

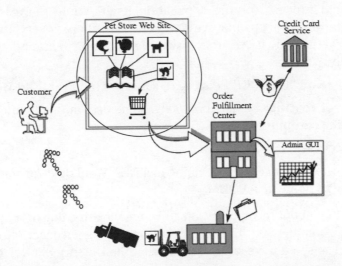

Figure 17.1 A model of the Petstore with our portion of the application circled.

The Petstore Web site will require us to validate business objects, data access components, and EJBs using asynchronous messaging. Figure 17.2 shows a UML UseCase diagram for the Petstore Web site.

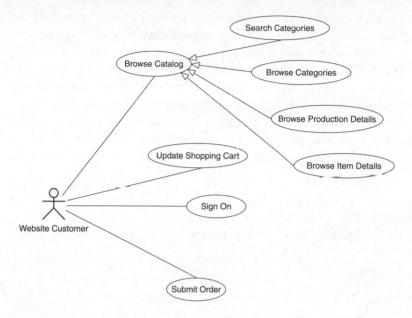

Figure 17.2 UML UseCase diagram for the Petstore Web site.

Figure 17.2 indicates that from the Web site a user should be able to do the following:

- Search the catalog
- Browse categories
- Browse product details
- Browse item details
- Update shopping cart
- Sign on
- Submit order

This list of functionality can and will be used as a baseline for our TestSuite. It is important here to emphasize that our TestSuite does not exist to test the user experience in any way. These tests are designed to evaluate the functionality of the underlying methods used to drive this functionality on the Web site. We will not be writing tests for a Web page that displays a list of categories. Instead, we will write tests that evaluate the behavior of the classes used to return a list of categories to the view layer of the application.

This approach has two key advantages to the application developer. When we integrate these tests into the build process, regression testing will become an integral and automated event. The developer will always know whether (in the current build configuration) the classes are still behaving in the intended fashion. In addition, this approach will allow the developer to decouple the behavior of these classes from the view layer of the application. If the category browsing component fails to return values in the presentation layer (JSP or servlet), by running this test the developer can verify the problem does not exist in pulling data from the database or populating the business objects. To this end we will focus on decoupling the testable processes from the presentation layer wherever possible (for example, DAOs will be decoupled from the EJB layer where they normally retrieve their database connections).

The main components of the application are catalog browsing, user authentication, and shopping cart management. Figure 17.3 displays a relationship diagram from J2EE Blueprints for these modules. These relationships will be fundamental to understanding how to construct the TestSuite for the application.

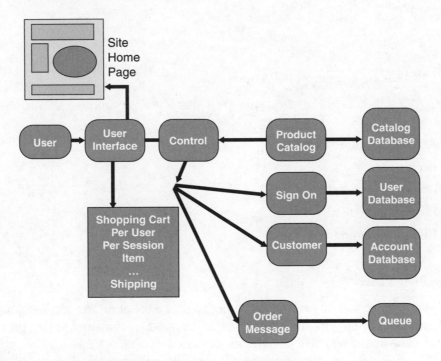

Figure 17.3 A relationship diagram from J2EE Blueprints for the modules.

CHAPTER 18

Design and Components of the Sample Application

A good scientist is a person with original ideas.
A good engineer is a person who makes a design that works
with as few original ideas as possible.

—*Freeman Dyson, physicist*

The purpose of this chapter is to identify the components that will make up our Petstore application TestSuite. In order to achieve this we will do the following:

1. Walk through the application itself.

2. Divide the application into components.

3. For each component:

   a. Identify testworthy units.

   b. Identify testworthy functions for integration testing.

   c. Plan functionality requirements for an end-to-end test.

1. Walking Through the Sample Application

In this section we examine the Petstore application's Web site to get a sense of the workflow and functions we'll need to test. We inspect the Web site one page at a time by walking through a typical user interaction. For each page we will identify the functions exposed by the functionality required by the page. However, before doing so we should define some of the domain specific terms used within the Web site.

First, the Petstore is considered to be a *catalog* Web site—it emulates a catalog in the real world by displaying information on similar products, grouped together in categories, and allows the customer an opportunity to purchase them. This is the core purpose for the Web site's existence. Some common terms used in describing the Petstore catalog Web site are the following:

- **Categories:** A grouping of related products within the Petstore catalog. For example, all canines would be in a category called dogs.

- **Products:** A type of purchasable item within a category. Within the dog category there may be a product called Saint Bernard.

- **Items:** A specific instance of a product (a purchasable item). An inventoried item such as this: Male St. Bernard Dog (1yr) : neutered.

- **Shopping Cart:** A container where a customer can aggregate items for a single purchase.

- **User:** A person viewing the Petstore Web site.

Figure 18.1 shows a page that is the output of a search for all categories from the Petstore database. Each category displayed has both a textual and graphical link to a page that will search for all products in that category, given it's ID. Additionally on this page there is an interface to search for specific items in the database (see search page below), to retrieve a shopping cart (see shopping cart page below), and to authenticate a user (see login page below).

If a user clicks on the Birds category, they will be taken to the page displayed in Figure 18.2.

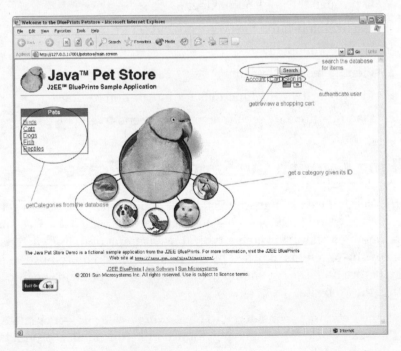

Figure 18.1 Main page of the J2EE Petstore.

Figure 18.2 Bird category page of the J2EE Petstore.

On the category page we have the output of a query to the database to get all Products for a category. In addition to the navigational elements identified in the main page, we also now have a drilldown link to view a product, given it's productId. If we click on one of these products, we are taken to the product page shown in Figure 18.3.

Figure 18.3 Product page of the J2EE Petstore.

On the product page we are shown the output of a query to show all items for a product. In addition to the navigational elements identified in the main page, we have a drilldown to view a specific item, given its id. Clicking on one of these links navigates the browser to the item page shown in Figure 18.4.

Figure 18.4 Item page of the J2EE Petstore.

On the item page is the output of the query to display details of a specific product item, given its id. In addition to the navigational elements identified on the main page, the item page includes a link to add this item to a shopping cart. By clicking on the Add to Cart link we are taken to the shopping cart page shown in Figure 18.5.

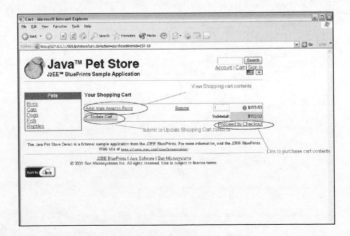

Figure 18.5 Shopping cart page of the J2EE Petstore.

The Your Shopping Cart page shows the output of a query to display the contents of a shopping cart. In addition to the navigational elements identified on the main page, this page includes a link to update the contents of the shopping cart and a link to purchase the contents of the shopping cart. Clicking on the Update Cart link will refresh this page with the updated shopping cart contents displayed; clicking on the Proceed to Checkout link to continue on and purchase the contents of the shopping cart will take the browser to the login page shown in Figure 18.6.

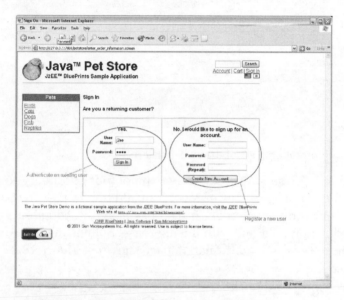

Figure 18.6 Login page of the J2EE Petstore.

In the login screen we are shown two forms: a login form for returning customers, and a login form that enables new users to create an account. The login screen is pre-populated with an anonymous user.

For the sake of simplicity (and since the system already provides for a default, anonymous user login) we are not going to test the process of creating a new user in our testsuite; instead we will focus on testing the user authentication process.

From this page the client's choices include:

- Clicking on the Sign In button with its pre-populated values

   or

- Typing a valid username/password combination into the form.

After clicking either the Sign In button or the Create New Account button, the client will be redirected to the billing information page shown in Figure 18.7.

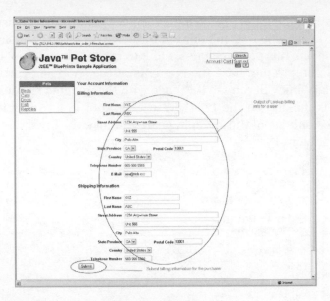

Figure 18.7 Billing information page of the J2EE Petstore.

The billing information screen shows the output of a query to look up billing information for a specific user record. In addition to the navigational elements identified in the main screen, it also has a button to submit updated billing information and continue with the purchase. Submitting this form will redirect the client to the order confirmation page shown in Figure 18.8.

Figure 18.8 Order confirmation page for the J2EE Petstore.

The order confirmation page contains the output of a query displaying an order confirmation number to the client; it also contains the navigational elements identified in the main screen.

Additionally, the item search page (Figure 18.9) will display the results of a query for items based on a search string; this page also displays the navigational elements identified in the main screen.

Figure 18.9 Item search page for the J2EE Petstore.

From the Web pages we've now identified as part of the application's frontend, we can identify several entities and methods we'll want to test. The first step in creating a testsuite is to identify each of the entities and methods we want to cover; our decisions will be based in large part on the walkthrough we just completed of the application. The units we'll be looking at are the datastructs (or javabeans) that represent the data in the database (like products and categories) and the classes that manipulate them (like DAOs and Controller EJBs).

First we will want to identify unit tests that represent the most granular elements of the underlying object model. These testcases will be useful for incremental development, repetitive build processes, and regression and integration testing. Next we will look for functions that use these objects (such as obtaining a listing of categories and then choosing one from it to inspect). Finally, we will want to develop one or more tests that will walk through all the functionality of our application by passing arguments to methods while remaining decoupled from the view layer. This will be our end-to-end test of the application.

2. Divide the Application into Components

Given our e-commerce/catalog site and a mandate to create a TestSuite, we must first identify units of testable code. Identification of these units depends upon having an object model and an understanding of the architecture.

Our application can be seen as consisting of three components:

- **Catalog Browsing:** The catalog-browsing component of the application deals with the viewing and manipulation of several business objects representing data that is stored in a relational database. The objects used in this component are Categories, Products, and Items. Additionally, this component defines a new data type called Pages. Pages hold chunks of products, categories, or items together so they can be grouped as logical pages of data in the view layer of the application. So the unit tests for this component will be based on evaluating the behavior of the catalog model and the catalog data access object (DAO).

- **User Authentication:** In the application itself this component consists of user registration and the authentication of existing users in the database—both are for the purpose of completing purchases through the PetStore Web site. For our test application, though, we will limit ourselves to testing the authentication of existing users. The rationale behind this is that the application comes configured with an anonymous user account that can be used for purchasing.

- **Shopping Cart:** The shopping cart component consists of the ability to add products to, edit products in, and remove products from a shopping cart. It also includes the ability to get an existing shopping cart for a user and complete the purchase of an order based on the contents of a shopping cart.

For Each Component

For each component of the application we must take the following steps:

- Identify Testworthy Units.
- Identify TestWorthy Functions for Integration Testing.
- Plan functionality requirements for an End-to-End Test.

Identify Testworthy Units

First we must identify units of code which require unit tests.

Catalog Component

The catalog component will be tested from two perspectives: the catalog data model (JavaBeans) and the catalog object mutators (Data Access Objects). After inspection of the Object model we were able to determine the units of code that require unit tests:

- com.sun.j2ee.blueprints.catalog.model.Category
- com.sun.j2ee.blueprints.catalog.model.Item
- com.sun.j2ee.blueprints.catalog.model.Page
- com.sun.j2ee.blueprints.catalog.model.Product
- com.sun.j2ee.blueprints.catalog.dao.CatalogPointBaseDaoImpl

User Authentication Component

For the user authentication component of the application we went back to the list of testable functions in Chapter 20 (from the J2EE Blueprints specification for the J2EE Petstore). The functionality we decided to test is user SignOn. By reviewing the object model and the architectural description in the J2EE blueprints book (our specification), the testable unit is determined to be:

- com.sun.j2ee.blueprints.signon.ejb.SignOnEJB

The testable functionality of the shopping cart will involve accessing and mutating attributes of a specific shopping cart instance, as well as completing a purchase based on the contents of the shopping cart. Based on an inspection of the object model and a review of the application description in the J2EE Blueprints book, the testable units were determined to be:

- com.sun.j2ee.blueprints.cart.model.CartItem
- com.sun.j2ee.blueprints.cart.model.ShoppingCartModel
- com.sun.j2ee.blueprints.cart.ejb.ShoppingCartLocalEJB

Identify Testworthy Functions for Integration Testing

Next we must identify testworthy functions for integration testing.

Catalog Component

The functions we will test in the catalog component are directly analogous to the functions identified for the catalog component in Chapter 20 of J2EE Blueprints. They are as follows:

- List all categories in the catalog (unit tested).
- List all products in a category (unit tested).
- List all items for a product (unit tested).

- View item details (unit tested).
- Search for an item by passing in a descriptive string of characters (unit tested).

But for a functional test we will group these together in a logical unit of work. If this were written up as a use case, it would probably look something like this:

> *A customer hits the homepage of the Web site which displays all the categories in the catalog. The customer drills down into the Dogs category and selects the Bulldog product. The customer then drills down into the Bulldog product and selects a female bulldog item. The customer then does a search on "female bulldog" from the search page so he can verify that he sees the same product from the search function.*

For the sake of identifying a functional test of the catalog component we will call this use case *granular product browsing verified against search results.*

User Authentication Component

There is one function we will test in the User Authentication component:

- Sign a user on.

Shopping Cart Component

The shopping cart component has the following testable functions:

- Get a new shopping cart and add an item.
- Add an item to an existing shopping cart.
- Remove an item from a shopping cart.
- Change the quantity of an item in a shopping cart.
- Purchase the contents of a shopping cart.

Plan Functionality Requirements for an End-to-End Test

Our end-to-end test should be an aggregation of unit tests wherever possible, but it should at a minimum include the functionality to perform the following:

- View all categories.
- Select a category to drill down to.
- Select a product from the category.
- Select an item from the product.
- Add the item to a shopping cart.
- Select a new category.

- Add an item from the products in that category to the existing cart.
- View the cart contents.
- Remove an item from the cart.
- Change the quantity for an item in the cart.
- Update account information for a user.
- Complete the purchase of the contents of the shopping cart.

The sample application's end-to-end test needs perform in such a way that it mimics, to the greatest degree possible, a customer's experience with the Petstore Web site.

Having done the initial discovery work on the application, we are now ready to move on to creating the unit tests, which is addressed in the next chapter of this book.

CHAPTER 19

Unit Tests for the Sample Application

So, naturalists observe, a flea
Has smaller fleas that on him prey;
And these have smaller still to bite 'em;
And so proceed ad infinitum.

—Jonathan Swift

Testing The Catalog Component

Testing the Catalog component of the Petstore application consists of testing both the Catalog model and the Catalog Data Access Objects.

Testing the Catalog Model

The business objects in the data model are Product, Category, Item, and Page. These objects are represented by JavaBeans in the application; consequently, their unit tests will require the testing of assessors and mutators (mutators are initialized in the constructors in this case) so that we can always ensure that if an object is initialized with a given value, it will return that value in its accessory method. These classes are grouped in the Petstore Application under the package *com.sun.j2ee.blueprints.catalog.model* (Figure 19.1).

Given this model, we will create (in our test branch) a package with the same name that will contain the following classes:

- CategoryTest.java (TestCase for Category)
- ProductTest.java (TestCase for Product)
- ItemTest.java (TestCase for Item)
- PageTest.java (TestCase for Page)
- AllTests.java (TestSuite for package)

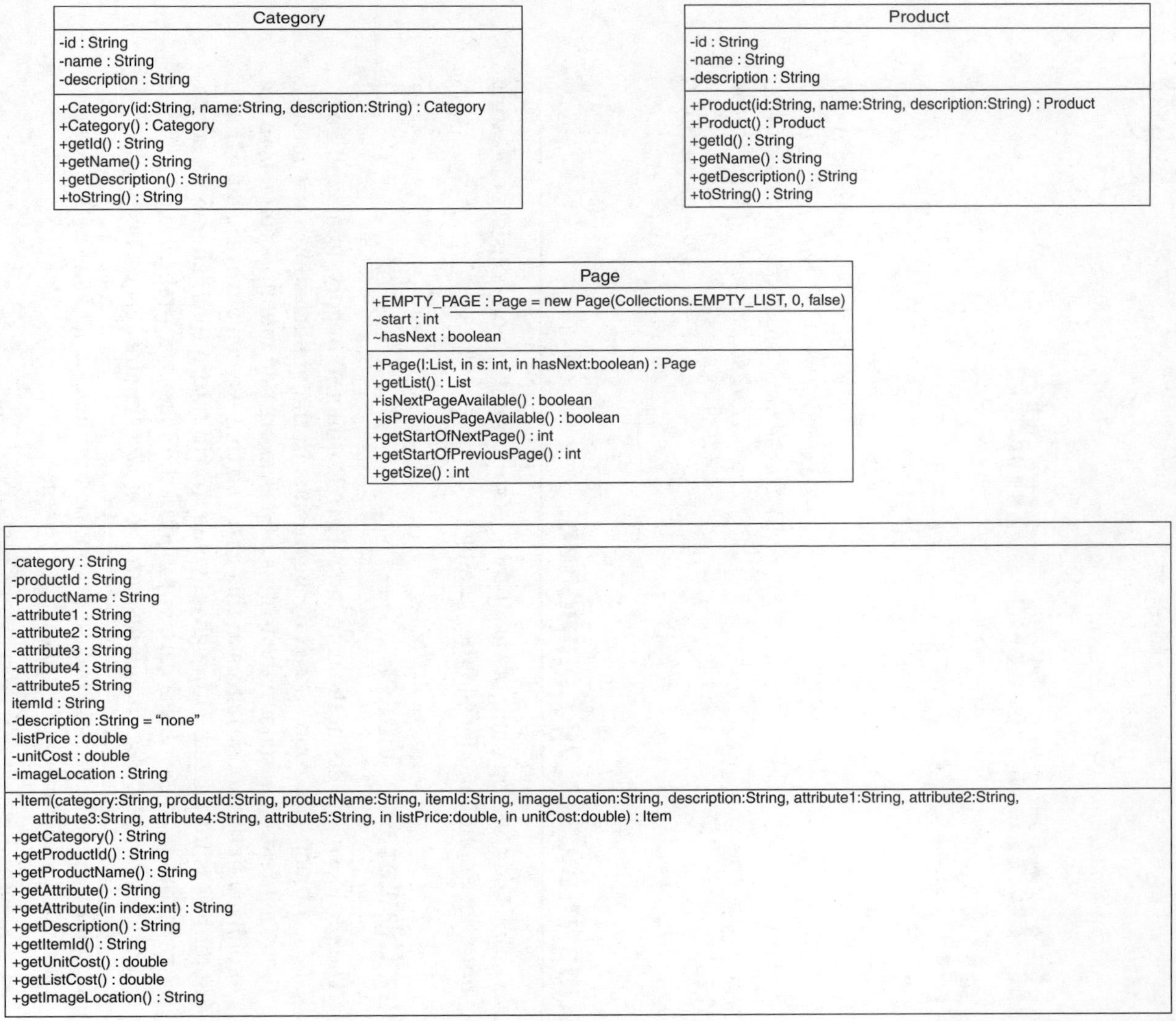

Category

-id : String
-name : String
-description : String

+Category(id:String, name:String, description:String) : Category
+Category() : Category
+getId() : String
+getName() : String
+getDescription() : String
+toString() : String

Product

-id : String
-name : String
-description : String

+Product(id:String, name:String, description:String) : Product
+Product() : Product
+getId() : String
+getName() : String
+getDescription() : String
+toString() : String

Page

+EMPTY_PAGE : Page = new Page(Collections.EMPTY_LIST, 0, false)
~start : int
-hasNext : boolean

+Page(l:List, in s: int, in hasNext:boolean) : Page
+getList() : List
+isNextPageAvailable() : boolean
+isPreviousPageAvailable() : boolean
+getStartOfNextPage() : int
+getStartOfPreviousPage() : int
+getSize() : int

-category : String
-productId : String
-productName : String
-attribute1 : String
-attribute2 : String
-attribute3 : String
-attribute4 : String
-attribute5 : String
itemId : String
-description :String = "none"
-listPrice : double
-unitCost : double
-imageLocation : String

+Item(category:String, productId:String, productName:String, itemId:String, imageLocation:String, description:String, attribute1:String, attribute2:String,
  attribute3:String, attribute4:String, attribute5:String, in listPrice:double, in unitCost:double) : Item
+getCategory() : String
+getProductId() : String
+getProductName() : String
+getAttribute() : String
+getAttribute(in index:int) : String
+getDescription() : String
+getItemId() : String
+getUnitCost() : double
+getListCost() : double
+getImageLocation() : String

Figure 19.1 The business objects in the data model.

Listing 19.1 contains the Category test CategoryTest.java, Listing 19.2 contains Product test ProductTest.java, Listing 19.3 contains the Item test ItemTest.java, Listing 19.4 contains the Page test PageTest.java, and Listing 19.5 contains the package test AllTests.java.

```java
package com.sun.j2ee.blueprints.catalog.model;

import junit.framework.TestCase;

public class CategoryTest extends TestCase {

    private Category cat;
    private String description,id,name;

    /**
     * Constructor for CategoryTest.
     * @param arg0
     */

    public CategoryTest(String arg0) {
            super(arg0);
    }


    /*
     * @see TestCase#setUp()
     */
    protected void setUp() throws Exception {
            super.setUp();
            description = "A really cool dog nobody knows about";
            name = "Leonberger";
            id = "LEON-DOG";
            cat = new Category(id,name,description);
    }


    /*
     * Test for void Category()
     */
    public void testCategory() {
    }

    public void testGetId() {
            assertEquals("The id was not the correct value in the
accessor.",cat.getId(),this.id);
    }
```

Listing 19.1 CategoryTest.java. (continues)

```
        public void testGetName() {
                assertEquals("The name was not the correct value in the
accessor.",cat.getName(),this.name);

        }

        public void testGetDescription() {
                assertEquals("The description was not the correct value in
the accessor.",cat.getDescription(),this.description);
        }


}
```

Listing 19.1 CategoryTest.java. (continued)

```
        package com.sun.j2ee.blueprints.catalog.model;

        import junit.framework.TestCase;

        public class ProductTest extends TestCase {

            private Product product;
            private String description, id, name;

            public ProductTest(String arg0) {
                    super(arg0);
            }

            protected void setUp() throws Exception {
                    super.setUp();
                    description = "A great dog nobody knows about.";
                    id = "LEON-DOG";
                    name = "Leonberger Dog";
                    product = new Product(id,name,description);
            }

            public void testGetId() {
                    assertEquals("the Product ID is not equal to the one set in
the constructor",product.getId(),this.id);
            }

            public void testGetName() {
                    assertEquals("the Product name is not equal to the one set
in the constructor",product.getName(),this.name);
            }
```

Listing 19.2 ProductTest.java. (continues)

```
        public void testGetDescription() {
                assertEquals("the Product description is not equal to the
one set in the constructor",product.getDescription(),this.description);
        }
}
```

Listing 19.2 ProductTest.java. (continued)

```
package com.sun.j2ee.blueprints.catalog.model;

import junit.framework.TestCase;

public class ItemTest extends TestCase {

    private String
attribute1,attribute2,attribute3,attribute4,attribute5,category,
description,imageLocation,itemId,productId,productName;
    private double unitCost,listPrice;
    private Item item;

    /**
     * Constructor for ItemTest.
     * @param arg0
     */
    public ItemTest(String arg0) {
            super(arg0);
    }

    /*
     * @see TestCase#setUp()
     */
    protected void setUp() throws Exception {
            super.setUp();
            attribute1="attr1";
            attribute2="attr2";
            attribute3="attr3";
            attribute4="attr4";
            attribute5="attr5";
            category="Dogs";
            description="Male Leonberger";
            imageLocation="/dev/null/leo.jpg";
            itemId="LEON-DOG-MALE";
            listPrice=1500.00;
            productId="LEON-DOG";
            productName="Leonberger";
            unitCost=300.00;
```

Listing 19.3 ItemTest.java. (continues)

```
                    item = new Item(        category,
                                                   productId,
                                                   productName,
                                                   itemId,
                                                   imageLocation,
                                                   description,
                                                   attribute1,
                                                   attribute2,
                                                   attribute3,

                                                   attribute4,
                                                   attribute5,
                                                   listPrice,
                                                   unitCost);
            }

        public void testGetCategory() {
                    assertEquals("The Category is not equal to the value set
    to in the constructor",item.getCategory(),this.category);
            }

        public void testGetProductId() {
                    assertEquals("The ProductId is not equal to the value set
    to in the constructor",item.getProductId(),this.productId);
            }

        public void testGetProductName() {
                    assertEquals("The ProductName is not equal to the value
    set to in the constructor",item.getProductName(),this.productName);
            }

        /*
         * Test for String getAttribute(int)
         */
        public void testGetAttributeint() {
                    for(int i=1;i<6;i++){
                            //TODO use reflection to figure this out
                            //assertEquals("The Attribute" + i + " is not equal
    to the value set to in the constructor",item.getAttribute(i));
                    }
            }

        public void testGetDescription() {
                    assertEquals("The Description is not equal to the value
    set to in the constructor",item.getDescription(),this.description);
            }
```

Listing 19.3 ItemTest.java. (continues)

```
    public void testGetItemId() {
            assertEquals("The Item Id is not equal to the value set to
in the constructor",item.getItemId(),this.itemId);
    }

    public void testGetUnitCost() {
            assertEquals("The Unit Cost is not equal to the value set
to in the constructor",item.getUnitCost(),this.unitCost,0.00);
    }

    public void testGetListCost() {
            assertEquals("The List Price is not equal to the value set
to in the constructor",item.getListCost(),this.listPrice,0.00);
    }

    public void testGetImageLocation() {
            assertEquals("The Image Location is not equal to the value
set to in the constructor",item.getImageLocation(),this.imageLocation);
    }

}
```

Listing 19.3 ItemTest.java. (continued)

```
package com.sun.j2ee.blueprints.catalog.model;

import java.util.ArrayList;
import java.util.List;
import junit.framework.TestCase;

public class PageTest extends TestCase {

    private Page page;
    private int start;
    private List objects;
    private boolean hasNext;

    public PageTest(String arg0) {
            super(arg0);
    }

    protected void setUp() throws Exception {
            start = 0;
            objects = new ArrayList();
            for (int i=0;i<3;i++){
```

Listing 19.4 PageTest.java. (continues)

```
        objects.add(new Page(new ArrayList(),0,i<2?true:false));
            }
            hasNext = true;
            page = new Page(objects,start,hasNext);
            super.setUp();
    }

    public void testGetList() {
            assertEquals("The List of objects is not equal to the one
set in the constructor",page.getList(),this.objects);
        }

    public void testIsNextPageAvailable() {
            assertEquals("The next page boolean is not equal to the
one set in the constructor",page.isNextPageAvailable(),this.hasNext);
        }

    public void testIsPreviousPageAvailable() {
            assertEquals("The previous page boolean is not equal to
the one set in the constructor",page.isPreviousPageAvailable(),false);
        }

    public void testGetStartOfNextPage() {
            assertEquals("The start of next page is not equal to the
one set in the constructor",page.getStartOfNextPage(),3);
        }

    public void testGetStartOfPreviousPage() {
            assertEquals("The start of previous page is not equal to
the one set in the constructor",page.getStartOfPreviousPage(),0);
        }

    public void testGetSize() {
            assertEquals("The size of the page is not equal to the one
set in the constructor",page.getSize(),this.objects.size());
        }
}
```

Listing 19.4 PageTest.java. (continued)

```
package com.sun.j2ee.blueprints.catalog.model;

import junit.framework.Test;
import junit.framework.TestSuite;

public class AllTests {

    public static Test suite() {
        TestSuite suite =
                new TestSuite("Test for com.sun.j2ee.blueprints.
                catalog.model");
        //$JUnit-BEGIN$
        suite.addTest(new TestSuite(CategoryTest.class));
        suite.addTest(new TestSuite(ItemTest.class));
        suite.addTest(new TestSuite(PageTest.class));
        suite.addTest(new TestSuite(ProductTest.class));
        //$JUnit-END$
        return suite;
    }
}
```

Listing 19.5 AllTests.java.

Testing the Catalog Data Access Objects

The model classes were essentially structs for data, but in our bottom-up testing strategy the next layer up will be the classes that actually populate these business objects. In the case of the CatalogComponent this is the Data Access Object (DAO). The BEA implementation of the TestStore comes with three different DAOs (one for each rdbms system supported by the implementation):

- The CloudScape DAO (from Sun's original reference implimentation (RI)
- The Oracle Implementation
- The PointBase implementation (we'll use this one for our unit test).

The tricky thing about the DAO layer (Model in the MVC) of the Petstore is that it is very tightly coupled to the EJB layer of the Application (Control layer in the MVC). This makes it very difficult to test the data access and bean population without going through the EJBs. To overcome this obstacle we are going to subclass the DAO and overwrite its getDataStore method to return one with a strict JDBC connection to the database (instead of a connection handled through the EJB). To accomplish this in the DAO we will use a Boolean attribute called isTestable and a factory method to decide which DataConnection to use. The Model for our test is shown in Figure 19.2.

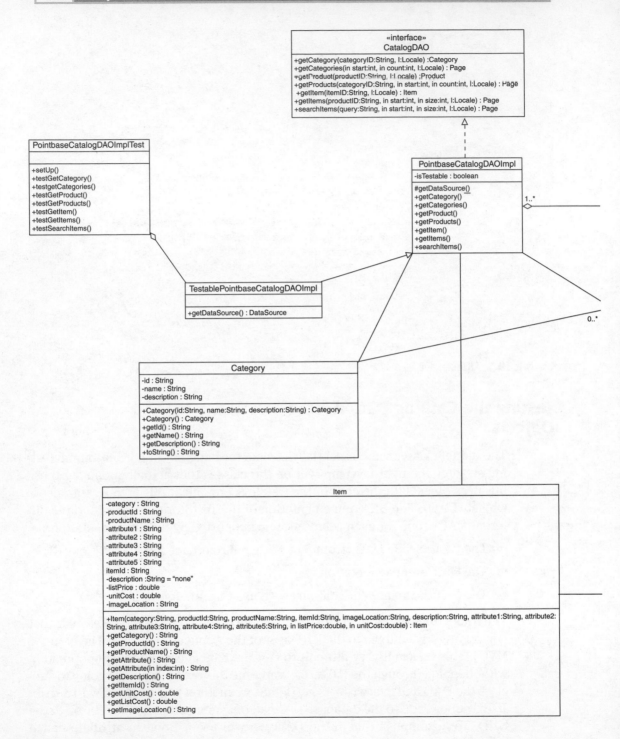

Figure 19.2 The model for our test.

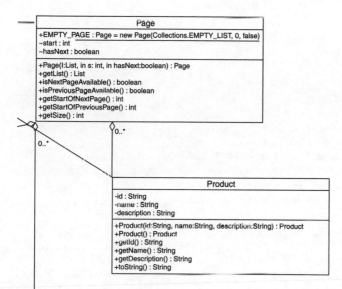

Page
+EMPTY_PAGE : Page = new Page(Collections.EMPTY_LIST, 0, false) ~start : int ~hasNext : boolean
+Page(l:List, in s: int, in hasNext:boolean) : Page +getList() : List +isNextPageAvailable() : boolean +isPreviousPageAvailable() : boolean +getStartOfNextPage() : int +getStartOfPreviousPage() : int +getSize() : int

0..*

0..*

Product
-id : String -name : String -description : String
+Product(id:String, name:String, description:String) : Product +Product() : Product +getId() : String +getName() : String +getDescription() : String +toString() : String

The classes/interfaces documented in this portion are the following:

- CatalogDao
- CatalogPointbaseDAOImpl
- TestableCatalogPointbaseDAOImpl class
- CatalogPointbaseDAOImplTest

Listing 19.6 contains CatalogDao, Listing 19.7 contains CatalogPointbaseDAO Impl, Listing 19.8 contains TestablePointbaseCatalogDAOImpl class, and Listing 19.9 contains CatalogPointbaseDAOImplTest.

```java
package com.sun.j2ee.blueprints.catalog.dao;

import java.util.Collection;
import java.util.Locale;

import com.sun.j2ee.blueprints.catalog.exceptions.CatalogDAOSysException;

import com.sun.j2ee.blueprints.catalog.model.Page;
import com.sun.j2ee.blueprints.catalog.model.Category;
import com.sun.j2ee.blueprints.catalog.model.Product;
import com.sun.j2ee.blueprints.catalog.model.Item;

public interface CatalogDAO {

    public Category getCategory(String categoryID, Locale l)
        throws CatalogDAOSysException;

    public Page getCategories(int start, int count, Locale l)
        throws CatalogDAOSysException;

    public Product getProduct(String productID, Locale l)
        throws CatalogDAOSysException;

    public Page getProducts(String categoryID, int start, int count,
Locale l)
        throws CatalogDAOSysException;

    public Item getItem(String itemID, Locale l)
        throws CatalogDAOSysException;

    public Page getItems(String productID, int start, int size, Locale
l)
        throws CatalogDAOSysException;

    public Page searchItems(String query, int start, int size, Locale l)
        throws CatalogDAOSysException;
}
```

Listing 19.6 CatalogDAO.

```
package com.sun.j2ee.blueprints.catalog.dao;

import java.sql.Connection;
import java.sql.ResultSet;
import java.sql.SQLException;
import java.sql.Statement;
import java.sql.PreparedStatement;
import java.util.*;
import javax.naming.InitialContext;
import javax.sql.DataSource;
import javax.naming.NamingException;

import com.sun.j2ee.blueprints.catalog.util.JNDINames;
import com.sun.j2ee.blueprints.catalog.model.Page;
import com.sun.j2ee.blueprints.catalog.model.Category;
import com.sun.j2ee.blueprints.catalog.model.Product;
import com.sun.j2ee.blueprints.catalog.model.Item;
import com.sun.j2ee.blueprints.catalog.util.DatabaseNames;
import com.sun.j2ee.blueprints.catalog.exceptions.CatalogDAOSysExcep-
tion;

import com.sun.j2ee.blueprints.util.tracer.Debug;

/**
 * This class implements CatalogDAO for oracle, sybase and cloudscape
DBs.
 * This class encapsulates all the SQL calls made by Catalog EJB.
 * This layer maps the relational data stored in the database to
 * the objects needed by Catalog EJB.
*/
public class CatalogPointbaseDAOImpl implements CatalogDAO {

    // Helper methods

    static boolean isTestable = true;

    protected static DataSource getDataSource()
        throws CatalogDAOSysException {
        if(isTestable == false){
                try {
                        InitialContext ic = new InitialContext();
                        return (DataSource) ic.lookup
                        (JNDINames.CATALOG_DATASOURCE);
                }
                catch (NamingException ne) {
                        throw new CatalogDAOSysException
                        ("NamingException while looking "

    + "up DB context : "
```

Listing 19.7 CatalogPointbaseDAOImpl class. (continues)

```
                + ne.getMessage());
                        }

        }else{
            return TestableCatalogPointbaseDaoImpl.getDataSource();
        }

    }
     // Business methods
            /**
             * TODO
             * subclass each method in the subclass if you have to to
get the right Datasource
             */

     public Category getCategory(String categoryID, Locale l)
         throws CatalogDAOSysException {
         Connection c = null;
         PreparedStatement ps = null;
         ResultSet rs = null;
         Category ret = null;

         try {
             System.out.println(this.getClass().getName() + ":About to
call getDataSource" );
             DataSource ds = getDataSource();
                 System.out.println(this.getClass().getName() + ":Got
DataSource it was a " + ds.getClass().getName() );
             c = ds.getConnection();

             ps = c.prepareStatement("select a.catid, name, descn "
                                 + "from category a join "
                                 + "category_details b on "
                                 + "a.catid=b.catid "
                                 + "where locale = ? "
                                 + "and a.catid = ?",
                                 ResultSet.TYPE_SCROLL_INSENSITIVE,
                                 ResultSet.CONCUR_READ_ONLY);
             ps.setString(1, l.toString());
             ps.setString(2, categoryID);
             rs = ps.executeQuery();
             if (rs.first()) {
                 ret = new Category(rs.getString(1).trim(),
                                 rs.getString(2),
                                 rs.getString(3));
             }
             rs.close();
             ps.close();
```

Listing 19.7 CatalogPointbaseDAOImpl class. (continues)

```
                    c.close();
                    return ret;
            }

        catch (SQLException se) {
            throw new CatalogDAOSysException("SQLException: "
                                        + se.getMessage());
        }
    }

    public Page getCategories(int start, int count, Locale l)
        throws CatalogDAOSysException {

        Connection c = null;
        PreparedStatement ps = null;
        ResultSet rs = null;
        Page ret = null;

        try {
            c = this.getDataSource().getConnection();

            // Count.
            ps = c.prepareStatement("select COUNT(*) "
                                    + "from category a join "
                                    + "category_details b on "
                                    + "a.catid=b.catid "
                                    + "where locale = ?",
                                    ResultSet.TYPE_SCROLL_INSENSITIVE,
                                    ResultSet.CONCUR_READ_ONLY);
            ps.setString(1, l.toString());
            rs = ps.executeQuery();
            rs.first();
            int total = rs.getInt(1);
            rs.close();
            ps.close();

            // Select.
            ps = c.prepareStatement("select a.catid, name, descn "
                                    + "from category a join "
                                    + "category_details b on "
                                    + "a.catid=b.catid "
                                    + "where locale = ? "
                                    + "order by name",
                                    ResultSet.TYPE_SCROLL_INSENSITIVE,
                                    ResultSet.CONCUR_READ_ONLY);
            ps.setString(1, l.toString());

            rs = ps.executeQuery();
            if (start >= 0 && start < total) {
```

Listing 19.7 CatalogPointbaseDAOImpl class. (continues)

```
                      List items = new ArrayList();
                      rs.absolute(start+1);
                      do {

                           items.add(new Category(rs.getString(1).trim(),
                                                   rs.getString(2),
                                                   rs.getString(3)));
                      } while (rs.next() && (--count > 0));
                      ret = new Page(items, start, total);
                  }
                  else {
                      ret = Page.EMPTY_PAGE;
                  }

                  rs.close();
                  ps.close();
                  c.close();

                  return ret;
              }
              catch (SQLException se) {
                  throw new CatalogDAOSysException("SQLException: "
                                                  + se.getMessage());

              }
         }

         public Product getProduct(String productID, Locale l)
              throws CatalogDAOSysException {

              Connection c = null;
              PreparedStatement ps = null;
              ResultSet rs = null;
              Product ret = null;

              try {
                  c = this.getDataSource().getConnection();

                  ps = c.prepareStatement("select a.productid, name, descn "
                                  + "from (product a join "
                                  + "product_details b on "
                                  + "a.productid=b.productid) "
                                  + "where locale = ? "
                                  + "and a.productid = ? ",
                                  ResultSet.TYPE_SCROLL_INSENSITIVE,
                                  ResultSet.CONCUR_READ_ONLY);
                  ps.setString(1, l.toString());
                  ps.setString(2, productID);
                  rs = ps.executeQuery();
                  if (rs.first()) {
```

Listing 19.7 CatalogPointbaseDAOImpl class. (continues)

```
                        ret = new Product(rs.getString(1).trim(),
                                           rs.getString(2),
                                           rs.getString(3));
                    }

                    rs.close();
                    ps.close();

                    c.close();
                    return ret;
                }
            catch (SQLException se) {
                throw new CatalogDAOSysException("SQLException: "
                                                 + se.getMessage());
            }
        }

        public Page getProducts(String categoryID, int start,
                                int count, Locale l)
            throws CatalogDAOSysException {

            Connection c = null;
            PreparedStatement ps = null;
            ResultSet rs = null;
            Page ret = null;

            try {
                c = this.getDataSource().getConnection();

                // Count.
                ps = c.prepareStatement("select COUNT(*) "
                                        + "from product a join "
                                        + "product_details b on "
                                        + "a.productid=b.productid "
                                        + "where locale = ? "
                                        + "and a.catid = ? ",
                                        ResultSet.TYPE_SCROLL_INSENSITIVE,
                                        ResultSet.CONCUR_READ_ONLY);
                ps.setString(1, l.toString());
                ps.setString(2, categoryID);
                rs = ps.executeQuery();
                rs.first();
                int total = rs.getInt(1);
                rs.close();
                ps.close();

                // Select.
                ps = c.prepareStatement("select a.productid, name, descn "
```

Listing 19.7 CatalogPointbaseDAOImpl class. (continues)

```
                                    + "from product a join "
                                        + "product_details b on "
                                        + "a.productid=b.productid "
                                        + "where locale = ? "
                                        + "and a.catid = ? "
                                        + "order by name",

                                        ResultSet.TYPE_SCROLL_INSENSITIVE,
                                        ResultSet.CONCUR_READ_ONLY);
                ps.setString(1, l.toString());
                ps.setString(2, categoryID);
                rs = ps.executeQuery();
                if (start >= 0 && start < total) {
                    List items = new ArrayList();
                    rs.absolute(start+1);
                    do {
                        items.add(new Product(rs.getString(1).trim(),
                                              rs.getString(2).trim(),
                                              rs.getString(3).trim()));
                    } while (rs.next() && (--count > 0));
                    ret = new Page(items, start, total);
                }
                else {
                    ret = Page.EMPTY_PAGE;
                }

                rs.close();
                ps.close();

                c.close();
                return ret;
            }
            catch (SQLException se) {
                throw new CatalogDAOSysException("SQLException: "
                                                + se.getMessage());
            }
        }

        public Item getItem(String itemID, Locale l)
            throws CatalogDAOSysException {

            Connection c = null;
            PreparedStatement ps = null;
            ResultSet rs = null;
            Item ret = null;

            try {
                c = this.getDataSource().getConnection();
```

Listing 19.7 CatalogPointbaseDAOImpl class. (continues)

```
                ps = c.prepareStatement("select catid, a.productid, name, "
                              + "a.itemid, b.image, b.descn,
                                 attr1, "
                              + "attr2, attr3, attr4, attr5, "
                              + "listprice, unitcost "
                              + "from item a, item_details b,
                                 product_details c, product d  "

                              + "where a.itemid=b.itemid "
                              + "and a.productid=c.productid "
                              + "and d.productid=c.productid and
                                 b.locale = c.locale "
                              + "and b.locale = ? and "
                              + "a.itemid = ?",
                              ResultSet.TYPE_SCROLL_INSENSITIVE,
                              ResultSet.CONCUR_READ_ONLY);
            ps.setString(1, l.toString());
            ps.setString(2, itemID);
            rs = ps.executeQuery();

            if (rs.first()) {
                int i = 1;
                ret = new Item(rs.getString(i++).trim(),
                               rs.getString(i++).trim(),
                               rs.getString(i++),
                               rs.getString(i++).trim(),
                               rs.getString(i++).trim(),
                               rs.getString(i++),
                               rs.getString(i++),
                               rs.getString(i++),
                               rs.getString(i++),
                               rs.getString(i++),
                               rs.getString(i++),
                               rs.getDouble(i++),
                               rs.getDouble(i++));
            }
            rs.close();
            ps.close();

            c.close();
            return ret;
        }
        catch (SQLException se) {
            throw new CatalogDAOSysException("SQLException: "
                                        + se.getMessage());
        }
    }
```

Listing 19.7 CatalogPointbaseDAOImpl class. (continues)

```
        public Page getItems(String productID, int start, int count, Locale l)
        throws CatalogDAOSysException {

        Connection c = null;
        PreparedStatement ps = null;
        ResultSet rs = null;
        Page ret = null;

        try {
            c = this.getDataSource().getConnection();

            ps = c.prepareStatement("select COUNT(*) "
                                + "from item a, item_details b,
product_details c, product d "
                                + "where a.itemid=b.itemid "
                                + "and a.productid=c.productid "
                                + "and d.productid=c.productid "
                                + "and b.locale = c.locale "
                                + "and b.locale = ? "
                                + "and a.productid = ?",
                                ResultSet.TYPE_SCROLL_INSENSITIVE,
                                ResultSet.CONCUR_READ_ONLY);
            ps.setString(1, l.toString());
            ps.setString(2, productID);

            rs = ps.executeQuery();
            rs.first();
            int total = rs.getInt(1);
            rs.close();
            ps.close();

            // Select.
            ps = c.prepareStatement("select catid, a.productid, name, "
                                + "a.itemid, b.image, b.descn,
                                  attr1, "
                                + "attr2, attr3, attr4, attr5, "
                                + "listprice, unitcost "
                                + "from item a, item_details b,
                                  product_details c, product d "
                                + "where a.itemid=b.itemid "
                                + "and a.productid=c.productid "
                                + "and d.productid=c.productid "
                                + "and b.locale = c.locale "
                                + "and b.locale = ? "
                                + "and a.productid = ?",
                                ResultSet.TYPE_SCROLL_INSENSITIVE,
                                ResultSet.CONCUR_READ_ONLY);
            ps.setString(1, l.toString());
            ps.setString(2, productID);
```

Listing 19.7 CatalogPointbaseDAOImpl class. (continues)

```
                    rs = ps.executeQuery();
                    if (start >= 0 && start < total) {
                        List items = new ArrayList();
                        rs.absolute(start+1);
                        do {
                            int i = 1;

                            items.add(new Item(rs.getString(i++).trim(),
                                               rs.getString(i++).trim(),
                                               rs.getString(i++),
                                               rs.getString(i++).trim(),
                                               rs.getString(i++).trim(),
                                               rs.getString(i++),
                                               rs.getString(i++),
                                               rs.getString(i++),
                                               rs.getString(i++),
                                               rs.getString(i++),
                                               rs.getString(i++),
                                               rs.getDouble(i++),
                                               rs.getDouble(i++)));
                        } while (rs.next() && (--count > 0));
                        ret = new Page(items, start, total);
                    }
                    else {
                        ret = Page.EMPTY_PAGE;
                    }

                    rs.close();
                    ps.close();

                    c.close();
                    return ret;
                }
                catch (SQLException se) {
                    throw new CatalogDAOSysException("SQLException: "
                                                    + se.getMessage());
                }
            }

            public Page searchItems(String searchQuery, int start,
                                int count, Locale l)
                throws CatalogDAOSysException {


                Collection keywords = new HashSet();
                StringTokenizer st = new StringTokenizer(searchQuery);
                while (st.hasMoreTokens()) {
                    keywords.add(st.nextToken());
                }
```

Listing 19.7 CatalogPointbaseDAOImpl class. (continues)

```
                    if (keywords.isEmpty()) {
                        return Page.EMPTY_PAGE;
                    }

                    Connection c = null;
                    PreparedStatement ps = null;

                    ResultSet rs = null;
                    Page ret = null;

                    try {
                        c = this.getDataSource().getConnection();

                        Iterator it;
                        int i;
                        StringBuffer sb = new StringBuffer();

                        sb.append("(select e.productid from ");
    //                     sb.append("(product e join product_details f on ");
                        //sb.append("e.productid=f.productid) ");
                        sb.append("product e, product_details f ");
                        sb.append("where e.productid=f.productid ");

                        int keywordsSize = keywords.size();
                        if (keywordsSize > 0) {
                            sb.append("AND  ( ( lower(f.name) like ? ");
                            for (i = 1; i != keywordsSize; i++) {
                                sb.append("OR lower(f.name) like ? ");
                            }
                            sb.append(") OR ( lower(e.catid) like ? ");
                            for (i = 1; i != keywordsSize; i++) {
                                sb.append("OR lower(e.catid) like ? ");
                            }
                            sb.append(") )");
                        }

                        sb.append(")");

                        // Count.
                        ps = c.prepareStatement("select COUNT(*) "
                                            + "from item a, item_details b,
                                              product_details c, product d "
                                            + "where a.itemid=b.itemid "
                                            + "and a.productid=c.productid "
                                            + "and d.productid=c.productid "
                                            + "and b.locale = c.locale "
                                            + "and b.locale = ? "
                                            + "and a.productid in "
                                            + sb.toString(),
```

Listing 19.7 CatalogPointbaseDAOImpl class. (continues)

```
                                       ResultSet.TYPE_SCROLL_INSENSITIVE,
                                       ResultSet.CONCUR_READ_ONLY);
    /*
                                     + "from (((item a join item_details
                                       b "
                                     + "on a.itemid=b.itemid) join "
                                     + "product_details c on "

                          + "a.productid=c.productid) join "
                                     + "product d on "
                                     + "d.productid=c.productid and "
                                     + "b.locale = c.locale) "
                                     + "where b.locale = ? "
                                     + "and a.productid in " +
                                       sb.toString(),
                                       ResultSet.TYPE_SCROLL_INSENSITIVE,
                                       ResultSet.CONCUR_READ_ONLY);
    */
            ps.setString(1, l.toString());

            // The two loops are necessary because of the way the
            // query was constructed.
            i = 2;
            for (it = keywords.iterator(); it.hasNext(); i++) {
                String keyword = ((String) it.next()).toLowerCase();
                ps.setString(i, "%" + keyword + "%");
            }
            for (it = keywords.iterator(); it.hasNext(); i++) {
                String keyword = ((String) it.next()).toLowerCase();
                ps.setString(i, "%" + keyword + "%");
            }

            rs = ps.executeQuery();
            rs.first();
            int total = rs.getInt(1);
            rs.close();
            ps.close();

            // Select.

            ps = c.prepareStatement("select catid, a.productid, name, "
                                 + "a.itemid, b.image, b.descn,
                                   attr1, "
                                 + "attr2, attr3, attr4, attr5, "
                                 + "listprice, unitcost "
                                 + "from item a, item_details b,
                                   product_details c, product d "
                                 + "where a.itemid=b.itemid "
```

Listing 19.7 CatalogPointbaseDAOImpl class. *(continues)*

```
                                  + "and a.productid=c.productid "
                                    + "and d.productid=c.productid "
                                    + "and b.locale = c.locale "
                                    + "and b.locale = ? "
                                    + "and a.productid in " +
                                      sb.toString(),
                                    ResultSet.TYPE_SCROLL_INSENSITIVE,
                                    ResultSet.CONCUR_READ_ONLY);

            ps.setString(1, l.toString());

            // The two loops are necessary because of the way the
            // query was constructed.
            i = 2;
            for (it = keywords.iterator(); it.hasNext(); i++) {
                String keyword = ((String) it.next()).toLowerCase();
                ps.setString(i, "%" + keyword + "%");
            }
            for (it = keywords.iterator(); it.hasNext(); i++) {
                String keyword = ((String) it.next()).toLowerCase();
                ps.setString(i, "%" + keyword + "%");
            }

            rs = ps.executeQuery();
            if (start >= 0 && start < total) {
                List items = new ArrayList();
                rs.absolute(start+1);
                do {
                    i = 1;
                    items.add(new Item(rs.getString(i++).trim(),
                                       rs.getString(i++).trim(),
                                       rs.getString(i++),
                                       rs.getString(i++).trim(),
                                       rs.getString(i++).trim(),
                                       rs.getString(i++),
                                       rs.getString(i++),
                                       rs.getString(i++),
                                       rs.getString(i++),
                                       rs.getString(i++),
                                       rs.getString(i++),
                                       rs.getDouble(i++),
                                       rs.getDouble(i++)));
                } while (rs.next() && (--count > 0));
                ret = new Page(items, start, total);
            }
            else {
                ret = Page.EMPTY_PAGE;
            }

            rs.close();
```

Listing 19.7 CatalogPointbaseDAOImpl class. (continues)

```
                ps.close();

                c.close();
                return ret;
            }
        catch (SQLException se) {
            throw new CatalogDAOSysException("SQLException: "
                                        + se.getMessage());
        }
    }
}
```

Listing 19.7 CatalogPointbaseDAOImpl class. (continued)

```
package com.sun.j2ee.blueprints.catalog.dao;

import java.io.PrintWriter;
import java.sql.Connection;
import java.sql.DriverManager;

import javax.sql.DataSource;

import com.sun.j2ee.blueprints.catalog.exceptions.CatalogDAOSys
Exception;


public class TestableCatalogPointbaseDaoImpl extends Catalog
PointbaseDAOImpl {

    protected static DataSource getDataSource()throws CatalogDAOSys
    Exception {
        TestableCatalogPointbaseDaoImpl me = new Testable
        CatalogPointbaseDaoImpl();
        System.out.println("TestableCatalogPointbaseDaoImpl:
        returning new PointbaseDataSource");
        return me.new PointbaseDataSource();
    }

    class PointbaseDataSource implements DataSource{

        public Connection getConnection(){
            Connection con = null;
            System.out.println("Getting connection from the
            testable class.");
            try{
                Class.forName("com.pointbase.jdbc.
```

Listing 19.8 TestablePointbaseCatalogDAOImpl class. (continues)

```
                                jdbcUniversalDriver");
                                String url = "jdbc:pointbase:server://
                                localhost/demo";
                                con = DriverManager.getConnection(url,
                                "petstore","petstore");
                        }catch(Exception e){
                                e.printStackTrace();
                        }
                        return con;
                }

                public Connection getConnection(String userName, String
                password){
                        return null;
                }

                public int getLoginTimeout(){
                        return -1;
                }

                public PrintWriter getLogWriter(){
                        return null;
                }

                public void setLoginTimeout(int timeout){}

                public void setLogWriter(PrintWriter out){
                        int i=1;
                }
        }
}
```

Listing 19.8 TestablePointbaseCatalogDAOImpl class. (continued)

```
package com.sun.j2ee.blueprints.catalog.dao;

import java.util.ListIterator;
import java.util.Locale;

import com.sun.j2ee.blueprints.catalog.model.Category;
import com.sun.j2ee.blueprints.catalog.model.Item;
import com.sun.j2ee.blueprints.catalog.model.Page;
import com.sun.j2ee.blueprints.catalog.model.Product;

import junit.framework.TestCase;
```

Listing 19.9 CatalogPointbaseDAOImplTest class. (continues)

```
public class CatalogPointBaseDAOImplTest extends TestCase {

    private TestableCatalogPointbaseDaoImpl dao ;
    private Locale loc;

    public void setUp(){
        System.out.println("Geting new TestableCatalog
        PointbaseDaoImpl");
        dao = new TestableCatalogPointbaseDaoImpl();
        loc = new Locale("en");
    }

    public CatalogPointBaseDAOImplTest(String arg0) {
        super(arg0);
    }

    public void testGetCategory() {
        String categoryId = "DOGS";
        Category cat = dao.getCategory(categoryId,loc);
        assertNotNull("testGetCategory:The category was
null.",cat);
        assertEquals(cat.getName(),"Dogs");
    }

    public void testGetCategories() {
        Page categories = dao.getCategories(0,0,loc);
        assertNotNull("testGetCategories:The page was null.",
        categories);
        while(categories.hasNextPage()){
            ListIterator innerPage = categories.getList()
            .listIterator();
            assertTrue("testGetCategories:There are no
            categories in the database",innerPage.hasNext());
            while(innerPage.hasNext()){
                Object obj = innerPage.next();
                assertEquals(obj.getClass().getName(),
                "Category");
            }
        }
    }

    public void testGetProduct() {
        String productId = "K9-BD-01";
        Product prod = dao.getProduct(productId,loc);
        assertNotNull("testGetProduct:The product was null",prod);
        assertEquals(prod.getDescription(),"Friendly dog from
England ");
```

Listing 19.9 CatalogPointbaseDAOImplTest class. (continues)

```
        }

        public void testGetProducts() {
                String categoryId = "DOGS";
                Page products = dao.getProducts(categoryId,0,2,loc);
                assertNotNull("testGetProducts:The page was null",products);
                while(products.hasNextPage()){
                        ListIterator innerPage = products.getList().
                        listIterator();
                        assertTrue("testGetProducts:There are no Products
in the database for the category with the id " + categoryId,innerPage.
hasNext());
                        while(innerPage.hasNext()){
                                Object obj = innerPage.next();
                                assertEquals(obj.getClass().getName(),
                                "Product");
                        }
                }
        }

        public void testGetItem() {
                String itemId = "EST-6";
                Item item = dao.getItem(itemId,loc);
                assertNotNull("testGetItem:The item was null",item);
                assertEquals(item.getDescription(),"Male Adult Bulldog");
        }

        public void testGetItems() {
                String productId = "K9-BD-01";
                Page items = dao.getItems(productId,0,2,loc);
                assertNotNull("testGetItems:The page was null",items);
                while(items.hasNextPage()){
                        ListIterator innerPage = items.getList().list
                        Iterator();
                        assertTrue("testGetItems:There are no Items in the
                        database for the product with the id " +
                        productId,innerPage.hasNext());
                        while(innerPage.hasNext()){
                                Object obj = innerPage.next();

assertEquals(obj.getClass().getName(),"Item");
                        }
                }
        }

        public void testSearchItems() {
                String searchQuery = "sn";
                Page items = dao.getItems(searchQuery,0,2,loc);
```

Listing 19.9 CatalogPointbaseDAOImplTest class. (continues)

```
        assertNotNull("testSearchItems:The page was null",items);
              assertEquals("testSearchItems:There were not two items in
    the search results as expected",items.getList().size(),2);
              while(items.hasNextPage()){
                    ListIterator innerPage = items.getList().list
                    Iterator();
                    assertTrue("testSearchItems:There are no Items in
                    the database for the search using '" + searchQuery +
                    "'",innerPage.hasNext());
                    while(innerPage.hasNext()){
                          Object obj = innerPage.next();

    assertEquals(obj.getClass().getName(),"Item");
                    }
              }
        }

    }
```

Listing 19.9 CatalogPointbaseDAOImplTest class. (continued)

Testing the User Authentication Component

Testing the User Authentication component consists of test the SignOn function.

Testing the SignOn Function

Based on the chart shown in Figure 19.3 it is evident that to unit test this process we will need to call on the SignOnEJB with two sets of arguments (one for a correct signon and one for an invalid signon), and then assert the return value to determine whether or not the signon was validated. We will pass the same information into the EJB as the view layer would, and we will validate the same output as the view layer would use to determine which page to send to the browser. In this way we will be able to test the functionality of the signon EJB completely decoupled from the view layer of the application.

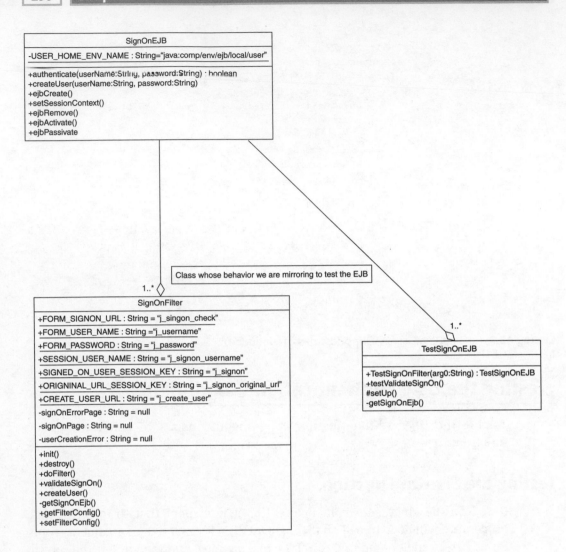

Figure 19.3 Class Diagram for LoginTest.

Figure 19.4 contains a use case diagram illustrating the functionality that needs to be tested for the signon process.

Figure 19.4 UML UseCase for Petstore SignOn.

The component that does this work is very straightforward: it is SignOnEJB in the SignOn component of the application. We will write a ServletTestCase within the Cactus framework so that we can test this component in container. Testing it in-container is necessary because of the intrinsic coupling of the signon process to the EJB container. It is also extremely simple to do once Cactus is installed and configured. Listing 19.10 shows the sample code for our ServletTestCase.

```
package com.sun.j2ee.blueprints.signon.ejb;

import javax.naming.InitialContext;
import javax.servlet.ServletException;

import org.apache.cactus.ServletTestCase;


public class TestSignOnEJB extends ServletTestCase {

     private String[][] userNames;
     private String[] passwords;
     public TestSignOnEJB(String arg0) {
          super(arg0);
     }

     public void testAuthenticate(){
          try{
               String username = null;
               String password = null;

               for(int i=0;i<userNames.length;i++){
                    username = userNames[i][0];
                    password = userNames[i][1];
```

Listing 19.10 Sample code for our ServletTestCase. (continues)

```
                            SignOnLocal signOn = getSignOnEjb();
                            boolean authenticated = signOn.authenti-
                            cate(username,password);
                            if(i==0){
                                    assertTrue("The User " + username +
                                    ":"+ password + "is NOT authenticated
                                    but should be.",authenticated);
                            }else if (i==1){
                                    assertEquals("The User " + username +
                                    ":"+ password + "is authenticated but
                                    should NOT be." ,false,authenticated);
                            }
                    }
            }catch(ServletException se){
                    fail("Failed on ServletException while getting a
                    signOn EJB.");
                    se.printStackTrace();
            }
    }

    /*
     * @see TestCase#setUp()
     */
    protected void setUp() throws Exception {
            super.setUp();
            SignOnLocal signOn = null;
             try {
            InitialContext ic = new InitialContext();
                    Object o = ic.lookup("java:comp/env/ejb/signon/
                    local/SignOn");
                    SignOnLocalHome home =(SignOnLocalHome)o;
                    signOn = home.create();
                    userNames = new String[][]{{"j2ee","j2ee"},
                    {"fail","fail"}};
             } catch (javax.ejb.CreateException cx) {
                    throw new ServletException("Failed to Create SignOn
                    EJB: caught " + cx);
             } catch (javax.naming.NamingException nx) {
                    throw new ServletException("Failed to Create SignOn
                    EJB: caught " + nx);
            }
    }

    private SignOnLocal getSignOnEjb() throws ServletException {
            SignOnLocal signOn = null;
            try {
                    InitialContext ic = new InitialContext();
```

Listing 19.10 Sample code for our ServletTestCase. (continues)

```
                    Object o = ic.lookup("java:comp/env/ejb/signon/
                    local/SignOn");
                    SignOnLocalHome home =(SignOnLocalHome)o;
                    signOn = home.create();
            } catch (javax.ejb.CreateException cx) {
                    throw new ServletException("Failed to Create SignOn
                    EJB: caught " + cx);
            } catch (javax.naming.NamingException nx) {
                    throw new ServletException("Failed to Create SignOn
                    EJB: caught " + nx);
            }

            return signOn;
        }

    }
```

Listing 19.10 Sample code for our ServletTestCase. (continued)

Testing The Shopping Cart Component

Testing the Shopping Cart component consists of testing the Shopping Cart model.

Testing the Shopping Cart Model

The business objects in the shopping cart data model are CartItem and ShoppingCartModel (Listing 19.5). These objects are represented by JavaBeans in the application; consequently, their unit tests will require the testing of assessors and mutators (mutators are initialized in the constructors in this case) so that we can always ensure that if an object is initialized with a given value it will return that value in it's accessory method. These classes are grouped in the Petstore Application under the package com.sun.j2ee.blueprints.cart.model.

The functionality to add and remove items from a cart is located in the Cart EJBAction, so that class will require a unit test as well. It is located in *com.sun.j2ee.blueprintspetstore.controller.ejb.actions*.

Finally, the functionality to order the contents of a cart exist in *OrderEJB Action* so they will also get a unit test.

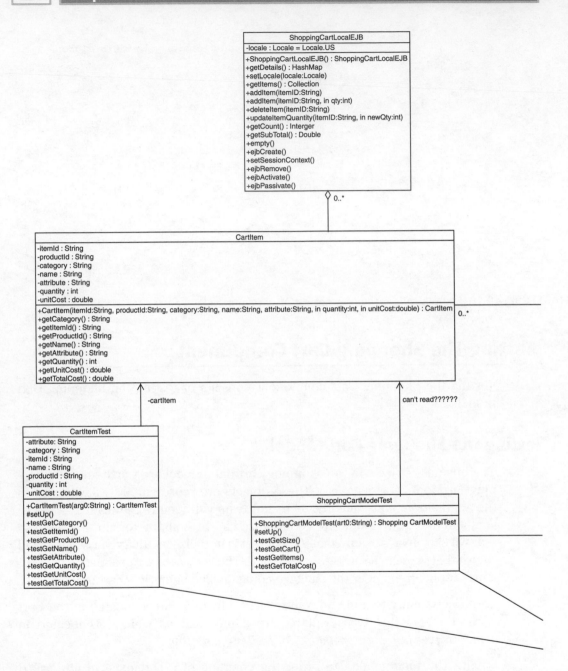

Figure 19.5 Shopping cart class diagram.

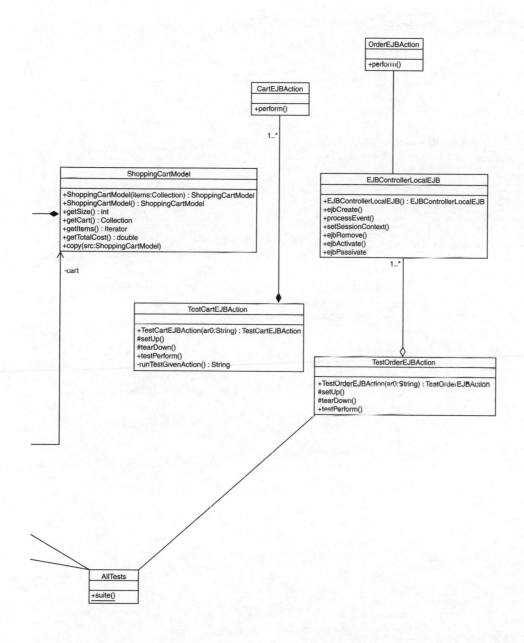

Listing 19.11 contains the CartItemTest class, Listing 19.12 contains Shopping-CartModelTest class, Listing 19.13 contains TestCartEJBAction class, and Listing 19.14 contains TestOrderEJBAction Class.

```java
package com.sun.j2ee.blueprints.cart.model;

import junit.framework.TestCase;

public class CartItemTest extends TestCase {

    private CartItem cartItem;
    private String attribute,category,itemId,name,productId;
    private int quantity;
    private double unitCost;

    public CartItemTest(String arg0) {
            super(arg0);
    }

    protected void setUp() throws Exception {
            super.setUp();
            attribute = "attribute";
            category = "DOGS";
            itemId = "LEON-DOG-MALE";
            name = "Male Leonberger";
            productId = "LEON-DOG";
            quantity = 3;
            unitCost = 1500.00;
            cartItem = new
CartItem(itemId,productId,category,name,attribute,quantity,unitCost);
    }


    public void testGetCategory() {
            assertEquals("The Category is not equal to the value set in
            the constructor",cartItem.getCategory(),this.category);
    }

    public void testGetItemId() {
            assertEquals("The Item ID is not equal to the value set in
            the constructor",cartItem.getItemId(),this.itemId);
    }

    public void testGetProductId() {
            assertEquals("The Product ID is not equal to the value set
            in the constructor",cartItem.getProductId(),this.productId);
    }
```

Listing 19.11 CartItemTest class. (continues)

```
      public void testGetName() {
              assertEquals("The Name is not equal to the value set in the
              constructor",cartItem.getName(),this.name);
      }

      public void testGetAttribute() {
              assertEquals("The Attribute is not equal to the value set
              in the
              constructor",cartItem.getAttribute(),this.attribute);
      }

      public void testGetQuantity() {
              assertEquals("The Quantity is not equal to the value set in
              the constructor",cartItem.getQuantity(),this.quantity);
      }

      public void testGetUnitCost() {
              assertEquals("The Unit Cost is not equal to the value set
              in the constructor",cartItem.getUnitCost(),this.unit-
              Cost,0.00);
      }

      public void testGetTotalCost() {
              assertEquals("The Total Cost is not equal to the derived
              product of the values set in the constructor",cartItem.
              getTotalCost(),(this.quantity*this.unitCost),0.00);
      }

}
```

Listing 19.11 CartItemTest class. (continued)

```
package com.sun.j2ee.blueprints.cart.model;

import java.util.ArrayList;
import java.util.HashMap;
import java.util.Iterator;
import java.util.Vector;

import junit.framework.TestCase;

public class ShoppingCartModelTest extends TestCase {

    private ArrayList cartItems;
    private ShoppingCartModel cart;
    private CartItem first,second,third;
```

Listing 19.12 ShoppingCartModelTest class. (continues)

```
       public ShoppingCartModelTest(String arg0) {
             super(arg0);
       }

       protected void setUp() throws Exception {
             super.setUp();
             first = new CartItem("A","A","A","A","A",2,100.00);
             second = new CartItem("B","B","B","B","B",2,50.00);
             third = new CartItem("C","C","C","C","C",2,150.00);
             cartItems = new ArrayList();
             cartItems.add(first);
             cartItems.add(second);
             cartItems.add(third);
             cart = new ShoppingCartModel(cartItems);
       }


       public void testGetSize() {
             assertEquals("The shopping cart contains a different number
             of items than it was constructed with",cart.getSize(),3);
       }

       public void testGetCart() {
             assertEquals("The shopping cart contains a different
             collection than it was constructed with",cart.getCart(),
             cartItems);
       }

       public void testGetItems() {
             Iterator itemsIt = cart.getItems();
             assertEquals("The first cartItem is not equal to its
             constructed value.",(CartItem)itemsIt.next(),first);
             assertEquals("The second cartItem is not equal to its
             constructed value.",(CartItem)itemsIt.next(),second);
             assertEquals("The third cartItem is not equal to its
             constructed value.",(CartItem)itemsIt.next(),third);
       }

       public void testGetTotalCost() {
             double derivedCost = (first.getUnitCost()*first.get
             Quantity()) + (second.getUnitCost()*second.getQuantity()) +
             (third.getUnitCost() *third.getQuantity());
             assertEquals("The total cost of the cart was not equal to
             the derived cost from the items at contruction.",
             cart.getTotalCost(),derivedCost,0.00);
       }

   }
```

Listing 19.12 ShoppingCartModelTest class. (continued)

```
package com.sun.j2ee.blueprints.petstore.controller.ejb.actions;

import java.util.HashMap;

import org.apache.cactus.ServletTestCase;

import com.sun.j2ee.blueprints.petstore.controller.events.CartEvent;
import com.sun.j2ee.blueprints.waf.controller.ejb.EJBClientCon-
trollerEJB;
import com.sun.j2ee.blueprints.waf.event.EventException;
import com.sun.j2ee.blueprints.waf.event.EventResponse;

public class TestCartEJBAction extends ServletTestCase {

    private CartEvent event,event2,event3,event4;
    private EJBClientControllerEJB controller;


    public TestCartEJBAction(String arg0) {
        super(arg0);
    }

    protected void setUp() throws Exception {
        super.setUp();
        controller = new EJBClientControllerEJB();
        controller.ejbCreate();
        event = new CartEvent(CartEvent.ADD_ITEM,"EST-6");
        event2 = new CartEvent(CartEvent.DELETE_ITEM,"EST-6");
        event3 = new CartEvent(CartEvent.ADD_ITEM,"EST-6");
        HashMap map = new HashMap();
        map.put("0","EST-5");
        map.put("1","EST-6");
        event4 = CartEvent.createUpdateItemEvent(map);
    }

    protected void tearDown() throws Exception {
        super.tearDown();
    }

    public void testPerform() {
        StringBuffer errors = new StringBuffer();
        System.out.println("In " + this.getClass().getName() +
        ":" + "testPerform".toUpperCase());
        errors.append(runTestGivenAction(event));
        errors.append(runTestGivenAction(event2));
        errors.append(runTestGivenAction(event3));
        errors.append(runTestGivenAction(event4));
        if(errors.length()>0){
```

Listing 19.13 TestCartEJBAction class. (continues)

```
                                fail(errors.toString());
                }
        }

        private String runTestGivenAction(CartEvent event) throws
        RuntimeException{
                String failureString = "";
                try{
                        String actionType = "";
                        switch (event.getActionType()){
                                case 1:
                                actionType = "Insert";
                                break;
                                case 2:

                                actionType = "Delete";
                                break;
                                case 3:
                                actionType = "Update";
                        }
                        EventResponse er =  (EventResponse)controller.
                        processEvent(event);
                        if(er == null){
                                failureString ="The response to the " +
                                actionType + " Item Cart Event was null:";
                        }
                }catch(EventException ee){
                        ee.printStackTrace();
                        failureString ="Caught an eventexception while
                        evaluating perform on CartEJBAction with eventAction
                        of " + event.getActionType() + ":";
                }finally{
                        return failureString;
                }
        }

}
```

Listing 19.13 TestCartEJBAction class. (continued)

```
package com.sun.j2ee.blueprints.petstore.controller.ejb.actions;


import com.sun.j2ee.blueprints.waf.controller.ejb.EJBClientCon-
trollerEJB;
import com.sun.j2ee.blueprints.waf.event.Event;
import com.sun.j2ee.blueprints.waf.event.EventException;
import com.sun.j2ee.blueprints.customer.account.ejb.Address;
import com.sun.j2ee.blueprints.customer.account.ejb.ContactInfo;
import com.sun.j2ee.blueprints.customer.account.ejb.CreditCard;
import com.sun.j2ee.blueprints.petstore.controller.events.OrderEvent;
import com.sun.j2ee.blueprints.petstore.controller.events.OrderEvent
Response;


import org.apache.cactus.ServletTestCase;

public class TestOrderEJBAction extends ServletTestCase {

    private ContactInfo ci;
    private CreditCard cc;
    private OrderEvent oe;
    private EJBClientControllerEJB controller;

    public TestOrderEJBAction(String arg0) {
        super(arg0);
    }

    /*
     * @see TestCase#setUp()
     */
    protected void setUp() throws Exception {
        super.setUp();
        String email = null, familyName = null, givenName = null,
        telephone = null;
        String cardNumber=null, cardType=null,expiryDate=null;
        Address address = null;
        address = new Address("940 Rose
        Ave","","Washington","DC","00000","USA");
        email = "spam2@rabidMInnesotaVikingsFan.com";
        familyName="Snorbert";
        givenName="OxenShed";
        telephone="555-555-5555";
        cardNumber="777777777777";
        cardType="Visa";
        expiryDate="1/1/2005";
        ci = new ContactInfo(givenName,familyName,telephone,email,
        address);
        cc = new CreditCard(cardNumber,cardType,expiryDate);
```

Listing 19.14 TestOrderEJBAction Class. (continues)

```
            oe = new OrderEvent(ci,ci,cc);
            controller = new EJBClientControllerEJB();
            controller.ejbCreate();
    }

    /*
     * @see TestCase#tearDown()
     */
    protected void tearDown() throws Exception {
            super.tearDown();
    }

    public void testPerform() {
            try{
                    OrderEventResponse oer =  (OrderEventResponse)
                    controller.processEvent(oe);
                    assertNotNull("The response to the order was
                    null.",oer);
            }catch(EventException ee){
                    ee.printStackTrace();
                    fail("Caught an eventexception while evaluating
                    perform.");
            }
    }
}
```

Listing 19.14 TestOrderEJBAction Class. (continued)

CHAPTER 20

Functional Tests for the Sample Application

Those who do not want to imitate anything, produce nothing.

—Salvador Dali

We have determined a set of requirements for the Petstore and have identified the application's three main components (the Catalog, User Authentication, and Shopping Cart), which allowed us to compile a list of testable functions for our Petstore Application TestSuite. The Catalog component functions are the following:

- List all categories in the catalog.
- List all products in a category.
- List all items for a product.
- View item details.
- Search for an item by passing in a descriptive string of characters.

In Chapter 18 we grouped these functions into a single use case-based functional test called *"granular product browsing verified against search results."* In this chapter we use JUnit to build the TestSuites used in functional testing of each of these requirements. To prepare, let's review the use case to plan our functional test:

> *A customer hits the homepage of the Web site which displays all the categories in the catalog. The customer drills down into the Dogs category and selects the Bulldog product. The customer then drills down into the Bulldog product and selects a female bulldog item. The customer then does a search on "female bulldog" from the search page so he can verify that he sees the same product from the search function.*

We want to mimic the functionality of many of our tests, but we will use the output from each test to drive the testFixture of the next. For example, we will run a test based on CatalogPointBaseDAOImplTest.testGetCategories; we will take the results, locate the category with the description "Dogs," and inspect its ID field. This field will become the fixture for a testcase based on CatalogPoint-BaseDAOImplTest.testGetCategory that will take an argument for the ID field (in fact we will probably override this test with a version that takes an argument). Then we will take the output of that second test and find a Product that meets the needs of the usecase, and so on. The end result will be structured along the lines of the diagram shown in Figure 20.1.

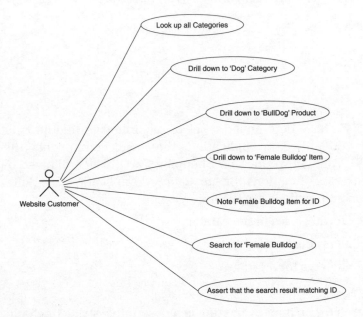

Figure 20.1 Partial diagram of our functional test.

Listing 20.1 contains the code for the CatalogFunctionalTest class.

```
package com.sun.j2ee2blueprints.catalog.dao;

import java.util.List;
import java.util.ListIterator;
import java.util.Locale;

import com.sun.j2ee.blueprints.catalog.dao.CatalogPointBaseDAOImplTest;
import com.sun.j2ee.blueprints.catalog.dao.TestableCatalogPoint
baseDaoImpl;
import com.sun.j2ee.blueprints.catalog.model.Category;
```

Listing 20.1 CatalogFunctionalTest class. (continues)

```java
import com.sun.j2ee.blueprints.catalog.model.Item;
import com.sun.j2ee.blueprints.catalog.model.Page;
import com.sun.j2ee.blueprints.catalog.model.Product;

import junit.framework.TestCase;

public class CatalogFunctionalTest extends TestCase {

    private TestableCatalogPointbaseDaoImpl test;
    private Locale loc;

    public CatalogFunctionalTest(String arg0) {
            super(arg0);
    }

    protected void setUp() throws Exception {
            super.setUp();
            test = new TestableCatalogPointbaseDaoImpl();
            System.out.println("Geting new TestableCatalogPoint-
            baseDaoImpl");
            loc = new Locale("en_US");
    }

    protected void tearDown() throws Exception {
            super.tearDown();
    }

    public void testGranularProductBrowsingVerifiedAgainstSearch
    Results(){
            ListIterator innerPage=null;
            String categoryId=null,productId=null,itemId=null;
            Page categories=null, products=null, items=null;
            categories = test.getCategories(0,5,loc);
            boolean breakMe = false;
            List categoryList = categories.getList();
            if(!categories.hasNextPage()){
                    fail("No Categories were found in the database
(Outer loop).");
            }
            while(categories.hasNextPage()){
                    innerPage = categories.getList().listIterator();
                    if(!innerPage.hasNext()){
                            fail("No Categories were found in the
                            database  (Inner loop).");
                    }
                    while(innerPage.hasNext()){
                            Category cat = (Category)innerPage.next();
                            System.out.println("About to assign the
                            CategoryId");
```

Listing 20.1 CatalogFunctionalTest class. (continues)

```
                            if(cat.getId().equalsIgnoreCase("DOGS")){
                                    categoryId = cat.getId();
                                    break;
                            }
                            else{
                                    System.out.println("The category id
                                    we found was " + cat.getId());
                            }
                    }
            }
            if(categoryId == null){
                    fail("The 'Dogs' category could not be found from
                    the database.");
            }else{
                    products = test.getProducts(categoryId,0,20,loc);
                    while(products.hasNextPage()){
                            innerPage = products.getList().list
                            Iterator();
                            while(innerPage.hasNext()){
                                    Product prod =
                                    (Product)innerPage.next();
                                    if(prod.getId().equalsIgnoreCase
                                    ("K9-BD-01")){
                                            productId = prod.getId();
                                            breakMe = true;
                                            break;
                                    }
                            }
                            if(breakMe == true){
                                    break;
                            }
                    }
                    if(productId == null){
                            fail("The 'BullDog' product could not be
                            found from the database.");
                    }else{
                            items = test.getItems(productId,0,0,loc);
                            while(items.hasNextPage()){
                                    innerPage = items.getList().list
                                    Iterator();
                                    while(innerPage.hasNext()){
                                            Item item =
                                            (Item)innerPage.next();
                                            if(item.getItemId().equals
                                            IgnoreCase("EST-7")){
                                                    itemId =
                                                    item.getItemId();
```

Listing 20.1 CatalogFunctionalTest class. (continues)

```
                                                breakMe = true;
                                                break;
                                        }
                                }
                                if(breakMe == true){
                                        break;
                                }
                        }
                        if(itemId == null){
                                fail("The 'Female BullDog' item could
                                not be found from the database.")
                                ;
                        }else{

                                Item item = test.getItem
                                ("EST-7",loc);
                                assertEquals("The 'browsed to' item
                                was not the same as the 'searched to'
                                item.",itemId,item.getItemId());
                        }
                }
        }
    }
}
```

Listing 20.1 CatalogFunctionalTest class. (continued)

User Authentication Component Functions

For the user authentication component, we have decided to test the functionality that involves enabling a user to sign on. Since this use case is defined by a unit test, we'll just refer to the unit test here for this functionality.

A Website Customer logs into the Petstore using the default user information (j2ee/j2ee). In order to accomplish this we will want to run a TestCase that evaluates TestSignOnEJBAction.testPerfom. Figure 20.2 shows use case diagram for SignOnAndChangeBillingAddressFunctionTest. This test is documented in Chapter 16.

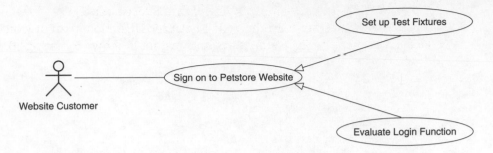

Figure 20.2 Use case diagram for SignOnAndChangeBillingAddressFunctionTest.

Shopping Cart Component Functions

For the shopping cart component, we want to test the following functionality:

- Get a new shopping cart and add an item.
- Add an item to an existing shopping cart.
- Remove an item from a shopping cart.
- Change the quantity of an item in a shopping cart.
- Purchase the contents of a shopping cart.

In Chapter 16 we identified this function for testing as based on the UseCase called "Customer Shopping Experience." Let's revisit it now:

A Website Customer chooses a pet from the petstore catalog and adds it to his Shopping Cart. He then proceeds to checkout the item and purchase it. Figure 20.3 shows the customer shopping experience use case.

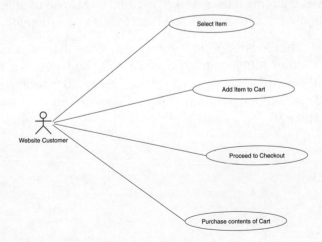

Figure 20.3 Customer shopping experience use case.

In order to accomplish this we'll use a slightly refactored version of TestCart EJBAction and tie it together logically with TestOrderEJBAction, both of which are defined in Chapter 17. The actual functional test for is shown in Listing 20.2.

```java
package com.sun.j2ee.blueprints.petstore.controller.ejb.actions;

import org.apache.cactus.ServletTestCase;

import com.sun.j2ee.blueprints.customer.account.ejb.Address;
import com.sun.j2ee.blueprints.customer.account.ejb.ContactInfo;
import com.sun.j2ee.blueprints.customer.account.ejb.CreditCard;
import com.sun.j2ee.blueprints.petstore.controller.events.CartEvent;
import com.sun.j2ee.blueprints.petstore.controller.events.OrderEvent;
import com.sun.j2ee.blueprints.petstore.controller.events.OrderEvent
Response;
import com.sun.j2ee.blueprints.waf.controller.ejb.EJBClientControllerEJB;
import com.sun.j2ee.blueprints.waf.event.EventException;
import com.sun.j2ee.blueprints.waf.event.EventResponse;


public class TestCustomerShoppingExperience extends ServletTestCase {

    private ContactInfo ci;
    private CreditCard cc;
    private OrderEvent oe;
    private EJBClientControllerEJB controller;
    private CartEvent event;

    public TestCustomerShoppingExperience(String arg0) {
        super(arg0);
    }

    protected void setUp() throws Exception {
        super.setUp();
        /*
         * INITIALIZE THE ORDER FIXTURES
         */
        String email = null, familyName = null, givenName = null,
telephone = null;
        String cardNumber=null, cardType=null,expiryDate=null;
        Address address = null;
        address = new Address("940 Rose
Ave","","Washington","DC","00000","USA");
        email = "spam2@rabidMInnesotaVikingsFan.com";
        familyName="Snorbert";
        givenName="OxenShed";
        telephone="555-555-5555";
```

Figure 20.2 TestCustomerShoppingExperience class. (continues)

```
                      cardNumber="777777777777";
                      cardType="Visa";
                      expiryDate-"1/1/2005";
                      ci = new ContactInfo(givenName,familyName,telephone,email,
                      address);
                      cc = new CreditCard(cardNumber,cardType,expiryDate);
                      oe = new OrderEvent(ci,ci,cc);

                      /*
                       * INITIALIZE THE CART FIXTURES
                       */
                      event = new CartEvent(CartEvent.ADD_ITEM,"EST-6");
                      controller = new EJBClientControllerEJB();
                      controller.ejbCreate();
              }

        public void testCustomerShoppingExperience(){
                      try{
                              EventResponse er =
                              (EventResponse)controller.processEvent(event);
                      }catch(EventException ee){
                              fail("Caught an event exception while adding an item
                              to the cart.");
                      }
                      try{
                              OrderEventResponse oer =  (OrderEventResponse)
                              controller.processEvent(oe);
                      }catch(EventException ee){
                              fail("Caught an event exception while purchasing the
                              contents of the cart.");
                      }
              }

        protected void tearDown() throws Exception {
                      super.tearDown();
              }
      }
```

Figure 20.2 TestCustomerShoppingExperience class. (continued)

CHAPTER 21

Integrating Unit Tests into Ant

Go to the ant, thou sluggard; consider her ways, and be wise.

—Samuel Johnson

Two central tenets of Extreme Programming are continuous integration and iterative build processes. The Petstore sample application is built using the Apache Ant Framework (discussed extensively in Appendix B). Ant works by defining builds and abstracting them into buildfiles (the naming convention for these files is build.xml by default).

The application is built from the top layer down, one component at a time. The source directories fall into the following structure:

- **components**
  - address
  - asyncsender
  - cart
  - catalog
  - contactinfo
  - creditcard
  - customer
  - encodingfilter
  - lineitem
  - mailer
  - processmanager
  - purchaseorder

- servicelocator
- signon
- supplierpo
- uidgen
- util
- xmldocuments

- **apps**
  - admin
  - opc
  - petstore
  - supplier

- **webservices**
  - apps
    - admin
    - opc
    - petstore
    - supplier
  - waf

Each directory above has a sourcefile directory which is composed of the source .java files for all of it's elements. Additionally, each folder listed here (at the lowest level for each branch) contains a build.xml file that defines the building of that component.

In the preceding chapters we identified and built unit tests for some of the core classes in the Petstore sample application. This served two purposes: It showed us how to identify integral application units needing testing, and it showed an example of how to create these unit tests and apply patterns to them.

Ideally, though, our application would have a unit test for each class in the source directories. These would either be created using the XP test first methodology, or they would be built after the fact to retrofit an existing application.

Given that a test was written for each task, we could now implement a tag in our build script that would rum each test in the application and report on it's success or failure. Then each time the application is built, we can easily verify that the classes are in working order. A first wave of developer-driven regression testing can be accomplished within the application build itself.

The Build Script

As we noted earlier, each source directory in the sample application includes a build script (build.xml). At the top level of the Petstore application source there is a build.xml file used by the application to recurse through the build scripts in each component of the application. In order to add testing to our build, we will use two JUnit extensions for Ant and an email extension. We will create a new <target> tag in the buildfile that calls each of the JUnit tests and handles reporting. We will make this tag dependent upon the init target, and we will make the default tag of the build core dependent on our new tag itself.

For purposes of discussion, we break up the resulting <petstore>/src/build.xml file into code segments:

```xml
<?xml version="1.0"?>

<!-- =================================================================
-->
<!-- $Id: build.xml,v 1.13 2001/10/25 01:25:45 inder Exp $
-->
<!-- =================================================================
-->

<project name="blueprints" default="core" basedir=".">

  <target name="init">
    <!-- include top-level common properties -->
    <property file="build.properties"/>

    <property name="petstore.javadocs.dir" value="docs/api"/>
  </target>
```

In the next code segment we define our run_tests target. It will only run after init has completed (depends='init'). We also print out a banner to the syslogger to indicate to an observer at what point the build script is.

```xml
<target name = "run_tests" depends = "init" description = "Run JUnit
tests for Petstore Sample Application">
      <echo>+----------------------------------------+</echo>
      <echo>+      JUNIT Testing Components          +</echo>
      <echo>+----------------------------------------+</echo>
```

In the following line of code we set a timestamp for the start of the JUnit testing process:

```xml
<tstamp description = "Building a timestamp for the JUnit Report" />
```

In the next code segment we initialize a new JUnit test task to run in a separate JVM. We must set the classpath to include the variables necessary for the test-cases and tell this task to format its output using XML. If we set the junit attribute 'haltonerror' = 'yes' we can stop the build process in the event of any junit failure. Instead, we will allow the process to continue and email the test results to an administrator at the end.

```
<junit fork="yes">
        <classpath>
                <pathelement path =
                "${java.class.path};components/catalog/src"/>
        </classpath>
        <formatter type="xml" />
```

In the following lines of code we tell the junit task to recurse through the application's entire directory path and execute any class following the naming convention *Test.class (this is JUnit's TestCase-TestSuite naming convention.

```
        <batchtest>
        <fileset dir=".">
          <include name="**/*Test.class" />
        </fileset>
      </batchtest>
    </junit>
```

Now we'll initialize a new JUnit Report task to handle the output from these junit test runs. It will look in the current directory for files named Test-*.xml (this is the file naming convention used by the XMLFormatter we specified above). It will format the output using an XSLT Template called noframes.xslt in the Reports subdirectory.

```
    <junitreport>
     <fileset dir=".">
       <include name="TEST-*.xml"/>
     </fileset>
     <report format="noframes" styledir="Reports"/>
    </junitreport>
     <taskdef name="mimemail"
  classname="org.apache.tools.ant.taskdefs.optional.net.MimeMail"/>
     <tstamp/>
```

And finally, we will send an email outlining the testResults of our junit task.

```
    <mail messageMimeType="text/html"
              messageFile="overview-summary.html"
              tolist="jon@thomasfamily-net.com"
              mailhost="smtp.west.cox.net"
              subject="JUnit Test Results: ${TODAY}"
              from="zachsdaddy@cox.net">
       <fileset dir=".">
         <include name="TESTS-*.xml"/>
       </fileset>
     </mail>
   </target>
```

In the next code segment, the target "core" is used to call the buildfiles within the application itself by calling the buildfiles in the apps, components, and waf/src subdirectories. Each of these buildfiles will in turn recurse through all the lower level buildfiles within the components. By making our target run_tests a dependency of core, we can ensure that core's functionality will not be executed until after run_tests' at any time. If we wanted to add functionality to run_tests that would cause the buildfile to fail if any of the tests failed, we could easily do so here by using the Ant junit task's failOnError attribute.

```
<target name="core" depends="init, run_tests">
  <ant dir="components" target="core"/>
  <ant dir="waf/src" target="core"/>
  <ant dir="apps" target="core"/>
</target>
```

From here out there are no further modifications to this or any other lower level buildfile. That is all we had to do!

```
<target name="deploy" depends="init">
  <property name="j2ee.classpath"
value="${j2ee.home}/lib/j2ee.jar:${j2ee.home}/lib/system/cloudscape.jar:
${j2ee.home}/lib/system/tools.jar:${j2ee.home}/lib/cloudscape/RmiJdbc.jar:
${j2ee.home}/lib/cloudscape/cloudclient.jar:${j2ee.home}/lib/classes:
${j2ee.home}/classes:${j2ee.home}/lib/locale:${j2ee.home}/lib/jhall.jar"/>
  <java classname="com.sun.enterprise.tools.deployment.main.Main"
    fork="yes">
    <classpath path="${j2ee.classpath}"/>
    <sysproperty key="com.sun.enterprise.home" value="${j2ee.home}"/>
    <sysproperty key="org.omg.CORBA.ORBInitialPort" value="1050"/>
    <sysproperty key="java.security.policy"
    value="${j2ee.home}/lib/security/java.policy"/>
    <arg line="-deploy apps/petstore/build/petstore.ear local"/>
  </java>
  <java classname="com.sun.enterprise.tools.deployment.main.Main"
    fork="yes">
    <classpath path="${j2ee.classpath}"/>
    <sysproperty key="com.sun.enterprise.home" value="${j2ee.home}"/>
    <sysproperty key="org.omg.CORBA.ORBInitialPort" value="1050"/>
    <sysproperty key="java.security.policy"
    value="${j2ee.home}/lib/security/java.policy"/>
    <arg line="-deploy apps/opc/build/opc.ear local"/>
  </java>
  <java classname="com.sun.enterprise.tools.deployment.main.Main"
    fork="yes">
    <classpath path="${j2ee.classpath}"/>
    <sysproperty key="com.sun.enterprise.home" value="${j2ee.home}"/>
    <sysproperty key="org.omg.CORBA.ORBInitialPort" value="1050"/>
    <sysproperty key="java.security.policy"
    value="${j2ee.home}/lib/security/java.policy"/>
    <arg line="-deploy apps/supplier/build/supplier.ear local"/>
  </java>
```

```
        <java classname="com.sun.enterprise.tools.deployment.main.Main"
      fork="yes">
        <classpath path="${j2ee.classpath}"/>
        <sysproperty key="com.sun.enterprise.home" value="${j2ee.home}"/>
        <sysproperty key="org.omg.CORBA.ORBInitialPort" value="1050"/>
        <sysproperty key="java.security.policy"
      value="${j2ee.home}/lib/security/java.policy"/>
        <arg line="-deploy apps/admin/build/petstoreadmin.ear local"/>
      </java>
    </target>

    <target name="docs" depends="init, core">
      <echo message="Generating API Javadocs...."/>
      <mkdir dir="${petstore.javadocs.dir}"/>
      <javadoc packagenames="com.sun.j2ee.blueprints.*"
               destdir="${petstore.javadocs.dir}"
               author="false" version="true" use="true"
               windowtitle="Java Pet Store Demo API"
               doctitle="Java Pet Store Demo"
               bottom="Copyright &#169; 2001 Sun Microsystems Inc. All
               Rights Reserved.">
        <classpath>
          <pathelement path="/junit3.8.1/junit.jar"/>
          <pathelement path="/jakarta-cactus-13-20030715/lib/cactus-
          20030715.jar"/>
          <pathelement path="${j2ee.home}/lib/j2ee.jar"/>
          <pathelement path="components/address/build/classes"/>
          <pathelement path="components/asyncsender/build/classes"/>
          <pathelement path="components/cart/build/classes"/>
          <pathelement path="components/catalog/build/classes"/>
          <pathelement path="components/contactinfo/build/classes"/>
          <pathelement path="components/creditcard/build/classes"/>
          <pathelement path="components/customer/build/classes"/>
          <pathelement path="components/mailer/build/classes"/>
          <pathelement path="components/purchaseorder/build/classes"/>
          <pathelement path="components/signon/build/classes"/>
          <pathelement path="components/util/tracer/build/classes"/>
          <pathelement path="components/util/shared/build/classes"/>
          <pathelement path="components/xmldocuments/build/classes"/>
          <pathelement path="apps/admin/build/classes"/>
          <pathelement path="apps/opc/build/classes"/>
          <pathelement path="apps/petstore/build/classes"/>
          <pathelement path="apps/supplier/build/classes"/>
          <pathelement path="waf/build/classes"/>
        </classpath>
        <sourcepath>
          <pathelement path="components/address/src"/>
          <pathelement path="components/asyncsender/src"/>
          <pathelement path="components/cart/src"/>
          <pathelement path="components/catalog/src"/>
          <pathelement path="components/contactinfo/src"/>
```

```
              <pathelement path="components/creditcard/src"/>
              <pathelement path="components/customer/src"/>
              <pathelement path="components/mailer/src"/>
              <pathelement path="components/purchaseorder/src"/>
              <pathelement path="components/signon/src"/>
              <pathelement path="components/util/tracer/src"/>
              <pathelement path="components/util/shared/src"/>
              <pathelement path="components/xmldocuments/src"/>
              <pathelement path="apps/admin/src"/>
              <pathelement path="apps/opc/src"/>
              <pathelement path="apps/petstore/src"/>
              <pathelement path="apps/supplier/src"/>
              <pathelement path="waf/src"/>
          </sourcepath>
      </javadoc>
    </target>

    <target name="clean" depends="init">
      <ant dir="components" target="clean"/>
      <ant dir="waf/src" target="clean"/>
      <ant dir="apps" target="clean"/>
      <delete dir="${petstore.javadocs.dir}"/>
    </target>

    <target name="all" depends="core, docs"/>
  </project>
```

Through a few simple modifications to an existing (though somewhat intricate)
Ant build process, we were able to integrate a full application's worth of unit
tests so that each and every time the application itself is built, it is evaluated
and the results of all tests are reported. The output of the report email will follow a format similar to the one below:

```
Summary
Tests Failures          Errors  Success Rate    Time(s)
100    25        0      75%     0.725


Packages
Name Tests   Errors  Failures       Time(s)
com.sun.j2ee.blueprints.catalog.model        5       0       0       .0125
… more packages


Package com.sun.j2ee.blueprints.catalog.model
Name Tests   Errors  Failures       Time(s)
ProductTest  1       0       0       .0125
ItemTest     2       0       0       0.185
… more tests


…next package
```

A Guide to JUnit

JUnit is a testing package written in Java and based on the xUnit testing framework created by Kent Beck and Erich Gamma. JUnit is distributed under IBM's common public license. A bounty of information on JUnit is available through www.junit.org and www.xprogramming.com.

How JUnit Works

JUnit is a framework, so it does not require an installation per se. It is a grouping of Java packages that, once downloaded, can be added to the class path of any Java project and used within any existing code base. While there are many extensions for Java 2 Enterprise Edition (J2EE), JUnit is coupled only to the Java 2 Platform Standard Edition (J2SE) and so can be used for testing both enterprise and non-enterprise Java applications.

JUnit works with three concepts we have covered in this book and that are foundational to its use:

- **TestCase:** A class designed to test a unit of code.
- **TestSuite:** An aggregation of TestCases.
- **TestFixture:** A static classifier or object used within the scope of running a test. When creating TestCases in JUnit, TestFixtures are usually declared as uninitialized class members and then initialized in the setup method (which you'll see in a moment).

JUnit classes extend a class within the framework called TestCase (within the Junit.jar, this class is located at JUnit.framework.TestCase). From this class they inherit a Constructor that takes an array of arguments as well as two important methods. The first method

```
public void setup()
```

is used to initialize test fixtures for the testRun. If, for instance, one of the test fixtures used by your class (declared as a class member) is a Vector called vectorFixture, then in the setup() method you would probably include code to initialize its state and composition:

```
vectorFixture = new Vector();
    vectorFixture.add(someObjectNeededForTests);
    vectorFixture.add(someOtherObjectNeededForTests);
    vectorFixture.add(someThirdObjectNeededForTests);
```

Then when a test is called, the Vector is prepared for use.

NOTE

The setup() method is run before every test method in a TestCase, so you cannot depend on fixtures retaining state between test methods. This is a common misconception. Also, note that there is no correlation between the order of tests in a class and the order in which tests will execute. These tests are stored internally in a Vector and the order they run in will be Java Virtual Machine (JVM) dependent.

The teardown method—public void teardown()—can be used to deallocate or destroy fixtures used by a test. A good example of this is a test fixture that utilizes system resources and could result in a memory leak if resources are not released. If, for example, you have a database connection testFixture declared as a class member and initialized in setup(), then you could close it in (java.sql.Connection instance.close()) teardown and ensure that the resource will always be released.

How JUnit Runs Tests

To run actual test methods, JUnit uses reflection to inspect TestCase implementations for public void methods following the naming convention test<*some name*>. When designing unit tests, many developers follow the pattern of naming the test methods test<*methodName*> and often for functional or use case testing, many will use the pattern test<*behaviorOrUseCaseName*>. The important thing to know is that the JUnit framework will automatically run all methods whose names start with "test" that it finds in classes extending TestCase.

Downloading/Installing JUnit

JUnit is available from JUnit.org (www.junit.org). As of this writing, the current version is 3.8.1. Downloading the latest version will leave you with a ZIP file, which you can extract to your system in a location where class paths can reference it. As a rule of thumb I generally set this on Windows machines to *<system Drive>*:/JUnit and on Unix machines to /usr/local/JUnit. For the sake of documentation, we'll refer to the installation directory as *<JUnit_home>*. You can also set up an environment variable (JUNIT_HOME) to point to this directory.

Once it has been downloaded and the zip file is extracted, you will want to add the junit.jar file to the class path of your environments. These environments may include the following:

- System class path
- J2EE Application Server startup scripts
- IDE or project-specific class paths
- Source control systems that applications are built from

Note that by adding the junit.jar file to your source control system you ensure that it can be updated by any developer getting code from source control and then utilized by build scripts within source control, thus saving a great deal of time in bringing new developers up to speed with IDEs and projects.

At this point, you should be able to write and exercise a unit test with JUnit.

Writing TestCases

In addition to creating a framework for creating test classes, JUnit makes a great deal of testing functionality available to developers writing TestCases.

Assertions

Through its superclass Assert, TestCase offers a great deal of functionality that uses the Assertion pattern we discussed in Chapter 6. The Assert implementations allow you to test states that will fail if they are not met, and include a mechanism for passing custom messages to the TestRunner written by you (the testWriter) indicating a failure has occurred. The implementations of Assert included in TestCase are as follows.

assertTrue

```
public static void assertTrue(java.lang.String message,
                              boolean condition)
```

This method asserts that the Boolean argument passed in is true and fails the TestCase if it is not. This is useful in evaluating Boolean return values. This method allows you to create a message that will be sent to the TestRunner in the event that the assertion fails.

assertTrue

```
public static void assertTrue(boolean condition)
```

This is the same method as assertTrue(java.lang.String message, boolean condition) except that it does not include the custom failure message.

assertFalse

```
public static void assertFalse(java.lang.String message,
                               boolean condition)
```

This method asserts that the Boolean argument passed in is false and fails the TestCase if it is not. It is useful in evaluating Boolean return values. This method allows you to create a message that will be sent to the TestRunner in the event that the assertion fails.

assertFalse

```
public static void assertFalse(boolean condition)
```

This is the same method as assertFalse(java.lang.String message, boolean condition) except that it does not include the custom failure message.

assertEquals

```
public static void assertEquals(java.lang.String message,
                                java.lang.Object expected,
                                java.lang.Object actual)
```

This method asserts that two object references are equal and fails the TestCase if they are not. It also includes a mechanism for passing a custom error message to the TestRunner in the event of failure.

assertEquals

```
public static void assertEquals(java.lang.Object expected,
                                java.lang.Object actual)
```

This method asserts that two object references are equal and fails the TestCase if they are not.

assertEquals

```
public static void assertEquals(java.lang.String message,
                                java.lang.String expected,
                                java.lang.String actual)
```

This method asserts that two String values are equal and fails the TestCase if they are not. It also includes a mechanism for passing a custom error message to the TestRunner in the event of failure.

assertEquals

```
public static void assertEquals(java.lang.String expected,
                                java.lang.String actual)
```

This method asserts that two String values are equal and fails the TestCase if they are not.

assertEquals

```
public static void assertEquals(java.lang.String message,
                                double expected,
                                double actual,
                                double delta)
```

This method asserts that two double values are equal (within the range of a given delta) and fails the TestCase if they are not. It also includes a mechanism for passing a custom error message to the TestRunner in the event of failure.

If the expected value is infinity, then the delta value is ignored.

assertEquals

```
public static void assertEquals(double expected,
                                double actual,
                                double delta)
```

This method asserts that two double decimal values are equal (within the range of a given delta) and fails the TestCase if they are not.

If the expected value is infinity, then the delta value is ignored.

assertEquals

```
public static void assertEquals(java.lang.String message,
                                float expected,
                                float actual,
                                float delta)
```

This method asserts that two floating-point decimal values are equal (within the range of a given delta) and fails the TestCase if they are not. It also includes a mechanism for passing a custom error message to the TestRunner in the event of failure.

If the expected value is infinity, then the delta value is ignored.

assertEquals

```
public static void assertEquals(float expected,
                                float actual,
                                float delta)
```

This method asserts that two floating-point decimal values are equal (within the range of a given delta) and fails the TestCase if they are not.

If the expected value is infinity, then the delta value is ignored.

assertEquals

```
public static void assertEquals(java.lang.String message,
                                long expected,
                                long actual)
```

This method asserts that two long integer values are equal and fails the Test-Case if they are not. It also includes a mechanism for passing a custom error message to the TestRunner in the event of failure.

assertEquals

```
public static void assertEquals(long expected,
                                long actual)
```

This method asserts that two long integer values are equal and fails the Test-Case if they are not. It also includes a mechanism for passing a custom error message to the TestRunner in the event of failure.

assertEquals

```
public static void assertEquals(java.lang.String message,
                                boolean expected,
                                boolean actual)
```

This method asserts that two Boolean values are equal and fails the TestCase if they are not. It also includes a mechanism for passing a custom error message to the TestRunner in the event of failure.

assertEquals

```
public static void assertEquals(boolean expected,
                                boolean actual)
```

This method asserts that two Boolean values are equal and fails the TestCase if they are not.

assertEquals

```
public static void assertEquals(java.lang.String message,
                                byte expected,
                                byte actual)
```

This method asserts that two byte values are equal and fails the TestCase if they are not. It also includes a mechanism for passing a custom error message to the TestRunner in the event of failure.

assertEquals

```
public static void assertEquals(byte expected,
                                byte actual)
```

This method asserts that two byte values are equal and fails the TestCase if they are not.

assertEquals

```
public static void assertEquals(java.lang.String message,
                                char expected,
                                char actual)
```

This method asserts that two character values are equal and fails the TestCase if they are not. It also includes a mechanism for passing a custom error message to the TestRunner in the event of failure.

assertEquals

```
public static void assertEquals(char expected,
                                char actual)
```

This method asserts that two character values are equal and fails the TestCase if they are not.

assertEquals

```
public static void assertEquals(java.lang.String message,
                                short expected,
                                short actual)
```

This method asserts that two short integer values are equal and fails the Test-Case if they are not. It also includes a mechanism for passing a custom error message to the TestRunner in the event of failure.

assertEquals

```
public static void assertEquals(short expected,
                                short actual)
```

This method asserts that two short integer values are equal and fails the Test-Case if they are not.

assertEquals

```
public static void assertEquals(java.lang.String message,
                                int expected,
                                int actual)
```

This method asserts that two integer values are equal and fails the TestCase if they are not. It also includes a mechanism for passing a custom error message to the TestRunner in the event of failure

assertEquals

```
public static void assertEquals(int expected,
                                int actual)
```

This method asserts that two integer values are equal and fails the TestCase if they are not.

assertNotNull

```
public static void assertNotNull(java.lang.Object object)
```

This method asserts that an object reference is not null and fails the TestCase if it is.

assertNotNull

```
public static void assertNotNull(java.lang.String message,
                                 java.lang.Object object)
```

This method asserts that an object reference is not null and fails the TestCase if it is. It also includes a mechanism for passing a custom error message to the TestRunner in the event of failure.

assertNull

```
public static void assertNull(java.lang.Object object)
```

This method asserts that an object reference is null and fails the TestCase if it is not.

assertNull

```
public static void assertNull(java.lang.String message,
                              java.lang.Object object)
```

This method asserts that an object reference is null and fails the TestCase if it is not. It also includes a mechanism for passing a custom error message to the TestRunner in the event of failure.

assertSame

```
public static void assertSame(java.lang.String message,
                              java.lang.Object expected,
                              java.lang.Object actual)
```

This method asserts that two object references refer to the same location on the stack and fails the TestCase if they do not. It also includes a mechanism for passing a custom error message to the TestRunner in the event of failure.

assertSame

```
public static void assertSame(java.lang.Object expected,
                              java.lang.Object actual)
```

This method asserts that two object references refer to the same location on the stack and fails the TestCase if they do not.

assertNotSame

```
public static void assertNotSame(java.lang.String message,
                                 java.lang.Object expected,
                                 java.lang.Object actual)
```

This method asserts that two object references do not refer to the same location on the stack and fails the TestCase if they do. It also includes a mechanism for passing a custom error message to the TestRunner in the event of failure

assertNotSame

```
public static void assertNotSame(java.lang.Object expected,
                                 java.lang.Object actual)
```

This method asserts that two object references do not refer to the same location on the stack and fails the TestCase if they do.

Failures

Failing is a mechanism in the JUnit framework that allows you to terminate a TestCase at any point an unacceptable condition occurs. You can utilize either fail method:

- fail(String message);

  which fails the TestCase and sends the custom error message "message" to the TestRunner.

- fail():

  which fails the TestCase without the custom error message.

TestRunners

TestRunners are the user interfaces to JUnit. Three are built into JUnit:

- **JUnit.awtui.TestRunner:** Views the TestRunner using graphical controls native to the operating system.

- **JUnit.swingui.TestRunner:** Views the TestRunner using graphical controls implemented by Java Swing.

- **JUnit.textui.TestRunner:** Views the TestRunner as text output.

The TestRunners are designed to show the same information using different implementations. Extensions are also available to JUnit that you can use to extend TestRunner to other delivery methods and platforms. Figure A.1 shows an example of a successful test in one of the graphical TestRunners.

Figure A.1 TestRunner on a successful TestCase.

The TestRunner shows the name of the class under test (CUT), how many tests were run, how many failed, and how many resulted in errors. It also shows the duration of the test in seconds and a console window for testing output and stack traces. These elements are common to all GUIs for JUnit. If tests fail, the bar at the bottom of the graphical user interface (GUI) will be red instead of green.

The text-based TestRunner shows you simple information directly in the standard out of the JVM. TestCases can choose which TestRunner to implement in code.

Writing a JUnit Test

The steps to writing a JUnit test are simple:

- Extend JUnit.framework.TestCase.
- Set up test fixtures as class members.
- Write a setup() method to initialize test fixtures.
- Write test methods named testSomething using assertions.

The following listings contain JUnit test samples. Listing A.1 is a sample Test-Case, Listing A.2 shows sample TestCase that implements a class-level unit test, and Listing A.3 is a sample class under test.

```java
import JUnit.framework.TestCase;

public class SampleTest extends TestCase{

    private String id;

    public SampleTest(String[] args){
        super(args);
    }

    public void setup(){
        id = "Now is the time for all good men to ….";
    }


    public void testSampleMethod(){
        assertEquals("The ID was not set to the initialized value",id, "
Now is the time for all good men to ….");
    }


}
```

Listing A.1 Sample TestCase.

```
import JUnit.framework.TestCase;

public class PersonTest extends TestCase{

    private Person him;
    private int age;
    private String name;

    public PersonTest(String args){
        super(args);

    }

    public void setup(){
        him = new Person();
        name = "Jon-Jon";
        age = 1;
    }


    public void testSetName (){
        him.setName(name);
        assertEquals(him.getName(),name);
    }

    public void testSetAge(){
        him.setAge(age);
        assertEquals(him.getAge(),age);
    }

}
```

Listing A.2 Sample TestCase implementing a class-level unit test.

```
public class Person{
    private String name;
    private int age;

  public String getName(){
    return this.name;
  }

  public int getAge(){
    return this.age;
  }
```

Listing A.3 Sample class under test. (continues)

```
      public void setName(String name){
        this.name = name;
      }

      public void setAge(int age){
        this.age=age;
      }

  }
```

Listing A.3 Sample class under test. (continued)

More Information

As mentioned earlier, a vast amount of information on JUnit is available at JUnit.org as well as Xprogramming.com. The many extensions of JUnit (including Cactus, which we used in this book) can be invaluable to all Enterprise Java developers who want to unit-test their work.

Ant Reference

A nt is a widely used Java-based build tool. Due to its popularity, Ant has recently moved out from under the Jakarta umbrella and has become a top-level project at the Apache Software Foundation.

Ant allows the rules and properties of an application build to be defined in an XML file with specific tags. It then uses Java to parse the XML file and build, test, and deploy the application. At runtime Ant will look for a file in the working directory called build.xml.

There is a structure of elements within a buildfile that Ant uses to build an application. Those elements include the following:

- **Buildfile:** An XML file used to build applications.
- **Project:** A complete element of building for the buildfile (e.g., build application JAR files).
- **Property:** An element necessary for the build process (e.g., specific compiler or location of a certain directory for building files to).
- **Task:** An element of work completed by Ant (e.g., compile a file or directory, copy a file, delete a directory).
- **Attribute:** An element of information used to complete a task (e.g., the location of the file to be deleted).

Once the framework finds the buildfile, it will use the file to build your Java application.

Ant is platform independent and completely extensible in Java. It is an open-source project released under the Apache Software Foundation.

NOTE

It is not necessary within Ant to name your buildfile build.xml. Using the <antfile> attribute, you can pass the filename of your buildfile into Ant as an argument. This is useful when you're abstracting buildfile elements into functions or specific environments.

Downloading Ant

Ant can be downloaded from the download section at http://ant.apache.org/. As of this writing, the current version of Ant is 1.6.1. It can be downloaded as a binary (compiled) or source version. The source version exposes the Ant implementation files in precompiled format so that the framework can be extended. Downloading the latest version will leave you with a zip file.

Installing Ant

Because Ant is more of a framework than an application, installation is relatively simple. This file can be extracted to your system in a place that a class path can reference it. As a rule of thumb, I generally set this on Windows machines to *<system Drive>*:/Ant and on UNIX machines to /usr/local/ant. Ant also requires the existence of two environment variables: JAVA_HOME is a variable pointing to the installation directory of the J2SDK, and ANT_HOME should point to the directory that Ant was extracted to. Finally, the ANT_HOME/bin directory will need to be added to the PATH variable in your shell.

Using Ant to Build an Application

This section presents the key concepts and techniques required to build an application with Ant. We focus on two primary components of Ant: its tag reference and the buildfile.

Ant Tag Reference

Before we can build an XML file, it is important to get a sense of which tags are supported by Ant. Rather than attempting to discuss every tag available in Ant we focus on tags that are commonly used or necessary for the scope of the applications included in this book (Table B.1).

Table B.1 Ant Core Tasks (continues)

ANT TAG	PURPOSE
Ant	Makes a call against a project in another buildfile
AntCall	Makes a call against another project in this buildfile
Apply	Executes a system command
BUnzip2	Extracts a gzip or bzip archive
BZip2	Compresses a file using the Gzip or Bzip2 algorithm
Checksum	Generates a checksum for files
Chmod	Performs chmod on a filesystem object
Concat	Concatenates a number of files into a single file
Copy	Copies a file or file set to a new location
Cvs	Executes a command against a Concurrent Versioning System repository
CvsTagDiff	Generates an XML diff between two separate tags in a CVS repository
Delete	Deletes a file or file set
Dependset	Manages dependencies between files
Dirname	Determines the filesystem location of a file
Ear	Builds Java enterprise archives
Echo	Prints a message to the syslogger
Exec	Executes a system command
Fail	Exits the current build and throws a Java exception
FixCRLF	Used to localize character sets in a file
Get	Gets a file from a URL
GUnzip	Same as BUnzip2
GZip	Same as BZip2

Table B.1 Ant Core Tasks (continues)

ANT TAG	PURPOSE
Input	Prompts user for input
Jar	Builds a Java archive
Java	Executes a Java class
Javac	Executes the Java compiler
Javadoc/*Javadoc2*	Generates Java documentation
LoadFile	Loads a text file as a property
LoadProperties	Loads Java properties
Mail	Sends SMTP mail
Manifest	Builds manifest for a Java archive
Mkdir	Makes a new directory
Move	Moves a file set to a new location
Parallel	Run several tasks in concurrent threads
Patch	Applies a diff to files
Property	Sets a Java property
Record	A listener/logger for a buildfile
Replace	String replacer
Rmic	Compiles using RMIC
Sequential	Used within a parallel task to define execution of threads
SignJar	Signs Java archives
Sleep	Puts the current thread to sleep
Sql	Executes a SQL command
Style	Parses XSLT
Tar	Builds a tar archive
Tempfile	Sets a property name to a temporary file
Touch	Changes the last modified time of a file
TStam	Sets a timestamp
Unjar	Extracts a Java archive
Untar	Extracts a tar archive

Table B.1 Ant Core Tasks (continued)

ANT TAG	PURPOSE
Unwar	Extracts a Java Web application archive
Unzip	Extracts a zip archive
Waitfor	Blocks execution until some condition is met
War	Builds a Java Web application archive
XmlProperty	Loads properties from an XML file
Xslt	Processes a set of XSLT documents
Zip	Builds a zip archive

In addition to the tasks listed in Table B.1, you should be aware of a set of advanced Ant tasks located in Optional.jar. These tasks are commonly used in application development but are not part of Ant's core framework. Included are tasks for, but not limited to:

- Extended archive types
- Extended compilers
- Deployment tasks like FTP
- EJB tasks like EJBC
- Extended execution tasks
- Extended mail tasks
- JUnit tasks
- Remote tasks like Telnet
- IDE-specific tasks

Sample Ant Buildfile

This section contains one of the many buildfiles for the J2EE Petstore sample application introduced in Chapter 17. It uses many of the tags listed in Table B.1 and is designed to give you a sense of how a buildfile can be structured. To run this buildfile, navigate your shell to the working directory and execute Ant. To run on a specific target, call ant –targetName.

For purposes of discussion, we are going to break up this buildfile and insert explanations of key code segments.

```
<?xml version="1.0"?>

<!--
Copyright 2002 Sun Microsystems, Inc. All rights reserved.
```

In the following line the project is defined using the project tag. This is the top hierarchical level within this buildfile

```
<project name="petstore" default="core" basedir=".">
```

Here is the init target. By convention this is used to prepare the build and is called as a dependency by other top-level targets to ensure the project has been properly set up. Often you will find the global properties initialized in this target:

```
<target name="init">
  <!-- include user specific build properties first -->
  <property file="${user.home}/petstore.properties"/>
  <!-- include top-level common properties -->
  <property file="../../../build.properties"/>

  <property name="deploytool"
  value="${j2ee.home}/bin/deploytool${j2ee-script-suffix}"/>
  <property name="verifier" value="${j2ee.home}/bin/verifier$
  {j2ee-script-suffix}"/>

  <!-- JSTL -->
  <property name="jstl.lib" value="../../../lib/jstl"/>

  <property name="petstore.application.name" value="PetStoreEAR"/>

  <!-- The root directory of the workspace -->
  <property name="petstore.home" value=".."/>

  <!-- The destination directory for the builds -->
  <property name="petstore.build" value="${petstore.home}/build"/>
  <property name="petstore.buildjardir"
  value="${petstore.home}/build/ejbjar"/>
  <property name="petstore.build.war"
  value="${petstore.home}/build/war"/>

  <property name="petstore.src" value="${petstore.home}/src"/>
  <property name="petstore.lib" value="${petstore.home}/src/lib"/>

  <!-- The destination directory for all the compiled classes. -->
  <property name="petstore.classbindir"
  value="${petstore.build}/classes"/>

  <!-- The root directory of all the components. -->
  <property name="petstore.components.basedir" value="../../../
  components"/>

  <property name="petstore.docroot" value="${petstore.src}/docroot"/>
  <property name="petstore.war.lib" value="${petstore.build.war}/
  WEB-INF/lib"/>
  <property name="petstore.war.classes"
  value="${petstore.build.war}/WEB-INF/classes"/>

  <!-- The destination directory for all the javadocs. -->
  <property name="petstore.javadocs.dir"
  value="${petstore.build}/docs/api"/>

  <!-- WAF -->
  <property name="petstore.waf.home" value="../../../waf/"/>
  <property name="petstore.waf.classbindir"
  value="${petstore.waf.home}/build/classes"/>
```

```xml
<property name="petstore.waf.docroot"
value="${petstore.waf.home}/src/docroot"/>
<property name="petstore.waf.lib"
value="${petstore.waf.home}/src/lib"/>
<property name="petstore.waf.web.jar"
value="${petstore.waf.home}/build/waf-web.jar"/>
<property name="petstore.waf.ejbjar"
value="${petstore.waf.home}/build/waf-ejb.jar"/>
<property name="petstore.waf.ejbjar.client"
value="${petstore.waf.home}/build/waf-ejb-client.jar"/>

<!-- Tracer Component -->
<property name="petstore.tracer.home"
value="${petstore.components.basedir}/util/tracer"/>
<property name="petstore.tracer.client"
value="${petstore.tracer.home}/build/tracer.jar"/>

<!-- Service Locator Component -->
<property name="petstore.servicelocator.home" value="${petstore.
components.basedir}/servicelocator"/>
<property name="petstore.servicelocator.client"
value="${petstore.servicelocator.home}/build/servicelocator.jar"/>

<!-- XML Documents Component - this contains the PO/Invoice classes
-->
<property name="petstore.xmldocuments.home" value="${petstore.
components.basedir}/xmldocuments"/>
<property name="petstore.xmldocuments.client" value="${petstore.
xmldocuments.home}/build/xmldocuments.jar"/>

<!-- SignOn Component -->
<property name="petstore.signon.home"
value="${petstore.components.basedir}/signon"/>
<property name="petstore.signon.classbindir"
value="${petstore.signon.home}/build/classes"/>
<property name="petstore.signon.ejbjar"
value="${petstore.signon.home}/build/signon-ejb.jar"/>
<property name="petstore.signon.ejbjar.client"
value="${petstore.signon.home}/build/signon-ejb-client.jar"/>

<!-- Encoding Filter Component -->
<property name="petstore.encodingfilter.home" value="${petstore.
components.basedir}/encodingfilter"/>
<property name="petstore.encodingfilter.classbindir" value="$
{petstore.encodingfilter.home}/build/classes"/>

<!-- UniqueIdGenerator Component -->
<property name="petstore.uidgen.home"
value="${petstore.components.basedir}/uidgen"/>
```

```
<property name="petstore.uidgen.ejbjar"
value="${petstore.uidgen.home}/build/uidgen-ejb.jar"/>
<property name="petstore.uidgen.ejbjar.client"
value="${petstore.uidgen.home}/build/uidgen-ejb-client.jar"/>


<!-- Async Component -->
<property name="petstore.asyncsender.home" value="${petstore.
components.basedir}/asyncsender"/>
<property name="petstore.asyncsender.ejbjar"
value="${petstore.asyncsender.home}/build/asyncsender-ejb.jar"/>
<property name="petstore.asyncsender.ejbjar.client" value="$
{petstore.asyncsender.home}/build/asyncsender-ejb-client.jar"/>

<!-- Catalog Component -->
<property name="petstore.catalog.home" value="${petstore.
components.basedir}/catalog"/>
<property name="petstore.catalog.ejbjar"
value="${petstore.catalog.home}/build/catalog-ejb.jar"/>
<property name="petstore.catalog.ejbjar.client"
value="${petstore.catalog.home}/build/catalog-ejb-client.jar"/>

<!-- Cart Component -->
<property name="petstore.cart.home"
value="${petstore.components.basedir}/cart"/>
<property name="petstore.cart.ejbjar"
value="${petstore.cart.home}/build/cart-ejb.jar"/>
<property name="petstore.cart.ejbjar.client"
value="${petstore.cart.home}/build/cart-ejb-client.jar"/>

<!-- Customer Component -->
<property name="petstore.customer.home" value="${petstore.
components.basedir}/customer"/>
<property name="petstore.customer.ejbjar" value="${petstore.
customer.home}/build/customer-ejb.jar"/>
<property name="petstore.customer.ejbjar.client"
value="${petstore.customer.home}/build/customer-ejb-client.jar"/>

<!-- Petstore Components -->
<property name="petstore.war" value="petstore.war"/>
<property name="petstore.ear" value="petstore.ear"/>
<property name="petstore.ejbjar" value="petstore-ejb.jar"/>

<!-- Purchase Order Components -->
<property name="petstore.po.home"
value="${petstore.components.basedir}/purchaseorder"/>
<property name="petstore.po.ejbjar.client"
value="${petstore.po.home}/build/po-ejb-client.jar"/>
```

```
<!-- The classpath for J2EE classes. -->
<property name="j2ee.classpath"
value="${j2ee.home}/lib/j2ee.jar:${j2ee.home}/lib/locale:${j2ee.home
}/lib/j2eetools.jar"/>

<!-- Classpaths -->
<property name="petstore.classpath" value="${petstore.signon.
classbindir}:${petstore.uidgen.ejbjar.client}:${petstore.async-
sender.ejbjar.client}:${petstore.xmldocuments.client}:${petstore.
customer.ejbjar.client}:${petstore.cart.ejbjar.client}:${petstore.
catalog.ejbjar.client}:${petstore.tracer.client}:${petstore.waf.
classbindir}:${petstore.po.ejbjar.client}:${petstore.service
locator.client}:${petstore.classbindir}:${j2ee.classpath}"/>

</target>

<target name="compile" depends="init">
  <mkdir dir="${petstore.classbindir}"/>
  <!-- Petstore Classes -->
  <javac srcdir="${petstore.src}"
         destdir="${petstore.classbindir}"
         classpath="${petstore.classpath}"
         includes="com/**"/>
</target>
```

Here is a target used to build a Web application archive:

```
<target name="war" depends="init">
  <!-- Combine the waf and the petstore docroots -->
  <mkdir dir="${petstore.build.war}"/>
  <copy todir="${petstore.build.war}" >
   <fileset dir="${petstore.waf.docroot}">
    <exclude name="**.jsp"/>
    <exclude name="**/WEB-INF/*.xml"/>
   </fileset>
   <fileset dir="${petstore.docroot}"/>
  </copy>
  <!--combine the waf and petstore classes -->
  <mkdir dir="${petstore.war.lib}"/>
  <mkdir dir="${petstore.war.classes}"/>
  <copy file="${petstore.waf.web.jar}" todir="${petstore.war.lib}" />
  <copy todir="${petstore.war.classes}">
   <fileset dir= "${petstore.classbindir}">
    <exclude name="**/ejb/ShoppingClientControllerEJB.class"/>
    <exclude name="**/ejb/ShoppingClientFacadeLocalEJB.class"/>
    <exclude name="**/ejb/StateMachine.class"/>
    <exclude name="**/ejb/actions/**"/>
   </fileset>
  </copy>

  <!--Add In the JSTL Libraries and Classes -->
```

```xml
      <copy file="${jstl.lib}/standard.jar" todir="${petstore.war.lib}" />
      <copy file="${jstl.lib}/jstl.jar" todir="${petstore.war.lib}" />
      <copy file="${jstl.lib}/c.tld" todir="${petstore.build.war}/WEB-INF" />
      <copy file="${jstl.lib}/fmt.tld" todir="${petstore.build.war}/
      WEB-INF" />
      <!--Add the encoding fitler to petstore classes -->
      <copy todir="${petstore.war.classes}">
       <fileset dir= "${petstore.encodingfilter.classbindir}"/>
      </copy>
      <!--add the signon to the petstore classes -->
      <copy todir="${petstore.war.classes}">
       <fileset dir= "${petstore.signon.classbindir}">
        <!--exclude CreateUserServlet because we use an Action -->
        <exclude name="**/CreateUserServlet.class"/>
        <exclude name="**/ejb/**"/>
       </fileset>
      </copy>
      <!-- combination complete -->
      <!-- copy in the ejb client jars -->
      <copy file="${petstore.tracer.client}" todir="${petstore.war.lib}" />
      <copy file="${petstore.servicelocator.client}"
      todir="${petstore.war.lib}" />
      <copy file="${petstore.customer.ejbjar.client}"
      todir="${petstore.war.lib}" />
      <copy file="${petstore.waf.ejbjar.client}"
      todir="${petstore.war.lib}" />
      <copy file="${petstore.cart.ejbjar.client}"
      todir="${petstore.war.lib}" />
      <copy file="${petstore.signon.ejbjar.client}"
      todir="${petstore.war.lib}" />
      <copy file="${petstore.catalog.ejbjar.client}"
      todir="${petstore.war.lib}" />
      <copy file="${petstore.po.ejbjar.client}"
      todir="${petstore.war.lib}" />
      <delete file="${petstore.build}/${petstore.war}" quiet="true"/>
      <jar jarfile="${petstore.build}/${petstore.war}" basedir="$
      {petstore.build.war}" excludes="cvs" />
      <delete dir="${petstore.build}/${petstore.build.war}"/>
 </target>

 <target name="ejbjar" depends="init">
    <delete dir="${petstore.buildjardir}" quiet="true"/>
    <mkdir dir="${petstore.buildjardir}"/>
    <!-- copy in the petstore ejb action classes -->
    <copy todir="${petstore.buildjardir}" >
     <fileset dir= "${petstore.classbindir}">
      <include name="**/ejb/**"/>

      <include name="**/exceptions/**"/>
      <include name="**/events/**"/>
```

```
            <exclude name="**/web/**"/>
            <exclude name="**/view/**"/>
            <exclude name="**/test/**"/>
            <exclude name="**/util/tracer/**"/>
        </fileset>
    </copy>
    <unjar src="${petstore.waf.ejbjar}" dest="${petstore.buildjardir}"
/>
    <delete dir="${petstore.buildjardir}/META-INF" quiet="true"/>
    <delete dir="${petstore.buildjardir}/com/sun/j2ee/blueprints/util/
    tracer"/>
    <mkdir dir="${petstore.buildjardir}/META-INF"/>
    <copy file="ejb-jar.xml" tofile="${petstore.buildjardir}/
    META-INF/ejb-jar.xml" />
    <jar jarfile="${petstore.build}/${petstore.ejbjar}" basedir="$
    {petstore.buildjardir}" manifest="ejb-jar-manifest.mf"/>
    <delete dir="${petstore.buildjardir}"/>
</target>

<target name="ear" depends="init">
    <mkdir dir="${petstore.buildjardir}"/>
    <mkdir dir="${petstore.buildjardir}/META-INF"/>
    <copy file="${petstore.src}/application.xml"
    todir="${petstore.buildjardir}/META-INF/" />
    <copy file="${petstore.src}/sun-j2ee-ri.xml"
    todir="${petstore.buildjardir}/META-INF/" />
    <!-- Copy in the EJB jars -->
    <copy file="${petstore.customer.ejbjar}" todir="${petstore.
    buildjardir}" />
    <copy file="${petstore.build}/${petstore.ejbjar}" todir="$
    {petstore.buildjardir}" />
    <copy file="${petstore.signon.ejbjar}" todir="${petstore.
    buildjardir}" />
    <copy file="${petstore.asyncsender.ejbjar}" todir="${petstore.
    buildjardir}" />
    <copy file="${petstore.uidgen.ejbjar}" todir="${petstore.
    buildjardir}" />
    <copy file="${petstore.build}/${petstore.war}"
    todir="${petstore.buildjardir}" />
    <copy file="${petstore.catalog.ejbjar}" todir="${petstore.
    buildjardir}" />
    <copy file="${petstore.cart.ejbjar}" todir="${petstore.buildjardir}"
    />
    <!-- Copy in the client jars -->
    <copy file="${petstore.servicelocator.client}"
    todir="${petstore.buildjardir}" />

    <copy file="${petstore.customer.ejbjar.client}"
    todir="${petstore.buildjardir}" />
```

```
    <copy file="${petstore.signon.ejbjar.client}"
    todir="${petstore.buildjardir}" />
    <copy file="${petstore.uidgen.ejbjar.client}"
    todir="${petstore.buildjardir}" />
    <copy file="${petstore.catalog.ejbjar.client}"
    todir="${petstore.buildjardir}" />
    <copy file="${petstore.asyncsender.ejbjar.client}" todir="$
    {petstore.buildjardir}" />
    <copy file="${petstore.po.ejbjar.client}" todir="${petstore.
    buildjardir}" />
    <copy file="${petstore.cart.ejbjar.client}" todir="${petstore.
    buildjardir}" />
    <copy file="${petstore.tracer.client}" todir="${petstore.
    buildjardir}" />
    <copy file="${petstore.xmldocuments.client}"
    todir="${petstore.buildjardir}" />
    <!-- Delete the old Jar and rebuild -->
    <delete file="${petstore.build}/${petstore.ear}" quiet="true"/>
    <jar jarfile="${petstore.build}/${petstore.ear}" basedir="$
    {petstore.buildjardir}" />
    <delete dir="${petstore.buildjardir}"/>
  </target>
```

In a clean target, the contents of the build directory are deleted, by convention, to ensure a clean build:

```
<target name="clean" depends="init">
  <delete dir="${petstore.build}"/>
  <delete dir="${petstore.javadocs.dir}"/>
</target>
```

The following code verifies the validity of an enterprise archive:

```
<target name="verify" depends="init">
  <exec executable="${verifier}">
    <arg line="-w ${petstore.build}/${petstore.ear}"/>
  </exec>
</target>
```

In a deploy target, by convention, an application will be copied and deployed to a remote environment:

```
<target name="deploy" depends="init">
  <exec executable="${deploytool}">
      <arg line="-generateSQL ${petstore.build}/${petstore.ear}
${j2ee.server.name}" />
  </exec>
  <exec executable="${deploytool}">
      <arg line="-deploy ${petstore.build}/${petstore.ear}
${j2ee.server.name}" />
  </exec>
</target>
```

In an undeploy target, by convention, an application will be removed and undeployed from a remote environment:

```
<target name="undeploy" depends="init">
  <exec executable="${deploytool}">
      <arg line="-uninstall ${petstore.application.name}
${j2ee.server.name}" />
  </exec>
</target>


<target name="clean_all" depends="init,clean">
    <ant dir="${petstore.waf.home}/src" target="clean"/>
    <ant dir="${petstore.servicelocator.home}/src" target="clean"/>
    <ant dir="${petstore.tracer.home}/src" target="clean"/>
    <ant dir="${petstore.xmldocuments.home}/src" target="clean"/>
    <ant dir="${petstore.asyncsender.home}/src" target="clean"/>
    <ant dir="${petstore.customer.home}/src" target="clean"/>
    <ant dir="${petstore.catalog.home}/src" target="clean"/>
    <ant dir="${petstore.cart.home}/src" target="clean"/>
    <ant dir="${petstore.signon.home}/src" target="clean"/>
    <ant dir="${petstore.po.home}/src" target="clean"/>
    <ant dir="${petstore.encodingfilter.home}/src" target="clean"/>
    </target>
```

Here Ant is called on a number of subdirectories (looking for the project called *core* in each directory's build.xml):

```
<target name="components" depends="init">
    <ant dir="${petstore.servicelocator.home}/src" target="core"/>
    <ant dir="${petstore.tracer.home}/src" target="core"/>
    <ant dir="${petstore.xmldocuments.home}/src" target="core"/>
    <ant dir="${petstore.waf.home}/src" target="core"/>
    <ant dir="${petstore.asyncsender.home}/src" target="core"/>
    <ant dir="${petstore.customer.home}/src" target="core"/>
    <ant dir="${petstore.catalog.home}/src" target="core"/>
    <ant dir="${petstore.cart.home}/src" target="core"/>
    <ant dir="${petstore.signon.home}/src" target="core"/>
    <ant dir="${petstore.uidgen.home}/src" target="core"/>
    <ant dir="${petstore.po.home}/src" target="core"/>
    <ant dir="${petstore.encodingfilter.home}/src" target="core"/>
    </target>
```

By convention a target called docs is used to build and place the API docs for the application:

```
<target name="docs" depends="init, core">
    <mkdir dir="${petstore.javadocs.dir}"/>
    <javadoc packagenames="com.sun.j2ee.blueprints.*"
             destdir="${petstore.javadocs.dir}"
             author="false" version="true" use="true"
             windowtitle="Java Pet Store Application API"
             doctitle="Java Pet Store Application"
             bottom="Copyright &#169; 2001 Sun Microsystems Inc. All
             Rights Reserved.">
    <classpath>
        <pathelement path="${j2ee.home}/lib/j2ee.jar"/>
        <pathelement path="${petstore.waf.home}/build/classes"/>
        <pathelement
path="${petstore.servicelocator.home}/build/classes"/>
        <pathelement path="${petstore.tracer.home}/build/classes"/>
        <pathelement
path="${petstore.xmldocuments.home}/build/classes"/>
        <pathelement path="${petstore.asyncsender.home}/build/classes"/>
        <pathelement path="${petstore.customer.home}/build/classes"/>
        <pathelement path="${petstore.catalog.home}/build/classes"/>
        <pathelement path="${petstore.cart.home}/build/classes"/>
        <pathelement path="${petstore.signon.home}/build/classes"/>
        <pathelement path="${petstore.uidgen.home}/build/classes"/>
        <pathelement path="${petstore.po.home}/build/classes"/>
        <pathelement path="${petstore.classbindir}"/>
    </classpath>
    <sourcepath>
        <pathelement path="${petstore.waf.home}/src"/>
        <pathelement path="${petstore.tracer.home}/src"/>
        <pathelement path="${petstore.xmldocuments.home}/src"/>
        <pathelement path="${petstore.asyncsender.home}/src"/>
        <pathelement path="${petstore.customer.home}/src"/>
        <pathelement path="${petstore.catalog.home}/src"/>
        <pathelement path="${petstore.cart.home}/src"/>
        <pathelement path="${petstore.signon.home}/src"/>
        <pathelement path="${petstore.uidgen.home}/src"/>
        <pathelement path="${petstore.po.home}/src"/>
        <pathelement path="${petstore.encodingfilter.home}/src"/>
        <pathelement path="."/>
    </sourcepath>
    </javadoc>
</target>
```

The banner target is used to print a build header out to the syslogger:

```
<target name="banner">
    <echo>+--------------------------------------+</echo>
    <echo>+    Building Petstore Application     +</echo>
    <echo>+--------------------------------------+</echo>
</target>
<target name="small" depends="compile, ejbjar, war, ear" />
<target name="core" depends="components, banner, compile, ejbjar, war,
ear" />
<target name="all" depends="components, core, docs" />
</project>
```

Additional Resources

A wealth of information is available on the Ant Web site at http://ant.apache.
org/ (especially a great article called "Ant in Anger"). The book *Professional
Java Tools for Extreme Programming*, written by Rick Hightower, et al. and
published by Wrox, contains a fantastic amount of detail about using Ant with
other tools (like XDoclet) to build Web components, EJBs, Struts applications,
and more. And finally, *Java Development with Ant*, by Erik Hatcher and Steve
Loughran (Manning Publications, 2002), is a great resource for anyone looking
to get the most from Ant.

DbUnit Reference

M ost enterprise applications are constructed with a database in mind. Databases, however, create interesting dependency scenarios when it comes to effective white box testing. At one level, isolating application code from a data store is an effective means of testing such code. As demonstrated earlier, the Mock DAO pattern and the Test Database pattern can be quite powerful in isolating code from a database.

Nevertheless, this level of code segregation is not always easy. Unit testing of EJB Entity beans is practically impossible without a container and an associated data store. Furthermore, applications using JDO-like frameworks also have slight difficulties in creating isolation levels without databases.

At another level, one can simply split code into subsystems and attempt to create various degrees of isolation. One common subsystem is a database and its associated access layer. Ideally, testing this sub-system would entail controlling the database as much as possible so as to isolate and test the code lying directly above the store.

Controlling a data store apart from any associated code, however, would require the database's state to be known at all times. Before any test was run, the database would need to contain all expected data; furthermore, after the test was complete, the database would probably contain some altered set of data.

As a database is simply a static store of records, ensuring the existence and validity of its contents for a test would imply some mechanism for loading a desired data set and possibly retrieving a data set.

Let's explore an example subsystem, and, in the process, determine an ideal mechanism for managing a database.

Example

Imagine a dictionary application having an interface named WordDAO, which communicates with a data store containing a WORD table, a DEFINITION table, and a SYNONYM table. WordDAO specifies the usual CRUD business methods, which interact with a database creating words, finding words, updating and deleting words. Figure C.1 shows a diagram of our simple application, and Listing C.1 contains the WordDAO interface code.

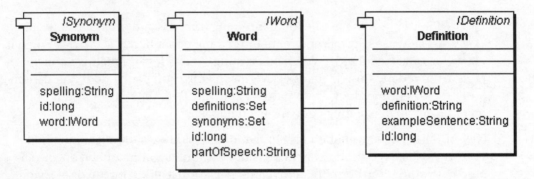

Figure C.1 The dictionary application.

```
public interface WordDAO {

    void updateWord(IWord word) throws UpdateException;

    void removeWord(IWord word) throws RemoveException;

    IWord findWord(String word) throws FindException;

    void createWord(IWord word) throws CreateException;
}

CREATE TABLE definition (
  DEFINITION_ID bigint(20) NOT NULL default '0',
  DEFINITION text NOT NULL,
```

Listing C.1 WordDAO interface. (continues)

```
    WORD_ID bigint(20) NOT NULL default '0',
    EXAMPLE_SENTENCE text,
    PRIMARY KEY  (DEFINITION_ID)
)

CREATE TABLE synonym (
    SYNONYM_ID bigint(20) NOT NULL default '0',
    WORD_ID bigint(20) NOT NULL default '0',
    SPELLING varchar(100) NOT NULL default '',
    PRIMARY KEY  (SYNONYM_ID)
)

CREATE TABLE word (
    WORD_ID bigint(20) NOT NULL default '0',
    PART_OF_SPEECH varchar(100) NOT NULL default '',
    SPELLING varchar(100) NOT NULL default '',
    PRIMARY KEY  (WORD_ID),
    UNIQUE KEY UniqueWord (SPELLING)
)
```

Listing C.1 WordDAO interface. (continued)

As we are interested in testing WordDAO's functionality, we will write a few tests for the object's business methods. CRUD business methods, however, undoubtedly depend on a predefined set of records in a database. For example, to find a record in the WORD table, the word and its various relationships (definitions and synonyms) must exist in the database. Moreover, deleting a word assumes its existence in a table, as does updating a word. Creating a word *may* require some subset of data in the database, such as static lookup values, perhaps representing the parts of speech (nouns, adjectives, etc).

- Before running our findWordTest, some mechanism would load data into WordDAO's corresponding tables (WORD, DEFINITION, and SYNONYM) such that our test could ensure the find operation worked properly. What's more, when we move on to test the create operation, we may not be too concerned on the data in the database before our test (unless we wanted to verify the create could handle an update scenario if the data already existed in the store); however, we would certainly want to guarantee the existence of properly loaded records in the WORD, DEFINITION, and SYNONYM tables after the test ran.

- Effective testing, additionally, requires tests be completely self-contained and not depend on previous tests. Nor should tests rely on outside dependencies existing in a known state.

- For example, imagine a test suite containing a test case which finds a record, in our case, a word. The test suite also contains a test case which removes the same word. If the database were loaded with our sample dataset *before* running any tests and our remove test ran *before* the find test, it's easy to see that the proceeding find test will fail. Consequently, this possible occurrence implies that a database's state should be controlled at a fine grained level, most likely at the test case.

Database Controller Use Case

Our use case, thus far, stipulates three requirements for a database controlling framework for component testing. First, managing records in a database before a test is absolutely necessary. We can not write a test without the confidence of knowing that any required data is present in the database. Second, having the ability to verify a database's contents at the completion of a test is essential to actually validating a test case. Lastly, the ability to manage database state should be exposed at the lowest level possible, ideally at an individual test case, so as to facilitate self-contained, non dependent tests.

The JUnit Model

Luckily, two of our requirements happen to fit quite well with the JUnit model of unit testing, as JUnit espouses the notion of test *fixtures*. Fixtures allow test cases to share a common set of objects or configurations through the process of overriding TestCase's setUp() and tearDown() lifecycle methods.

The fixture model meets requirement one, in that before each test case, the setUp() method could load a desired data set. Furthermore, tearDown() could be used to clean the database after test case completion.

What's more, requirement three has also been met, as JUnit's fixture model allows a fine grained level of control over test cases. Each test case can be configured within the context of a test suite and not depend on, for example, the database having been properly seeded by some previous method in a build process.

Data Format

One aspect we have not attempted to consider thus far is how to represent our desired record set. There are various options available; for example, we could have files containing SQL insert statements.

```
INSERT INTO definition VALUES (10,'Combative in nature;
belligerent.',1,'The pugnacious youth had no friends left to
pick on.'),(11,'Performed with a natural, offhand ease',2,'Joey
had a glib conversation with the principle- it surprised all of
```

```
us.'),(12,'Marked by ease and fluency of speech or writing that
often suggests or stems from insincerity, superficiality, or
deceitfulness',2,'The glib waiter received no tip.'),(14,'To
move unsteadily; to totter, waver, roll, etc.',3,NULL),(15,'To
feel nausea.',3,NULL);


INSERT INTO synonym VALUES (20,1,'belligerent'),(21,1,'aggres-
sive'),(30,2,'artful'),(31,2,
'suave'),(32,2,'insincere'),(33,2,'urbane');

INSERT INTO word VALUES
(1,'Adjective','pugnacious'),(2,'Adjective','glib'),(3,'Verb','
wamble');
```

Creating SQL files can work; however, this mechanism may not be entirely portable between databases. Additionally, these files can become cumbersome if there is a lot of data defined.

What's needed is a portable representation of database records. CSV files are a standard format which could easily work; however, we can be far more expressive of a data model with XML, as we can use elements to match table names and attributes to correspond with column names.

```xml
<?xml version='1.0' encoding='UTF-8'?>

<dataset>

<word WORD_ID="1" SPELLING="pugnacious"
PART_OF_SPEECH="Adjective"/>

<definition DEFINITION_ID="10"
            DEFINITION-"Combative in nature; belligerent."
            WORD_ID="1"
            EXAMPLE_SENTENCE="The pugnacious youth had no
friends left to pick on."/>

<synonym SYNONYM_ID="20" WORD_ID="1" SPELLING="belligerent"/>
<synonym SYNONYM_ID="21" WORD_ID="1" SPELLING="aqqressive"/>

</dataset>
```

Ideal Solution

With our high level requirements identified, we can begin to visualize our database management framework. The framework will integrate with JUnit and allow a database dataset to be controlled via the fixture model; moreover, the framework will provide an API for retrieving datasets. Lastly, the framework will allow the definition of XML file based datasets which can be read and processed via the framework.

Apparently, we are not the only ones who are in need of a database controlling framework for component testing. The open source DbUnit framework meets all our needs and more.

Working with DbUnit

DbUnit is an elegant database controlling framework; it can plug into JUnit quite nicely, and it allows for XML datasets. Moreover, DbUnit comes with a slick database export mechanism along with a pluggable Ant task for a further level of database management.

Seed File Creation

The first step to begin utilizing DbUnit involves the creation of datasets. DbUnit has multiple methods for representing datasets through its IDataSet interface, with the FlatXMLDataSet implementation the most commonly used.

The FlatXMLDataSet object represents a dataset in an intuitive manner, as table names match XML elements and a table's columns match the corresponding element's attributes.

For example, the DEFINITION table is defined with the following columns: definition_id, definition, word_id, and example_sentence. The corresponding DbUnit XML definition would have the following properties defined in DTD format:

```
<!ELEMENT dataset (
    definition*,
    synonym*,
    word*)>

<!ELEMENT definition EMPTY>
<!ATTLIST definition
    DEFINITION_ID CDATA #REQUIRED
    DEFINITION CDATA #REQUIRED
    WORD_ID CDATA #REQUIRED
    EXAMPLE_SENTENCE CDATA #IMPLIED >
```

Consequently, the XML would appear as follows:

```
<definition DEFINITION_ID="" DEFINITION=""
    WORD_ID="" EXAMPLE_SENTENCE=" "/>
```

Defining the XML format for a small database application, like our example Word application, with three tables and relatively few columns is easy; however, most enterprise systems have far more tables and columns.

Luckily, DbUnit provides a simple API for generating XML datasets with corresponding DTDs. The process involves three high level tasks: one, create a database connection using DbUnit's IDatabaseConnection class, two, create an IDataSet object, and lastly, write the subsequent IDataSet to a file. As we most likely will need to generate XML datasets often, let's create a simple utility to facilitate the creation of these files.

Conceptually, connecting to a database will require the standard connection information such as database location, user name, password, and database driver. Additionally, as we will be creating files, we'll need a file name and location. Since DbUnit's database export API allows one to select desired tables, we will also want to represent a collection of table names. We can represent this data in a JavaBean as shown in Listing C.2.

```java
public class DBUnitConfiguration {
  private String driver;
  private String databaseURL;
  private String user;
  private String password;
  private String fileLocation;
  private String schemaName;
  private String[] tables;

public DBUnitConfiguration() {
  super();
}

public String getDatabaseURL() {
  return databaseURL;
}

public String getDriver() {
  return driver;
}

public String getPassword() {
  return password;
}

public String[] getTables() {
  return tables;
}
```

Listing C.2 DBUnitConfiguration. (continues)

```
        public String getUser() {
        return user;
        }

        public void setDatabaseURL(final String string) {
         databaseURL = string;
        }

        public void setDriver(final String string) {
         driver = string;
        }

        public void setPassword(final String string) {
         password = string;
        }

        public void setUser(final String string) {
         user = string;
        }

        public void setTables(final String[] tables) {
         this.tables = tables;
        }

        public String getFileLocation() {
         return fileLocation;
        }

        public String getSchemaName() {
         return schemaName;
        }

        public void setFileLocation(final String string) {
         fileLocation = string;
        }

        public void setSchemaName(final String string) {
         schemaName = string;
        }


        }
```

Listing C.2 DBUnitConfiguration. (continued)

Next, let's define an object called DBUnitSeedFileCreator, which takes our
DBUnitConfiguration object and implements the three tasks defined above.

Creating an IDatabaseConnection object is trivial; in fact, it is simply a wrapper around a normal JDBC Connection object (Listing C.3).

```
private static IDatabaseConnection getDBUnitConnectionType(
    final DBUnitConfiguration dbConfig) throws
ClassNotFoundException, SQLException{

 Class.forName(dbConfig.getDriver());
 final Connection jdbcConnection =
 DriverManager.getConnection(dbConfig.getDatabaseURL(),
    dbConfig.getUser(), dbConfig.getPassword());
 return new DatabaseConnection(jdbcConnection);
}
```

Listing C.3 IDatabaseConnection.

Next, we create an IDataSet from our IDatabaseConnection object. As one can create a dataset from a subset of tables, we create simple conditional testing for the existence of the tables array:

```
final IDatabaseConnection conn =
 DBUnitSeedFileCreator.getDBUnitConnectionType(dbConfig);
IDataSet fullDataSet = null;
if(dbConfig.getTables() != null) {
    fullDataSet = conn.createDataSet(dbConfig.getTables());
}else {
    fullDataSet = conn.createDataSet();
}
```

Subsequently, we write the retrieved IDataSet to a file, creating both an XML file and its equivalent DTD.

```
final FileWriter xmlWrtr =
DBUnitSeedFileCreator.getFullyQualifiedXMLFileWriter(dbConfig);

FlatXmlDataSet.write(fullDataSet, xmlWrtr);

final FileWriter dtdWrtr = DBUnitSeedFileCreator.getFullyQualifiedDTD-
FileWriter(dbConfig);
// write DTD file
IDataSet dataset = null;
if(dbConfig.getTables() != null) {
  dataset = conn.createDataSet(dbConfig.getTables());
}else {
  dataset = conn.createDataSet();
}

FlatDtdDataSet.write(dataset, dtdWrtr);
```

Lastly, we create a specialized exception type, DBUnitSeedFileException to capture the range of possible exceptions that can be thrown during our processing, giving us our DBUnitSeedFileCreator (Listing C.4). With these two classes in place, we can now generate XML datasets quite easily.

```java
public class DBUnitSeedFileCreator {


private DBUnitSeedFileCreator() {
  super();
}

public static void createDBUnitLoadFile(final DBUnitConfiguration dbCon-
fig) throws DBUnitSeedFileException{
 try{

final IDatabaseConnection conn
DBUnitSeedFileCreator.getDBUnitConnectionType(dbConfig);
IDataSet fullDataSet = null;
if(dbConfig.getTables() != null) {
   fullDataSet = conn.createDataSet(dbConfig.getTables());
}else {
  fullDataSet = conn.createDataSet();
}

final FileWriter xmlWrtr =
DBUnitSeedFileCreator.getFullyQualifiedXMLFileWriter(dbConfig);

FlatXmlDataSet.write(fullDataSet, xmlWrtr);

final FileWriter dtdWrtr =
DBUnitSeedFileCreator.getFullyQualifiedDTDFileWriter(dbConfig);
// write DTD file
IDataSet dataset = null;
if(dbConfig.getTables() != null) {
 dataset = conn.createDataSet(dbConfig.getTables());
}else {
  dataset = conn.createDataSet();
}

FlatDtdDataSet.write(dataset, dtdWrtr);

}catch(ClassNotFoundException e){
throw new DBUnitSeedFileException("ClassNotFoundException occured while
trying to generate a seed file", e);
```

Listing C.4 DBUnitSeedFileCreator. (continues)

```
    }catch(SQLException e1){
    throw new DBUnitSeedFileException("SQLException occured while trying to
    generate a seed file", e1);
    }catch(IOException e2){
    throw new DBUnitSeedFileException("IOException occured while trying to
    generate a seed file", e2);
    }catch(DataSetException e3){
    throw new DBUnitSeedFileException("DataSetException occured while trying
    to generate a seed file", e3);
     }
    }

    private static FileWriter getFullyQualifiedXMLFileWriter(
      final DBUnitConfiguration dbConfig) throws IOException{
      final String fullName = DBUnitSeedFileCreator.getFileName(dbConfig,
    ".xml");
      return new FileWriter(fullName);
    }

    private static FileWriter getFullyQualifiedDTDFileWriter(
      final DBUnitConfiguration dbConfig) throws IOException{
     final String fullName = DBUnitSeedFileCreator.getFileName(dbConfig,
    ".dtd");
     return new FileWriter(fullName);
    }

    private static String getFileName(
      final DBUnitConfiguration dbConfig, final String extention){

     return dbConfig.getFileLocation() + System.getProperty("file.separa-
    tor") +
        dbConfig.getSchemaName() + " seed" + extention;
    }

    private static IDatabaseConnection getDBUnitConnectionType(
       final DBUnitConfiguration dbConfig) throws ClassNotFoundException,
    SQLException{

      Class.forName(dbConfig.getDriver());
      final Connection jdbcConnection =
       DriverManager.getConnection(dbConfig.getDatabaseURL(),
    dbConfig.getUser(), dbConfig.getPassword());
      return new DatabaseConnection(jdbcConnection);
     }
    }
```

Listing C.4 DBUnitSeedFileCreator. (continued)

Database Operations

DbUnit supports a wide range of database operations which effectively work on datasets. Found in the DatabaseOperation class, these operations take the form of standard SQL commands such as INSERT, and DELETE; however, DbUnit augments these commands with an elegant level of sophistication to enhance testing.

As of DbUnit 2.1, DatabaseOperation contains eleven operations, which work on XML datasets, with the most commonly utilized being DatabaseOperation .DELETE, DatabaseOperation.DELETE_ALL, DatabaseOperation.INSERT, DatabaseOperation.UPDATE, DatabaseOperation.REFRESH, DatabaseOperation .CLEAN_INSERT, and DatabaseOperation.NONE.

DatabaseOperation.DELETE removes all rows in a database table which correspond to dataset elements. This operation, however, does not delete additional data found in tables which are not found in an XML dataset. For example, if our dataset contained the following words

```
<word WORD_ID="1" SPELLING="pugnacious"
PART_OF_SPEECH="Adjective"/>
<word WORD_ID="2" SPELLING="glib" PART_OF_SPEECH="Adjective"/>
```

and our database contained an additional row containing word_id equal to three, following execution of DatabaseOperation.DELETE, the table would only contain one row with word_id equal to 3.

DatabaseOperation.DELETE_ALL is slightly less discriminating, as this operation will completely empty any table corresponding with any element found in a dataset. In the above example, all three rows in the WORD table would be removed leaving the table empty.

The DatabaseOperation.INSERT operation simply attempts to insert all data found in an XML dataset. This operation executes a blind insert and caution should be applied as data clashes can occur. DatabaseOperation .CLEAN_INSERT is a bit more cautious as it first executes a Database Operation.DELETE_ALL followed by a DatabaseOperation.INSERT. This circumspect action ensures no data clashing.

DatabaseOperation.UPDATE is much like a normal database update command, in that it assumes the data already exits in the database. When it finds a corresponding row matching in an XML dataset, the row is updated with the corresponding attributes.

Combining the logic of DatabaseOperation.INSERT and DatabaseOperation
.UPDATE, DatabaseOperation.REFRESH simply inserts any XML elements not
found in the database and updates any rows which do correspond to XML elements.

Interestingly enough, DatabaseOperation.NONE comes in quite handy once
one has mastered the test-database management life cycle as this operation is
conceptually a NOOP, allowing a database to be unchanged in a test life-cycle.

As you will quickly see, these operations are the fundamental building blocks
for utilizing DbUnit with JUnit as their execution affect the state of a database
in the context of a fixture.

Plugging DbUnit in with JUnit

With datasets defined and an understanding of DbUnit's DatabaseOperation
API, it becomes quite easy to see how one can effectively manage a database
with JUnit.

DbUnit offers three ways to incorporate its features into JUnit. One can simply extend from DbUnit's custom DatabaseTestCase, or one can delegate all
database operations in normal JUnit TestCase's via fixtures, or utilize DbUnit's
custom Ant tags to wrap test case execution.

Extending DatabaseTestCase

The DbUnit framework offers a custom test case called DatabaseTestCase
which extends JUnit's TestCase. With this class, it becomes incredibly simple
to take advantage of DbUnit's features within a test suite.

Central to the DatabaseTestCase's functionality is its adoption of the Template
Design pattern. There are two Abstract methods, getConnection() and get-
DataSet(), which essentially configure the test suite. Additionally, there are
two methods which can be overridden, getSetUpOperation() and getTear-
DownOperation(), which create a test case fixture to control the state of a
database.

The getConnection() method is required to create a connection to a desired
database and returns the IConnection object; moreover, the getDataSet()
method is where a dataset is constructed using any implementation of
IDataSet.

For example, the easiest way to create a FlatXmlDataSet is to pass in a File object. This File object, consequently, is the XML dataset.

```
protected IDataSet getDataSet() throws Exception {
   return new FlatXmlDataSet(new File("words.xml"));
}
```

The setUp() and tearDown() found in DatabaseTestCase's base class methods have been overridden to call the executeOperation() method. This method essentially acts upon the DatabaseOperation objects returned from the getSetUpOperation() and getTearDownOperation() methods. For example, the default implementation of DatabaseTestCase defines the following getSetUpOperation() and getTearDownOperation():

```
protected DatabaseOperation getSetUpOperation() throws
Exception {
        return DatabaseOperation.CLEAN_INSERT;
}

protected DatabaseOperation getTearDownOperation() throws
Exception
{
        return DatabaseOperation.NONE;
}
```

This sequence, consequently, will perform a CLEAN_INSERT in the set up phase of a fixture and leave the database untouched in the tear down phase as demonstrated below with both setup() and tearDown() calling executeOperation().

```
protected void setUp() throws Exception{
  super.setUp();
  executeOperation(getSetUpOperation());
}

protected void tearDown() throws Exception{
  super.tearDown();
  executeOperation(getTearDownOperation());
}

private void executeOperation(DatabaseOperation operation) throws
Exception{
    if (operation != DatabaseOperation.NONE) {
      IDatabaseConnection connection = getConnection();
      try{
         operation.execute(connection, getDataSet());
      }finally{
         closeConnection(connection);
      }
    }
}
```

Writing an actual test case using DatabaseTestCase is quite simple and should be familiar to anyone who has coded a normal JUnit test suite. Simply extend DatabaseTestCase, implement both getConnection() and getDataSet() and you are good to go.

For example, Listing C.5 is a test suite containing a test case which attempts to find a word in a configured database. Both getConnection() and getDataSet() have been implemented and the test suite leaves the default database lifecycle behavior.

```java
import java.io.File;
import java.sql.Connection;
import java.sql.DriverManager;
import java.util.Iterator;

import junit.framework.TestCase;

import org.aglover.words.bizobj.IDefinition;
import org.aglover.words.bizobj.IWord;
import org.aglover.words.dao.impl.WordDAOImpl;
import org.dbunit.DatabaseTestCase;
import org.dbunit.database.DatabaseConnection;
import org.dbunit.database.IDatabaseConnection;
import org.dbunit.dataset.IDataSet;
import org.dbunit.dataset.xml.FlatXmlDataSet;


public class DefaultWordDAOImplTest extends DatabaseTestCase {

    public void testFindVerifyDefinition() throws Exception{
        WordDAOImpl dao = new WordDAOImpl();
        IWord wrd = dao.findWord("pugnacious");

        for(Iterator iter = wrd.getDefinitions().iterator();
iter.hasNext();){
            IDefinition def = (IDefinition)iter.next();
            TestCase.assertEquals("size should be Combative in
nature; belligerent.",
                "Combative in nature; belligerent.",
def.getDefinition());
        }
    }

    protected IDatabaseConnection getConnection() throws
Exception {
        Class driverClass = Class.forName("org.gjt.mm.mysql.Driver");
```

Listing C.5 Test case that attempts to find a word in a configured database. (continues)

```
        Connection jdbcConnection =
            DriverManager.getConnection("jdbc:mysql://localhost/words",
                    "words", "words");

        return new DatabaseConnection(jdbcConnection);
    }

    protected IDataSet getDataSet() throws Exception {
        return new FlatXmlDataSet(
            new File("test/conf/words-seed.xml"));
    }

    public static void main(String[] args) {
    junit.textui.TestRunner.run(DefaultWordDAOImplTest.class);
    }

    public DefaultWordDAOImplTest(String arg0) {
        super(arg0);
    }
}
```

Listing C.5 Test case that attempts to find a word in a configured database. (continued)

Using DbUnit's Query API

While we have control over a database's state using the DatabaseOperation class, we also need the ability to assert various aspects of tests, like the contents of a table after an insert operation. To that extent, DbUnit provides a database query API and a comparison mechanism using a custom Assertion class in combination with the XML load files created earlier.

Essentially, to take advantage of this feature, we'll have to define a second "expected" dataset via XML and then compare that data with the data found in the database. As shown below, after we've created a new word in the database, we'd like to assert its existence in the WORD table.

We first define an expected dataset:

```
<?xml version='1.0' encoding='UTF-8'?>
<dataset>
<word WORD_ID="3" SPELLING="ancillary"
PART_OF_SPEECH="Adjective"/>
</dataset>
```

In our test case, testCreate(), we create the corresponding word, "ancillary" and then proceed to assert its existence in the WORD table.

```
public void testCreate() throws Exception{
   IWord word = new Word();
   word.setSpelling("ancillary");
   word.setPartOfSpeech(PartOfSpeechEnum.ADJECTIVE.getPartOfSpeech());

   Set definitions = this.getDefinitionsForWord(word);
   word.setDefinitions(definitions);
   Set syns = this.getSynonymsForWord(word);
   word.setSynonyms(syns);

   WordDAOImpl dao = new WordDAOImpl();
   dao.createWord(word);

    ITable actualJoinData = this.getConnection().
        createQueryTable("TestResult",
            "SELECT * FROM WORD WHERE WORD.SPELLING=\"ancillary\"");

    IDataSet expectedDataSet = new FlatXmlDataSet(
            new File("test/conf/expected-words.xml"));
    ITable actualTable = expectedDataSet.getTable("WORD");

    Assertion.assertEquals(actualJoinData, actualTable);

}
```

As shown above, to use the query API, one needs to create an ITable instance via the createQueryTable() method on the IConnection object. The expected dataset is created in the same way that the initial IDataSets are created. Lastly, the Assertion object provides two assertEquals methods which work just like the normal JUnit assertions.

Delegation with the DbUnit API

As the DbUnit framework offers a complete API for controlling the state of a database, which is abstracted away from pure JUnit functionality, it is possible to employ DbUnit via delegation rather than strictly inheriting from DatabaseTestCase. This elegant option allows one to combine various JUnit extensions to create powerful testing mechanisms.

As our requirements for controlling a database's lifecycle neatly fit the JUnit fixture model, to delegate behavior to DbUnit, we simply need to adopt a similar setUp()/tearDown() overriding pattern.

DbUnit's delegation flexibility becomes paramount when faced with other JUnit extensions which require a base class. One such framework which requires the use of its base class is the StrutsTestCase framework. As this framework simulates a servlet container, one must inherit from its MockStruts TestCase in order to gain the flexibility to test various Struts components via JUnit mechanisms. As Java is a single inheritance language, we are locked into using MockStrutsTestCase; however, we can employ the power of delegation to create our own DbUnit-MockStruts testing framework.

To construct this framework, we'll build upon what we've learned from examining DbUnit's DatabaseTestCase and enhance it slightly by constructing an IConnection object with greater ease; furthermore, we'll hide the creation of IDataSets. We'll define an abstract template method for defining the file name of XML seed files; additionally, we'll define another template method for defining a Properties object for database connection information. What's more, we'll reuse DbUnit's executeOperation(), getSetUpOperation(), and getTear-DownOperation() methods.

What we're left with is an abstract base class which combines the features of MockStrutsTestCase with the power of DbUnit (Listing C.6).

```java
import java.util.Properties;

import org.dbunit.DatabaseTestCase;
import org.dbunit.database.IDatabaseConnection;
import org.dbunit.dataset.IDataSet;
import org.dbunit.operation.DatabaseOperation;

import servletunit.struts.MockStrutsTestCase;

import com.vanward.resource.unittest.dbunit.util.DBUnitConfigurator;

public abstract class DefaultDBUnitMockStrutsTestCase extends
MockStrutsTestCase {

protected abstract Properties getConnectionProperties();

    protected abstract String getDBUnitDataSetFileForSetUp();

    public DefaultDBUnitMockStrutsTestCase(String testName) {
        super(testName);
    }

    public void setUp() throws Exception {
        super.setUp();
        this.executeOperation(this.getSetUpOperation());
    }
```

Listing C.6 Abstract base class which combines the features of MockStrutsTestCase with the power of DbUnit. (continues)

```java
        public void tearDown() throws Exception{
            super.tearDown();
            this.executeOperation(this.getTearDownOperation());
        }

        private void executeOperation(DatabaseOperation
    operation) throws Exception{
            if (operation != DatabaseOperation.NONE){
                IDatabaseConnection connection = this.getConnection();
                try{
                    operation.execute(connection,
    this.getDataSet());
                }finally{
                    connection.close();
                }
            }
        }

        protected IDatabaseConnection getConnection() throws
    Exception {
            Properties dbPrps = this.getConnectionProperties();
            DatabaseTestCase.assertNotNull("database properties
    were null",
    dbPrps);
            return DBUnitConfigurator.getDBUnitConnection(dbPrps);
        }

        protected DatabaseOperation getSetUpOperation() throws
    Exception {
            return DatabaseOperation.REFRESH;
        }

        protected DatabaseOperation getTearDownOperation() throws
    Exception {
            return DatabaseOperation.NONE;
        }

        protected IDataSet getDataSet() throws Exception {
            String fileName = this.getDBUnitDataSetFileForSetUp();
            DatabaseTestCase.assertNotNull("data set file was
    null", fileName);
            return DBUnitConfigurator.getDataSet(fileName);
        }
    }
```

Listing C.6 Abstract base class which combines the features of MockStrutsTestCase with the power of DbUnit. (continued)

As you can see, we've moved quite a bit of logic into the DBUnitConfigurator class, which attempts to hide the majority of DbUnit's API (Listing C.7). The object's two methods take normal Java objects we're most familiar with and return the objects required for DbUnit functionality.

```java
public class DBUnitConfigurator {


 public static IDatabaseConnection getDBUnitConnection(Properties props)
throws DBUnitConfigurationException{
      try{
        PropertiesAdaptor adptr = new PropertiesAdaptor(props);

        Class driverClass =

Class.forName(adptr.getProperty("connection.driver_class"));

        Connection jdbcConnection =
                          DriverManager.getConnection(adptr.getProp-
erty("connection.url"),
            adptr.getProperty("connection.username"),
            adptr.getProperty("connection.password"));

        return new DatabaseConnection(jdbcConnection);
    }catch(ClassNotFoundException e1){
          throw new DBUnitConfigurationException("ClassNotFoundExcep-
tion in
              getDBUnitConnection", e1);
    }catch(SQLException e2){
        throw new DBUnitConfigurationException("SQLException in
              getDBUnitConnection", e2);
    }
 }
 public static IDataSet getDataSet(String fileName) throws ResourceNot-
FoundException,
DBUnitConfigurationException {
      try{
        InputStream ins =
ResourceLocator.getInputStream(fileName);
        return new FlatXmlDataSet(new InputStreamReader(ins));
      }catch(IOException e1){
        throw new DBUnitConfigurationException("IOException in
getDataSet", e1);
      }catch(DataSetException e2){
        throw new DBUnitConfigurationException("DataSetException in
getDataSet",
```

Listing C.7 Updated DBUnitConfigurator. (continues)

```
        e2);
            }
        }
    }
```

Listing C.7 Updated DBUnitConfigurator. (continued)

Putting our hybrid DbUnit-MockStruts test case framework to work becomes effortless. We simply extend from our base class, provide implementations to our abstract methods, and we're in business.

Using DbUnit with Jakarta's Ant

As if extending from DbUnit's DatabaseTestCase or delegating database management to DbUnit's rich API wasn't enough, the DbUnit team has also provided a powerful set of Ant tasks for manipulating the state of a database, complete with database exporting. This Ant API is quite handy for various needs, such as placing a database into a known state before a larger set of system tests or for a fine grained approach to testing as we've explored above.

The first step required to use the various Ant tasks involves the usual task definition tag required by any custom Ant task.

```
<taskdef name="dbunit" classname="org.dbunit.ant.DbUnitTask"/>
```

Once the dbunit name has been associated with the class DbUnitTask, we are able to utilize the corresponding functionalities throughout our build.xml file. For example, to seed a database, we simply use the nested operation tag, passing in the desired database command type.

```
<dbunit driver="org.gjt.mm.mysql.Driver"
        url="jdbc:mysql://localhost/words"
        userid="words"
        password="words">
    <operation type="INSERT" src="words.xml"/>
</dbunit>
```

Incidentally, the valid command types map directly to the DatabaseOperation class.

This powerful Ant functionality creates the opportunity to create macro JUnit-like fixtures by mimicking the setUp() and tearDown() phases before and after a test case run. For example, Ant is able to run JUnit tests via its junit task; consequently, we can add a dependency target which updates a database before running any associated tests. After the tests are run, we can then clean things up by issuing a DELETE_ALL command.

```
<target name="test">
  <junit printsummary="yes" haltonfailure="no">
   <formatter type="xml"/>
     <batchtest fork="yes" todir="${test-results}/xml">
         <fileset dir="${src}">
        <include name="**/*Test*.java"/>
         </fileset>
     </batchtest>
  </junit>
</target>

<target name="insert">
  <dbunit driver="org.gjt.mm.mysql.Driver"
       url="jdbc:mysql://localhost/words"
       userid="words"
       password="words">
    <operation type="INSERT" src="words.xml"/>
  </dbunit>
</target>

<target name="remove">
  <dbunit driver="org.gjt.mm.mysql.Driver"
       url="jdbc:mysql://localhost/words"
       userid="words"
       password="words">
    <operation type="DELETE_ALL" src="words.xml"/>
  </dbunit>
</target>

<target name="run-tests" depends="insert, test, remove"/>
```

Kicking off our macro JUnit fixture is as easy as running the following command:

```
C:>ant run-tests
```

Notice how we've also decoupled DbUnit's functionality completely away from the code by moving database control into Ant tasks. This can be an effective manner to introduce DbUnit to an existing test suite.

DbUnit Best Practices

As you begin a meticulous methodology of component level testing with DbUnit, you'll find the following practices helpful in test case maintenance and construction.

Life Cycle Methodology

Via JUnit fixtures, a database's state is controlled by the execution of a database operation found in the DatabaseOperation class. There are many combinations of fixture strategies employed in both setUp() and tearDown(), the most common fixture for beginners being an INSERT in setUp() and a DELETE in tearDown() . The most effective strategy, however, employs a REFRESH in the beginning of the fixture followed by NONE in the tear down phase.

As each test case should ideally be independent of other test case executions, a REFRESH executed before a test case run normally handles the vast majority of desired database states. Additionally, as each other test case in a suite is independent and also is preceded by a REFRESH, there is really no need for a tear down operation. This strategy, consequently, also will enable test cases to execute more rapidly as we've effectively minimized the amount of database actives during a test suite run.

Seed File Strategies

Beginners to DbUnit often feel they need to create large XML datasets so as to properly seed a database for testing. In fact, if they've used other mechanisms for seeding databases before a large run of tests, they've probably *had* to create large data sets as so many tests depend on disparate data.

With DbUnit, however, one is usually able to focus test cases on precise subsets of data (i.e., database tables); consequently, XML seed files are able to be short and succinct.

For example, if Object A depended on tables PERSON and ADDRESS in a database containing 10 tables, then the seed file probably only needs to load data into those two tables. There may exist additional constraints and keys that may need to be satisfied; however, the complete schema most likely doesn't need to be properly seeded before a vast majority of tests. An obvious consequence of this strategy is that you'll find you have many small files.

Conclusion

Testing application code, which depends on a database, can be an arduous task as there are many facets which need consideration so as to minimize complexity and ensure reuse. Moreover, if automation is not consideration, any conceived database testing mechanism will fall short of delivering a quality solution.

DbUnit's facile yet powerful features enable effective and automatable component level tests. Developers can quickly understand and put to use DbUnit; moreover, its applicability is quite universal, leading to reusable frameworks.

Unified Modeling Language (UML)

U ML is an acronym for the Unified Modeling Language. The purpose of UML is to define and identify diagrams and diagram elements that can be used to model the processes required in object-oriented analysis design and development. Since its inception in late 1994 by Grady Booch, Ivar Jacobson, and James Rumbaugh, UML has gained great acceptance in the object-oriented development community at large and specifically in the Java community.

The goals of UML as defined by the UML Specification (version 1.5) are as follows:

- Provides users with a ready-to-use, expressive visual modeling language to develop and exchange meaningful models
- Furnishes extensibility and specialization mechanisms to extend the core concepts
- Supports specifications that are independent of particular programming languages and development processes
- Provides a formal basis for understanding the modeling language
- Encourages the growth of the object tools market
- Supports higher-level development concepts such as components, collaborations, frameworks, and patterns
- Integrates best practices

The UML is composed of eight standard diagram types:

1. Class
2. Component
3. Deployment
4. Use case
5. Sequence
6. Activity
7. Collaboration
8. StateChart

For each diagram type we use in this book, we include a key chart in this appendix. For charts that are part of the UML but are not used in this book, we include a brief description. Additional information on the UML can be found at http://www.uml.org/.

Class Diagram

A *class diagram* (see Figure D.1) is designed to model all the static identifiers in an object model. It includes classes, interfaces, packages, and the relationships between them. It is designed to model as well and has mechanisms for model instantions of static classes (objects). Although objects do exist in class diagrams, they are not used in this book and are not included in our key charts.

Component Diagram

A *component diagram* is designed to model the dependencies and relationships of software components in a system. This can include source files, class files (with inheritance), interfaces, property files, executables, and scripts. It is a listing of static classifiers, though, and does not include objects. Component diagrams are not used in this book.

Deployment Diagram

Deployment diagrams show the relationship between components as they exist at runtime within a system. This includes objects, code units, states, and properties. Deployment diagrams are not used within this book.

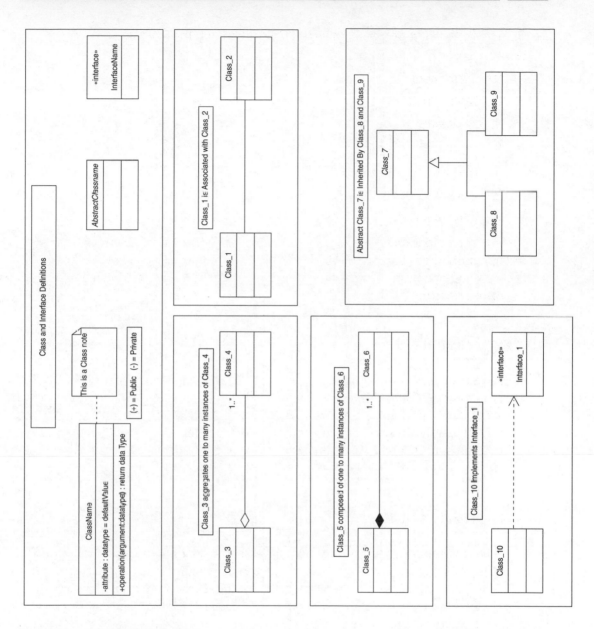

Figure D.1 Sample class diagrams.

Use Case Diagram

Use case diagrams (see Figure D.2) represent users of a system (or actors) and the elements with which they interact in the scope of a given UseCase.

Now let's take that map of a UseCase diagram and make it a bit more concrete for clarity's sake (see Figure D.3).

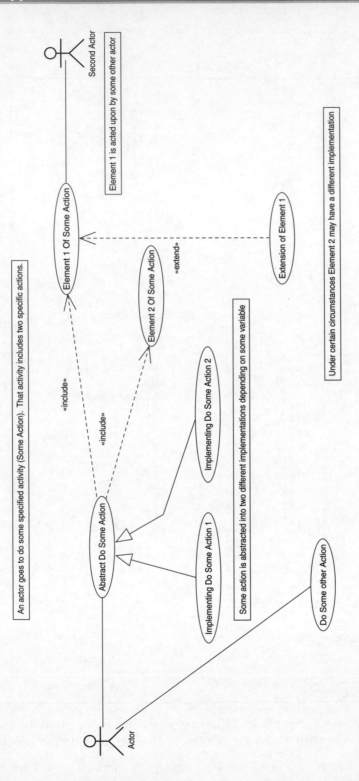

Figure D.2 Abstract model of a UseCase.

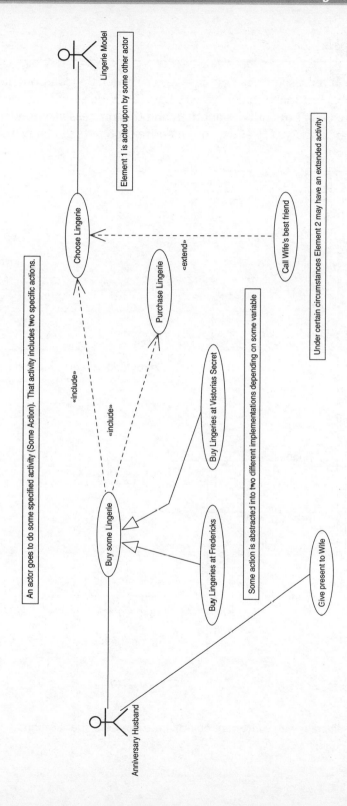

Figure D.3 Concrete model of a UseCase.

Sequence Diagram

A *sequence diagram* represents a set of messages between the components that compose a collaboration within a system. Each activity is modeled as extending from one object or entity to another, and this process is extended to model an element of activity, a UseCase, or an entire system (see Figure D.4).

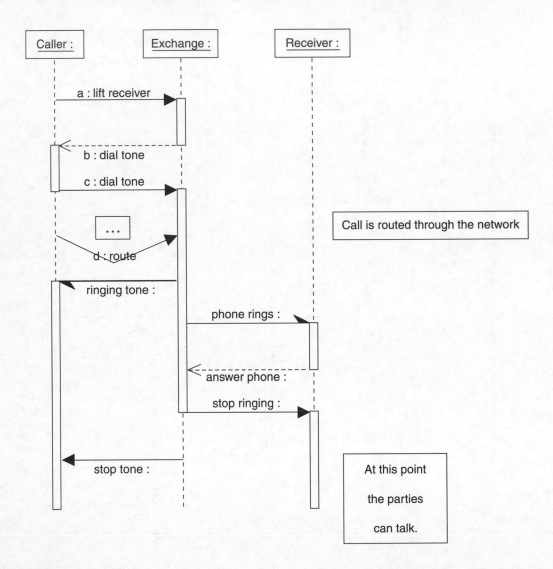

Figure D.4 Simple sequence diagram with concurrent objects from the UML Specification.

Activity Diagram

An *activity diagram* is a type of state-based flowchart in which each state is triggered by the completion of a previous state. Activity diagrams are not used in this book.

Collaboration Diagram

A *collaboration diagram* shows the collaborations of instantiated objects within a system at runtime. Collaboration diagrams are not used in this book.

StateChart Diagram

A *StateChart diagram* is designed to model a state machine. StateChart diagrams are not used in this book.

Aspect-Oriented Programming and Testing

What Is Aspect-Oriented Programming?

If you've seen any of the countless Internet programming sites, chances are you've run across the term *aspect-oriented programming* (AOP). It's been sold as everything from the replacement to object-oriented programming to the greatest way of thinking yet—the dessert topping and floor wax of the programming age. As a developer, although you might often engage in such academic debates as to the usefulness of such paradigm shifts, in the end you are the one who must get the job done. Okay, so what is this AOP tool and how can you use it?

Growing out of the shortcomings in the object-oriented paradigm, AOP is a new way of viewing a system. Instead of seeing components and objects and their interactions, AOP is focused on the idea of *concerns*. Take for instance, a hospital system application for viewing a patient's record (lab results, doctor's orders, medication profiles, etc.). From a basic analysis model, we can easily think of it as modeled like the one in Figure E.1.

We can see that the major functional components of the system are there, but what about all the other issues that are part of this—security, auditing, logging, persistence, business logic? Typically, these are relegated to *utility classes*, the object-oriented programming equivalent of the global function. If we want to maintain common security, auditing, and logging throughout the system, this starts to get a little messy and leads to spaghetti code that is both tough to understand and impossible to debug and repair. Just from the explosion of security system details we can see that we've gained quite a bit of complexity—not to mention that even with using standard design patterns such as

Visitor and chain of responsibility, we've segmented the code, separating all of our security code into classes that will be scattered throughout the system.

If we need to implement some common security feature, we have to possibly modify every last implementing SecurityHandler. Even if we create abstract base classes and push common functionality into them, we are just compounding our problem by scattering code that should be logically grouped together (see Figure E.2).

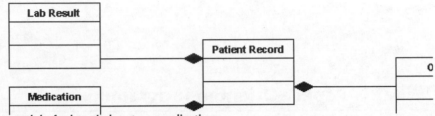

Figure E.1 Simple model of a hospital system application.

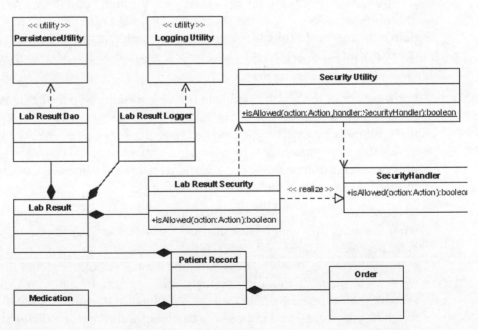

Figure E.2 A more complex and troublesome version of the hospital system application.

To remedy this situation and provide a new view of the system, we turn to AOP, which lets us look at a system not as a collection of objects and interactions but as a group of common concerns. Within this small example, we already see common concerns of security, logging, persistence, and business logic. The AOP way of addressing these issues is to look at the concerns of the system, address each separately, and recompose the concerns into a system. In the previous example, the Lab Results object wouldn't need to know that there is such a thing as security on its operations or that its actions were being logged or results persisted to a database. As a pure business object, Lab Results is concerned only with modeling the business relationships of a lab result and not with the system actions. The shift from OOP to AOP involves making an object less aware of the system and more aware of its individual contribution.

Up to this point, it sounds heavy on the analysis and design portion but not real practical for implementation. How would we assemble all these separate concerns without falling back to the OOP patterns that we've all come to know and love? That's where specialized AOP programming tools come into play—among those, AspectJ (http://www.aspectj.org) is a language that provides extensions to Java for supporting AOP concepts. This appendix isn't intended as a tutorial on AOP and AspectJ, but rather a brief introduction to the terminology and capabilities of the language with respect to testing. For indepth information on these topics, see *Mastering AspectJ* by Joseph Gradecki and Nicholas Lesiecki.

AspectJ introduces three new concepts that extend the AOP idea to Java:

- **Joinpoints:** Specific points in the runtime of a program. These can be thought of almost as breakpoints or watchpoints set within a program. As the code executes, these points may or may not be reached. While any point within a program may be considered a joinpoint, AspectJ exposes a limited set of joinpoints (accessors/mutators, pre/post-method execution, etc.).

- **Pointcuts:** Methods of specifying how to locate a joinpoint. Here is where the real power of AOP lies. Rather than just specifying a single point in an execution, the pointcut language allows you to specify groups and patterns to joinpoint locations. This can be useful for checking things like method calls that take three arguments, the last one being a Comparator. While the joinpoint set may be limited, the pointcut expression language allows you to be very sophisticated in finding locations or groups of locations.

- **Advices:** Actions to take upon approaching a joinpoint. An advice is basically the code you want to execute when the joinpoint is reached.

Think of the AspectJ tool as a way to watch over your program at execution time and ensure that common functionality is being performed. Using pointcut expressions, you specify the joinpoint locations that you want to affect and then include advices to execute actions when that point is reached. This way, you can weave concerns throughout your code and better maintain cohesive logic. For example, in the medical system example, we know that any access to our Lab Results object must first be checked by a security manager to see if it is "allowed." Furthermore, we want to create an audit log of all the user's failed actions. So our first attempt at writing the code would look similar to this:

```
public class LabResult{
    LabResultType type;
    Date dateRequested;
    boolean processed;
    Physician requestingPhysician;
    Patient patient;

    LabResultSecurity security =
SecurityUtility.createSecurityHandler( this );

    LabResultAuditor auditor =
        AuditorUtility.createAuditHandler( this );

    public LabResultType getType() throws SecurityException{
        Action typeAction = new Action( "getType", this );
        if( LabResult.security.isAllowed( typeAction ){
            return type;
        }
        else{
            auditor.auditEntry( typeAction, AuditorUtility.FAILURE
);
            throw new SecurityException("Unable to retrieve type" );
        }
    }
}
```

Okay, not bad—but we've got to do this for every last one of the accessors and mutators. And what about the long-term maintenance of this code? If we ever need to change the security policy, we'd have to go back through all the code that is using the LabResultsSecurity class. There is just too much potential for broken code when this type of programming is used. So how would this be any better with AOP?

First, we could create separate concerns for the three areas that we are addressing: business logic, security, and auditing. The business logic can be simply a POV (short for plain vanilla object—a simple JavaBean).

We haven't mixed in any security, logging, or anything other than straight business-level logic. Nothing new here—so where is the AOP stuff? Let's start to address the other concern, security. From our specification, we know that we want to invoke security when elements of Lab Results are accessed. In AOP terms, this translates to a joinpoint of calls to the LabResult class's accessor methods. We do this by creating an aspect file (typically denoted with an *.aj* extension) that specifies the pointcut language to find our joinpoints and the advice to take once that joinpoint is reached. That code would look something like this (we'll explain the contents a little later):

```
aspect LabResultSecurity implements SecurityHandler{

    pointcut accessors(LabResult lr): call( * LabResult.get*() ) &&
target(lr);

    before(LabResult lr) : accessors( lr ){
        String actionName = thisJoinPointStaticPart.getSignature().
getName();
        Action action = new Action( actionName, lr );
        if !( isAllowed( action ) ){
            throw new SecurityException("Unable to "  + actionName );
        }
    }

    // more code here, including implementation of isAllowed( action :
Action )
}
```

Okay, it sort of looks like a Java class declaration, and in fact it's very close to one. You can implement an interface or extend other classes just as you would with a class. (You can see that we're implementing the SecurityHandler interface in this case.) What is different is the pointcut declaration, so let's break this down a little more:

```
pointcut accessors(LabResult lr): call( * LabResult.get*() ) &&
target(lr);
```

In this code snippet, pointcut is simply a keyword that designates that we are writing a pointcut, in this case, a pointcut named accessors that has an argument of a LabResult object that will be referenced as *lr*. The call statement says that we are attempting to locate joinpoints that are calls matching a certain signature—specifically, a call with any return value (the first *) on a LabResult object starting with *get* (the second * signifies that we can accept any method call ending that starts with *get*, such as getX(), getTypes(), or getto()). We have further stipulated that the target of the call (the object on which the message is invoked) should be the same as lr (in fact, this will be used to get the called object inside the method call itself—a kind of *this* pointer within AOP). So in the end, we simply define a pointcut to locate joinpoints of calls to get…() made from the LabResult object—our accessor methods.

Now, on to the advice and the action of the aspect. We've specified something that looks like a method call with the before()... statement. In fact, this is an advice for the pointcut accessors() we defined earlier. You can see that we've extracted the LabResult object from the pointcut by specifying the formal parameter LabResults lr. We didn't have to name it the same as the formals used in the pointcut, but for consistency we did. From here on out, the body looks strikingly similar to a method declaration in Java. In fact, except for the special form of thisJoinPointStaticPart that allows you to access metadata (signatures, variables, types, exceptions, context, etc.) about the joinpoint, it *is* a Java method. So, just as we did in our first attempt, we get the name of the method, create an action, and if we are not allowed to perform the action, we throw an exception. Of course, all this assumes that we wrote the original method to throw a SecurityException. But what if we didn't? Well, we can actually weave that into our business logic as well.

What did we change? We changed the type of advice so that rather than acting before the statement, it acts "around" the statement. We also added a return type (since our actual method does return a value) of Object. It's okay to return an object even if a primitive value is called for (int, float, double, etc.), since it will be automatically converted to its object type. The last thing we did was add a return statement with a call to proceed(). This is the way that AspectJ allows us to call the actual method itself. We are letting the method proceed and return its normal value.

But this will only put security on calls to getXXXX()—what about any internal uses of the property? Well, as you can imagine, AspectJ has a way to handle this as well. By changing the pointcut description to the following:

```
pointcut accessors(LabResult lr): call( * LabResult.get*() ) &&
    target(lr) &&
    get( private * LabResult.* )
```

we can intercept all attempts to access the property from calls to LabResult.getType() to reference to the type property (i.e., if(type.equals(LabResult.BloodTest))). All in all, the language of pointcuts is very expressive and allows you to find almost every type of joinpoint that you need to affect your code.

As far as our auditing concern goes, our initial specification called for auditing any security exceptions that were raised, so we set out to create a pointcut and advice for this as well:

```
aspect LabResultAuditing implements AuditHandler{
    pointcut allcalls( LabResult lr ) : call( * LabResults.*() ) &&
target(lr);

    after( LabResult result ) throwing( SecurityException ) : allcalls(
result ){
        String actionName = thisJoinPointStaticPart.getSignature().
getName();
        Action action = new Action( actionName, lr );
        auditEntry( action );
```

```
          }

          // more code here, including implementation of auditEntry( action :
     Action )
     }
```

Here, we've changed the pointcut definition slightly to accept any calls made on a LabResult object. The advice for this point now specifies that, after any call that actually throws a SecurityException (throwing(SecurityException)), the body should be executed. Just as before, the body creates the action from the actual method call name and calls a further method to create an audit entry. For this example, we limited the calls to LabResult objects, but even that isn't a requirement. We can easily specify a package or groups of packages, or even all classes within the system. Centralizing all the logic for logging into a single concern is also a possibility. With such a universal auditor, we can add auditing to all of our packages and even those for which we don't have the source code.

To explain that last statement requires a further explanation of what happens after you have an aspect file. Using the tools supplied by AspectJ, a compiler/weaver weaves your code throughout the applied codebase. That is, for your existing Java and already compiled class files, you can weave aspects throughout. As a matter of implementation, the AspectJ weaver will create any additional classes it finds necessary to implement, but the resulting execution will be as if the actual advice code was placed in the proper Java file and compiled into the code (or an off-the-shelf class file). So you might have additional classes to add to your JAR or class path—yet at the same time you'll have code that behaves just the way you want, but with a more logical packaging of concerns.

What this means is that you can write an advice to catch NullPointerExceptions and weave it through an off-the-shelf implementation where you had only class files. Or better yet, you could change such a package to throw only your specialized exceptions when any other exception was raised. The possibilities are endless. I hope that from this very quick drink from the fire hose of AOP that you can see the power that such a construct can have in programming.

How Can It Help Me Test?

So this all looks promising for logging and security, but this is a book on testing. How can this help you test code? To answer that, think of testing as a concern of the system as well. Rather than create huge testing frameworks with small, specialized classes that do much the same thing, we can create generalized tests for the entire system and better maintain a separation of concerns and concentration of functionality.

AOP can be applied to testing at various levels, from just basic interception of calls and checking for values through a complex construction of test harnesses. If you begin to think of testing as a concern of the system and not just as an afterthought to construction, you'll ultimately begin to classify AOP testing into these general categories:

- **Generalized testing:** This form of AOP testing uses the interceptor features of AOP languages to define common joinpoints where testing can occur and execute a battery of tests based on the statement signature, context, or other factor.

  Think back to the Category-Partition pattern (Chapter 13) where we were trying to find combinations of values to break the system or, better yet, just supply the typical set of values that would be sent to a method. Wouldn't it be nice to keep those values and tests together, rather than have them scattered throughout the code? And better yet, you can have them always applied to methods, without having to remember to write a test for each one.

  While this doesn't cover all tests or all aspects of what would be required in testing, you can see that it goes a long way to creating a common test for all object parameters. With some thought and test planning (specific to your application and data sets), you can start to build up generalized testing methods. You can also see this extending to trapping methods that throw exceptions, checking getter/setter pairs, or other common but cookie-cutter testing.

- **Structural testing:** This is something that is not entirely addressed in this book as it's not so much a software unit test as it is an inspection test. Here, you are looking for enforcement of coding standards and practices rather than functionality of the application. Say you have a coding standard that requires all classes to implement a custom Persistable interface or some derivative thereof (i.e., it's okay to extend a class that implements Persistable). You could check through every module (and this isn't such a bad idea—code inspection is a good thing), but it might not be practical. Once again, AOP to the rescue.

```
aspect CheckStructure {

    declare error: withincode( *.new(..) ) && !target(Persistable)
    : "didn't implement persistable";

}
```

This code will throw a compiler error when it encounters a constructor that isn't implementing the Persistable interface. It is quite a bit easier to do this and run all your code through the compiler than to check all 10,000 class files by hand. (In fact, you can even just go ahead and create an advice that would inherit the interface for all classes that didn't.) But, as you can see, all kinds of structural checks could be performed, from checking that variables are given proper default values to ensuring that no one catches a generic exception instead of the specific exceptions thrown.

- **Testing harness assistance:** In this last category, we have tests that help you build the testing harness. Just from the patterns that we've discussed here, you can see that there are some tasks that just can't be tested (or at least not tested without a serious amount of work and high risk). If you have code that should be executed to destroy the rocket if it veers off course or want to simulate situations such as nuclear meltdown or system overheating that would just be totally infeasible, AOP can help. Also, AOP can help you look inside other packages (such as off-the-shelf solutions) to check for errors, override values, and generate exceptions and conditions that you may not otherwise encounter.

AOP testing methods, if used wisely, can greatly improve your testing abilities and help you maintain a consistent set of tests with a common focus. To demonstrate this type of testing, let's reexamine one of the testing patterns that we previously encountered and see what AOP can do for the basic patterns.

Self-Shunt Revisited

As you might recall, the Self-Shunt pattern's basic premise was, that in a collaboration between objects, the test should become one of the collaborators, and if that isn't possible, it can at least pretend to be one (see Chapter 11). We used the example of a Pilot Control System (PCS) that is given to us as off-the-shelf software. We have code that will handle the errors generated by the PCS if an anomaly is detected. We only have the JAR file from the PCS vendor, so we can't change the package (or at least right now that's not being addressed as an option), not to mention the fact that it's being coupled with some hardware that's very expensive if we happen to exercise the wrong code values. As you recall, the basic structure of the application looks like that shown in Figure E.3.

We're checking to see that the correctSystems() method is being called if and when an error occurs. You'll notice that we had two problems: first, how to verify that the correctSystems() method was actually called, and second, how to generate some of the critical system errors (overheating, gyroscopic controls that are misaligned, etc.) without destroying expensive pieces of hardware. We solved these problems originally using a delegate, but we could have just as easily used AOP to solve them (and in fact, it may be even better using AOP).

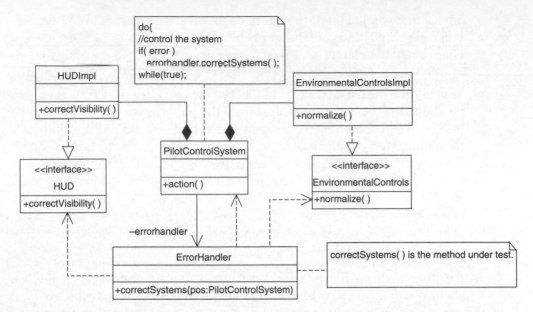

Figure E.3 Pilot Control System basic concept.

We start with the first issue—how to see that the correctSystems() method was called. We create a pointcut that intercepts any calls to the correct System() method and sets a corresponding flag.

Well, this certainly looks easier than the original solution, which required creating a proxy to do the job. We simply allow the AOP language to weave its advice into the code, setting a flag when the method is called. With minimal setup, we are able to implant our flag inside the vendor's code to let us know when a method is executed. Now on to our other issue: generating errors in the first place.

From the vendor's documentation, we see that the method adjustHeading() in the HUD controller throws an InvalidHeadingException. We further note that the system will recognize this exception as being an error state, which should trip our correctSystem() method again. But we've got a problem: We can't directly call the adjustHeading() method; it's private and can only be called by the constructor. So, we can use AOP to generate the error state for us (so that a team of programmers won't have to lift up the HUD sensors and move the display trying to generate improper headings). We simply expand upon the test framework that we already started.

At this point, you can probably see a whole set of problems that AOP can be used to solve. While most situations can still be addressed with traditional OOP methods, AOP can lead to a more compact, easier-to-maintain system for logically grouping testing functionality.

The Dangers of AOP

With power often comes danger, and AOP is not an exception. When dealing with AOP at any level in your coding or testing, here are some things to keep in mind:

- **AOP changes the code:** Although this is a small point, it is one you should not forget. The code that you are running with the weaving in place (unless you intend to leave it weaved for production modes) is not the code you are executing. In the case of the correctSystem() method call earlier, you are only setting a simple Boolean value; however, you could do anything that you want in this code, including changing values passed into methods that may not be readily apparent to the casual user. If my code is doing something (like the example of the InvalidHeadingException) and this code remains in place in production, you will always generate an InvalidHeadingException when the method is called. Someone can pore over the code time and time again and not see any reason for the exception to be raised. The code has been changed and there is no direct trail for it.

- **AOP isn't easy to debug or easy to understand:** Along these same lines, it's not so easy to debug and understand AOP code. While the examples that I showed are relatively easy, it is just as easy to get in over your head with pointcut language and advice that isn't as human readable, especially when wildcards are used. To compound this, multiple pointcuts in multiple aspects can refer to the same joinpoint and both offer advice. This becomes very tricky to debug and impossible to understand. Although tools are getting better at this type of work, most are still not at the level we've come to expect with other types of debugging tools.

- **AOP can get real messy real fast:** I was just casually playing around with using AOP in one of my recent projects, trying to trap all JDBC execute Statement() calls in an attempt to log the SQL statement to a database for monitoring and debugging purposes. (Not quite that simple—but the idea still holds.) I wrote a simple pointcut to trap calls to executeStatement().

When I ran this code, I was shocked to see that I got a StackOverFlow error and my database was full of records after making just one call. As you'll recall, pointcuts specify locations to find a joinpoint regardless of the location—including locations in your own advice. So it was catching the invocation of executeStatement() referred to by the proceed statement. This can be easily fixed by adding a !within(MyAspect), but that's not the point. The problem is that when aspects are weaved throughout your codebase, they can get out of control very fast and could potentially do some damage. You'll need to think and plan through all your advice and pointcuts prior to launching your application, especially in areas that might lead to critical errors (or at least costly ones).

What Does All This Mean?

Recently, a lot of attention has been paid to the emerging paradigm of aspect-oriented programming. Just like all new shifts in thinking, this has been touted as the be-all, end-all, silver-bullet solution that will revolutionize programming. AOP has promise. It provides a way to think about systems that better models our understanding of them. As we've shown in this appendix, it can be used to improve our testing strategies and to aid in our development of test cases. However, it is a model of the way we think and not a full and robust description in and of itself, and using it comes with a price. Will languages and tools be developed that make greater use of AOP? Almost certainly. Will AOP be the next big thing in computing? Maybe. Will there be a new way to look at computing and testing? Definitely.

AOP and JUnit and Cactus and MockEJB and countless other testing frameworks and tools are just that—today's models of understanding. As a systems engineer often dealing with models and simulations, I've learned to live by one rule of thumb that keeps it all in perspective:

> *AOP is just another tool in the set that you have in dealing with the issues of testing. Use it wisely and it will help you—misuse it and it will make your job even tougher. There are no silver bullets with respect to software.*

Index